Ho for California!

Ho for California!

Women's
Overland
Diaries
from the
Huntington
Library

EDITED & ANNOTATED BY
Sandra L. Myres

HUNTINGTON LIBRARY
SAN MARINO

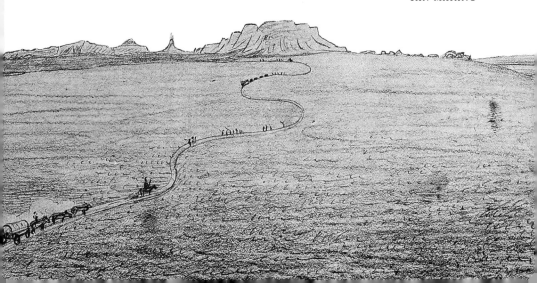

Henry E. Huntington Library and Art Gallery
1151 Oxford Road, San Marino, California 91108
Copyright 1980 by the Henry E. Huntington Library and Art Gallery
All rights reserved
Published 1980.
Sixth printing 1999
Printed in the United States of America

Library of Congress Cataloging-in-Publication Data

Ho for California! Women's overland diaries from the Huntington
 Library, edited & annotated by Sandra L. Myres. San Marino,
Huntington Library, 1980.

314 p. illus. 24 cm. ([Huntington Library publications])

Contents.--The Isthmus of Panama, 1849; A diary kept by Mrs. Jane
McDougal.--The California trail, 1850-1859; A journal of Mary Stuart
Bailey, 1852. A trip across the plains in an ox cart, 1857, by H.
Carpenter.--The Southwestern trails, 1869-1870; Diary of a young
girl, 1869, by H. Bunyard. Journal, 1870, by M. Shrode.

Bibliography: p. [297]-306.
1. Overland journeys to the Pacific--Collected works. 2. Voyages
to the Pacific Coast--Collected works. 3. Women--The West--Biog.--
Collected works. 4. Frontier and pioneer life--The West--Sources--
Collected works. I. Myres, Sandra Lynn, 1933- II. Henry E.
Huntington Library and Art Gallery, San Marino, Calif. III. Series.
5. The West--History--1848-1950--Sources--Collected works.

ISBN: O-87328-119-5   LC 79-28115 CIP
                                             km 6/80

Table of Contents

Illustrations

Unless otherwise noted, illustrations are from the Huntington Collections.

Acknowledgments

A S with any project of this kind, I have had a great deal of encouragement and assistance from others. The book was first conceived in discussions with Dr. Ray Allen Billington, Senior Research Associate of the Huntington Library, and his continuing encouragement and helpful advice have been of great assistance. I am especially grateful to the Huntington Library, the Newberry Library Family and Community History Center, and the Organized Research Fund of the University of Texas at Arlington which provided funds to help underwrite the research expenses incurred in completing the manuscript. Without this assistance it would have been impossible for me to complete the project. I would also like to thank the excellent reference librarians at the Huntington and Newberry libraries. They were all gracious and efficient and helped make my research pleasant as well as productive. Thanks are also due to Glenda Riley, the University of Northern Iowa, who read parts of the manuscript and offered a number of helpful suggestions. And my very special thanks to John Hudson, University Librarian, the University of Texas at Arlington, who not only read the manuscript and saved me from several serious errors, but whose continuing friendship and support encouraged me throughout the project.

SANDRA L. MYRES

CALIFORNIA TRAILS

-- Route of Mary Stuart Bailey, 1852
— Route of Helen Carpenter, 1857
— Alternate Routes

SOUTHWESTERN TRAILS

-- Route of Harriet Bunyard, 1869
— Route of Maria Shrode, 1870

Introduction

*Ho—for California—at last we are on the way. . . . We have really started,
and with good luck may some day reach the "promised land."*
                    Helen Carpenter, "A Trip Across the Plains"

*One was going on a pilgrimage whose every suggestion was of the familiar
sacred stories. One sought a romantic and far off golden land of promise, and
one was in the wilderness of this world. . . . Amid the jagged, broken and barren hills, amid the desolation of the lonely plains, amid the half-known but
always horrible dangers of the way, one met experiences. . . .*
                                        Josiah Royce, *California*

PERHAPS no mass movement in history has been better recorded than the great migration of Americans across the continent during the 1840s, 50s, and 60s. Beginning with the first
explorations of the Louisiana Territory, gaining momentum with the
opening of Oregon, swelling into a "rush" with the California gold
discoveries, thousands of Americans and foreign settlers and tourists
followed the major routes westward. Yet until recently little was written about women on the trails. "Westering" was supposed to be a
male enterprise, full of hardships, unsuitable for the "weaker" sex. But
women were part of the westward migration and their experiences,
recorded in diaries, letters, and reminiscences, are an important part of
the trail literature.

Of the hundreds of books written about the westering experience, a
few have become literary and historic classics, but none, with the
possible exception of those by Susan McGoffin and Sarah Royce, was
written by a woman. Our perceptions of westering women have been
shaped by male writers who did not read what women themselves
wrote about the west. Or, if they did read the many journals and reminiscences written by women, they chose to ignore them in favor of
more dramatic legends and myths. Thus westering women became the
protagonists of a stereotyped version of the west as false as that of the
Hollywood Indian. The redman rides into the sunset, tall, bronzed,
stoic, crowned with an eagle feather warbonnet. The white woman

strides westward with grim-faced determination, clad in gingham, wreathed in a sunbonnet, baby at breast, bravely awaiting unknown dangers while she yearns for home and hearth.[1] And, in recent years, a new picture of the westering woman has emerged from the writings of feminist historians. She is the trail drudge, reluctant companion, and overworked helpmate following wearily after the wagons. Pre-occupied with death, resentful of male-imposed rules, she performs unaccustomed tasks, gathers buffalo chips, and cooks and washes while her strong male companion lolls before the fire, smoking his pipe and "betting how many miles we had covered during the day."[2]

Neither stereotype is true. Women, like men, were neither saints nor sinners. Some did wear gingham and sunbonnets; others preferred bloomers and hunting shirts. Some had large families; some gave birth along the way; others were single and carefree. Some were resentful of performing new chores imposed by trail conditions; others embraced the new freedom from woman's "place." Different women experi-enced different conditions, reacted in different ways to the westward journey. Westering, as revealed in the diaries of both men and women, was neither a male adventure nor a female endurance test. It was a human experience in which all — men, women, and children — partici-pated as individuals. Women's perceptions of themselves and their companions are as varied as those of male writers.

The diaries which follow reflect five different women's experiences on three of the major westward routes — the Panama route, the Cali-fornia Trail, and the southern or Gila Trail. The introduction to each section briefly discusses the route, and the footnotes and annotations compare the diarists' comments with those of other travelers on the same route. Each trail had its own peculiar perils and pleasures. Each offered some magnificent scenery, some unexpected joys and respites from the dreary monotony of slow, daily travel. Each had its own hardships of terrain and climate which must be overcome. Together, these five diaries and the comparative comments present an overall woman's picture of the westering experience.

The most popular of the overland routes generally followed the Platte River to Fort Bridger, then turned north to Fort Hall where the Oregon road struck northward toward the Columbia River and the

Cascade range, and the California Trail branched south to the Humboldt River and the Sierra Nevada. Hundreds of thousands of Americans followed this "Great Platte River Road" westward between 1840 and 1865. During the "boom" years of the 1850s more than 200,000 men, women, and children crossed the continent along this route.[3] Unknown numbers returned by the same road. The Platte Road passed some of the nation's most interesting natural wonders, and travelers often took short side trips to Devil's Gate or Soda Springs or stopped briefly to admire the view or to scratch their names on Independence Rock or Chimney Rock. But most days were a dreary succession of steep hills, flat alkali plains, poor water, and clouds of dust. Stampedes, accidents, and disease extracted a heavy toll in human life and suffering but there were also pleasures — beautiful sunsets, the amusing antics of the prairie dogs, the discovery of a spring of clear, cold water, the first glimpse of the snow-capped coastal ranges. Many of the diaries and reminiscences of overlanders were written about the Platte Road (Mattes discovered more than seven hundred), and two of the diaries which follow, those of Mary Bailey and Helen Carpenter, relate experiences on this trail during the 1850s.

With the advent of the Pacific mail steamers in 1849 some California-bound travelers preferred the speed of a combined sea and land journey via Mexico, Panama, or, later, Nicaragua. Service via Panama was the quickest of the sea-land routes, but it was also the most expensive. Like the cross-continental trails, these routes had their dangers. Wagon breakdowns and stock losses were replaced by shipboard fires and occasional groundings. Steaming jungle heat replaced dry alkali dust. Panama travelers rarely encountered hostile natives but they were frequently exploited by unscrupulous agents and companions. Disease, especially cholera, was common to both routes, and Isthmian travelers also suffered from Panama fever, dysentery, and malaria. Like the Platte road, the Panama route had its pleasures and occasional luxuries, and some of these are described by Jane McDougal, a passenger on the first Pacific steamboat from Panama to California. The Isthmian routes were popular with returning California travelers, and it is of such a journey that Mrs. McDougal writes.

There was a second major overland trail approached by many roads through Arkansas, Louisiana, Texas, and New Mexico. These roads converged near Tucson where travelers joined the trail along the Gila River to Yuma, swung south into Mexico, and then turned northwest across the Forty Mile Desert to the southern California slopes. Like the Platte route, the Gila Trail had its perils — dust, heat, hostile Indians, difficult terrain. But it also had its pleasures — giant saguaro cactus, quaint Mexican villages, the hospitable Pima Indians who offered fresh vegetables and fruit to weary pilgrims. During the 1860s the southern route was a favorite with western stockmen who envisioned gold not in the California mines but in the profits from herds of cattle for restocking ranches and for sale to a meat-hungry, burgeoning California population. Both Maria Shrode and Hattie Bunyard wrote of the southern crossing in the post-Civil War years. Their diaries are of particular interest because they help to supplement the rather scanty literature, especially by women, about this least-documented trail.

Just as the trails varied in their pleasures and dangers, so different decades of westering brought different problems for travelers. Most of the troubles of the 1840s came from lack of experience in the skills of transcontinental travel. The early immigrants were often misguided and some even got lost. There was little literature to aid them, and what they had was often inaccurate. Travelers during the 1850s suffered more from overcrowding (and the subsequent scarcity of grass for their stock) and from polluted campgrounds than from Indian attacks or lack of guides and maps. The twin specters of cholera and dead stock haunted the trails while shipboard fever, bad food, and inadequate quarters took their toll of those crossing the Isthmus. Travelers during the 1860s often suffered more from the inconveniences and discomforts imposed by the soldiers sent to protect them than from the outrages of hostiles or from ravages of terrain and climate.

According to J. H. Kemble, "There is no such thing as a 'typical' California gold rush journal. Every journal and the experiences which formed the basis of every journal reflected individual and unique happenings and it would be pointless to try to select one which was a common denominator."[4] To some extent Kemble is right; there is no "typical" California journal. Thus the journals in this volume are perhaps not typical, but they are representative of the experiences of westering women, and they provide a basis for analyzing women's motives, adventures, experiences, and hopes along the routes to California.

Although all of the selections which follow were written by women, none conforms to either the "saint" or the "drudge" stereotype of women on the overland trails. In and of themselves, none of the journals is particularly significant. They are not literary in the tradition of Parkman or Bryant or historical in the tradition of Bridger or Whitman. Rather they are everyday experiences of ordinary people told in a blunt, often uninspiring prose frequently marred by poor spelling, bad grammar, and a singular lack of dramatic detail. They will never become literary classics or best sellers; they are not likely to become the basis for a movie or television script. There are no dramatic rescues, thrilling battles with Indians, heart-rending tragedies, or the bitterness and silent suffering of popular trail literature. There are simply day-by-day, matter-of-fact reports of what life was really like for the thousands of women who undertook the western journey and helped to open the continent to settlement.

---

[1]For different versions of this "sunbonnet saint," see Glenda Riley, *Women on the American Frontier*, The Forum Series (St. Louis: Forum Press, 1977); Riley, "Images of the Frontierswoman: Iowa as a Case Study," *Western Historical Quarterly* 8 (April 1977): 189–202; Beverly J. Stoeltje, " 'A Helpmate for Man Indeed' The Image of the Frontier Woman," *Journal of American Folklore* 88 (January–March 1975): 25–41; and Joan S. Reiter, *The Women* (Alexandria, Virginia, Time-Life Books, 1978), 17–37.

[2]Johnny Faragher and Christine Stansell, "Women and Their Families on the Overland Trail to California and Oregon, 1842-1867," *Feminist Studies* 2 (1975): 150–66. For a similar view of trail women, see Lillian Schlissel, "Women's Diaries on the Western Frontier," *American Studies* 18 (Spring 1977): 87–100.

[3]Merrill J. Mattes, *The Great Platte River Road: The Covered Wagon Mainline via Fort Kearny to Fort Laramie*, Nebraska State Historical Society Publications, 25 (Lincoln: Nebraska State Historical Society, 1969), 23.

[4]Albert G. Osbun, *To California and the South Seas, The Diary of Albert G. Osbun*, J. H. Kemble, ed. (San Marino: The Huntington Library, 1966), vii.

A Brief Note on Methodology

The diaries have been edited for readability rather than with an intent to replicate the originals. Since all five women were writing under difficult circumstances, it is understandable that their narratives lack many of the niceties of spelling, punctuation, and grammar. For example, Maria Shrode's daily entries are often one long sentence tied together with "ands" and "buts." Mary Bailey paid no attention to the use of periods or capital letters; both are thrown in higgledy piggledy. The same is true of the diary of Hattie Bunyard. Jane McDougal's and Helen Carpenter's journals are more correct in form, but even in these diaries there are frequent errors and inconsistencies in grammar and punctuation. Thus, I have attempted to make the text of each diary more readable by regularizing grammar, punctuation, and occasionally spelling.

In most cases, I have retained the original spelling except in cases where there were obvious slips of the pen, and I have changed misspellings which occurred only once or twice, with the word correctly spelled in the remainder of the text. I have not corrected words consistently misspelled by the writer. Thus, I have retained "travail" for "travel" which is used throughout one diary. I have kept the often strange spellings of Indian and Spanish words. The diarists' improper uses of common French or other foreign expressions also remain as they were written.

The paragraphing, especially in the Carpenter diary, is artificial and intended as a convenience to the reader. Where entry dates were missing or inconsistent, they have been changed to reflect the correct notation. I have also taken considerable editorial liberty with punctuation and capitalization. All of the women frequently used dashes to tie together long sentences and inserted commas in the most unlikely places. I have tried to regularize their use consistent with nineteenth-century style. The diaries have been edited without deletions from the original texts, and I have used only sparingly the scholarly notation, *sic*. In a few places I have recast sentences and where necessary for clarity or smoothness, a few words have been added. The latter are enclosed in brackets which I trust will not be overly disruptive.

Although editorial purists may disagree with the methodology, I believe it is justified. None of these women, after all, were literary or historical figures. Their journals are of interest from a narrative point of view, and every effort has been made to make them readable while preserving the flavor of the language and each author's individual style. The diaries are in the manuscript collections of the Huntington Library, San Marino, California.

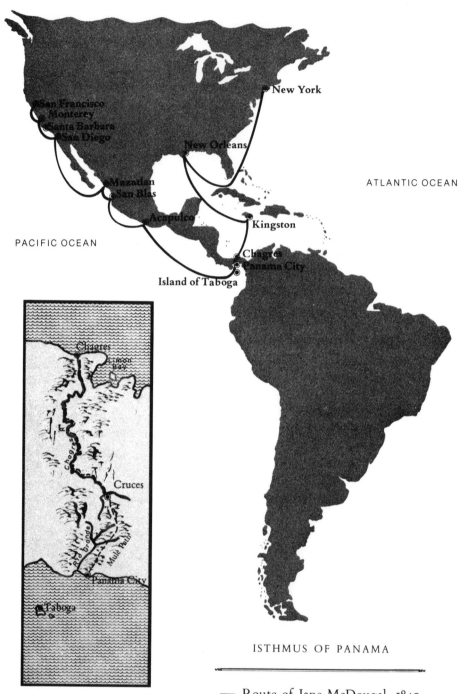

ATLANTIC OCEAN

New York

San Francisco
Monterey
Santa Barbara
San Diego

New Orleans

Mazatlan
San Blas

Acapulco

Kingston

PACIFIC OCEAN

Chagres
Panama City

Island of Taboga

Chagres

Chagres

Cruces

Panama City

Taboga

ISTHMUS OF PANAMA

— Route of Jane McDougal, 1849
-- Panama Route (Insert)

The Isthmus of Panama, 1849

It was an episode individual and peculiar; a part, and no small part, of the great uprising and exodus of the nations; it was the grand pathway of pilgrims from all parts of the eastern world; it was brim full of romance and comedy, of unnumbered woes and tragedy, enlivened now and then by a disaster which sent a thrill throughout the civilized world. It was a briny, boisterous idyl where courage bore along the slippery passage-ways, and love lounged upon the canopied decks, and sentiment in thin muslin cooed in close cabins, and vice and virtue went hand in hand as friends.

H. H. Bancroft, *California Inter Pocula*

OF the various routes to the gold fields, the Panamanian crossing was the quickest and the most expensive. Although the trip from New York could be made in about a month and a half (assuming good connections could be made in Panama), the price for a New York to San Francisco passage was $200 for first class and $185 for third class. And there were additional expenses incurred in crossing the Isthmus, ranging from thirty to sixty dollars for transportation, baggage handling, and food and accommodations along the way and in Panama City while waiting for a ship to San Francisco. Thus the route was potentially attractive for single people and even couples, but the cost for families was prohibitive.[1]

The Isthmus also had a reputation for disease, high prices, and bad food. One newspaper reminded potential travelers that Panama was the "pest hole of the world," and almost every traveler on the route contracted, or knew someone who contracted, cholera, yellow fever (commonly called Panama or Chagres fever), malaria, or similar

---

[1]John H. Kemble, *The Panama Route, 1848-1868* (Berkeley: University of California Press, 1943), 37; Rodman Paul, *California Gold: The Beginning of Mining in the Far West* (Cambridge: Harvard University Press, 1947), 31. Ware's *Guide* estimated a higher price of $280 for the trip from New Orleans to San Francisco. Joseph E. Ware, *The Emigrant's Guide to California*, reprint ed. (Princeton: Princeton University Press, 1932), 55.

"tropical" maladies. Many blamed the combination of tropical fruits (such as plantains) and alcoholic drinks taken in large quantity to ward off disease, for the ills which afflicted travelers, especially young men. However, some of the illnesses such as cholera were contracted before leaving the States and simply spread rapidly and widely in the crowded conditions prevalent on the ships and in Panama City.

Adding to the problems of the Panamanian route was the difficulty in taking large amounts of goods and baggage. Since everything had to be taken off at the Atlantic side, carried across the Isthmus, and reloaded on the Pacific side, less baggage could be taken. One newspaper cautioned that "nothing over 150 pounds weight can be carried with safety,"[2] and other travelers warned of lost, stolen, and abandoned luggage all along the overland crossing. Some gold seekers went via Panama and sent their baggage via the Cape Horn route, but most simply preferred to brave the monotony of the longer voyage which usually took four to six months and cost $300 for first class and $100 for third class.[3]

During the first years of gold fever, the route over the Isthmus was not particularly popular. There were 30,675 arrivals in San Francisco between March 31 and December, 1849. Of these "12,237 came from U.S. ports via Cape Horn, 6,000 via Panama, and 2,600 via San Blas and Mazatlán, and the rest from other quarters."[4] After 1851, the Panamanian crossing became more popular, particularly for return trips. Faster ships with better accommodations, "hotels," or at least stopping places along the land route, and the completion of the railroad from Aspinwall to Panama, which eliminated most of the dangerous and difficult river and land trip, increased the speed and comfort of the trip and reduced the cost slightly.

In 1849, however, such amenities were not available. Jane McDougal, whose diary follows, was a passenger on the steamer *Falcon* which left New Orleans on December 18, 1848, and reached Panama on December 27, with a cargo of excited gold seekers. Several weeks later, after crossing the Isthmus, the *Falcon*'s passengers boarded

---

[2]New York *Herald*, December 13, 1848, quoted in William McCollum, *California As I Saw It*, Dale Morgan, ed. (Los Gatos: Talisman Press, 1960), 38–39.

[3]Paul, *California Gold*, 32; Oscar Lewis, *Sea Routes to the Gold Fields: The Migration by Water to California, 1849-1852* (New York: Knopf, 1949), 117.

[4]McCollum, *California*, 44–45.

the steamer *California* for her maiden voyage to San Francisco. Unfortunately, McDougal did not leave a diary of her outbound trip, but her diary of the return trip is still typical of the reminiscences of other travelers on the Panamanian route in 1849.

Many diaries and reminiscences were written by the Argonauts of '49, for as Oscar Lewis comments, "those who traveled by sea found in their journals a welcome relief from the tedium of the weeks aboard ship."[5] For many, too, this was the adventure of a lifetime and they wanted to record their experiences and their impressions of the strange and exotic places they visited. Whether sea travelers chose the Horn route or the shorter Panamanian trip, long, boring hours at sea forced passengers to find pastimes and amusement to while away the long hours. Chess, checkers, backgammon, and card games; sewing, mending, or polishing gear; fishing, reading, and visiting and gossiping with friends all helped to pass the time and are mentioned in various journals. Practical jokes and horseplay and mock trials, such as those described by Mrs. McDougal, also seem to have been favorite pastimes of the passengers. Parties, teas, impromptu song fests, and amateur theatricals were also frequent occurrences. Church services, usually the Episcopal service read by the Captain, were held regularly on most ships.

The less pleasant aspects of the trip described by McDougal are also typical of most journals. Seasickness the first few days was common among passengers, both male and female. Bancroft recommended brandy as a remedy, as did Mrs. McDougal. He also noted that "some find relief in iced champagne. . . ."[6] If this treatment was effective, the passengers on the *California* evidently suffered little from the malady. Once recovered from their initial *mal de mer*, most passengers complained about the food. Panama steamer passengers had less cause for complaint since they could usually obtain fresh fruits and other provisions at the frequent ports of call, a luxury denied to those on sailing vessels which ran much farther out to sea and rarely stopped between Panama and San Francisco. Not only was the food "indifferent" if not bad, accommodations were crowded, and although

---

[5]Lewis, *Sea Routes*, v.
[6]H. H. Bancroft, *California Inter Pocula* (San Francisco: History Publishing Company, 1888), 141.

McDougal seems to have found her stateroom fairly pleasant, the rooms were small, and there were frequent complaints that cleanliness was not one of the virtues of the ships.

In addition to poor food and crowded quarters, there were also dangers in steamship travel. The possibility of shipwreck was increased on the steamers since they sailed so close to the shore, and their machinery and fuel supplies made fire an ever-present danger. In the early years, mutinies by both passengers and crews were additional cause for alarm. The passengers, disgusted with the food and service or other real or imagined grievances against the captains or owners, talked of taking over the ship, and crews plotted to scuttle the ship and desert to the gold fields or steal the fortunes of returning gold seekers. Captain Cleveland Forbes, on Jane McDougal's trip, had real reason for alarm at the supposed mutiny reported in her diary. He had already had one mutiny among the firemen and passengers on the voyage to San Francisco and had lost one crew by desertion in February. There was also the possibility of running out of fuel, another occurrence which plagued the *California* and her sister steamers. The *California* had run short of coal on the trip from Panama to San Francisco, and the passengers had to assist the crew in cutting wood at Monterey. On the return trip, as fuel ran short, Captain Forbes was concerned that the ship would not make port. In fact, Mrs. McDougal did not seem to realize how narrowly the ship made anchor at Panama. "If I drift to Sea there is no telling when I will get back, perhaps never," Forbes recorded in his log. After anchoring he noted with relief, "Gave the ship 50 fms. chain & thus I have just saved myself."[7]

The crossing of the Isthmus was considered the greatest peril of the Panama route, although McDougal doesn't seem to dread it as much as other journalists of the period. She writes nothing of the maladies which frequently attacked the travelers and which are mentioned in almost every reminiscence. For example, Ida Fitzgerald remembered that her mother nearly died from "brain fever" during the crossing. Mrs. D. B. Bates wrote of burying three people during an eighteen-mile trip from Panama City to the railroad in 1852, and almost every

[7]John E. Pomfret, ed., *California Gold Rush Voyages, 1848–1849: Three Original Narratives* (San Marino: Huntington Library, 1954), 223.

male diarist, including Taylor, Dunbar, Stowell, and McCollum, recorded caring for some sick friend along the route.[8]

On the other hand, Jane McDougal's comments on the towns and villages of Panama and Mexico are typical of most of the journalists. The inhabitants of these strange and exotic places were considered inferior to the Anglos. The forty-niners, and those who followed, were "true-blue Americans" saturated with the propaganda of Manifest Destiny and eager to take up the "white man's burden" and bring culture and progress to their little brown brothers. Mary Jane Megquier described the Spanish families as "clean and neat," but, she continued, "their hands and feet are very small, but their faces are anything but handsome. . . ."[9] Ida Jeffries Fitzgerald noted that the natives of New Granada (of which Panama was then a part) "were intellectually little above the animals."[10] Almost all the men made similar comments, and most added an optimistic note about the salubrious effect Yankee enterprise would bring. "The dusky natives with their squalid children, their dogs and pigs, the monkeys, alligators, snakes, and all created things of the aligerous order," wrote Edward Dunbar, "were roused from their dreamy lethargy by this sudden irruption of the Northern white race."[11] "The business and general appearance of the city have undergone quite a change since the emigration to California commenced," William McCollum wrote of Panama City. "It will soon bear the mark of Yankee enterprise that will astonish the natives. . . ."[12] Most of the Anglos were also vehemently anti-Catholic. Megquier noted that "the priests gamble and enter into every species of vice and disappation [sic]. . . ." while

---

[8]Ida J. Fitzgerald, "Account of Life of Plummer Edwards Jefferis, including voyages from New York to California in 1850 and 1854," ms., Huntington Library; Mrs. D. B. Bates, *Incidents on Land and Water or Four Years on the Pacific Coast* (Boston: published for the author, 1860); Bayard Taylor, *Eldorado or Adventures in the Path of Empire*, 2 vols. (New York: George Putnam, 1850); Edward E. Dunbar, *The Romance of the Age or the Discovery of Gold in California* (New York: D. Appleton, 1867); Levi Stowell, "Bound for the Land of Canann, Ho! Diary of Levi Stowell," Marco G. Thorne, ed., *California Historical Society Quarterly* 27 (March 1948): 33-50.

[9]Robert G. Cleland, ed., *Apron Full of Gold: The Letters of Mary Jane Megquier From San Francisco, 1849-1856* (San Marino: Huntington Library, 1949), 11.

[10]Fitzgerald, "Account."

[11]Dunbar, *Romance of the Age*, 57.

[12]McCollum, *California*, 101.

Cleveland Forbes believed that the church would crumble "as the Roman Empire must do before civilization & Religion."[13] In a similar vein, Edward Dunbar wrote, "as usual in these Catholic countries, the poor Indian evinced a kind of stolid resignation to Fate, and resorted to religious ceremonies" in the face of a cholera epidemic contracted from the gold-rush travelers.[14]

Oscar Lewis noted that most of the travelers over the Panama route were men. He contended that "the voyage by sailing ship, either round the Horn or via Panama, was so severe an ordeal that few women had the hardihood to undertake it."[15] Yet, of the 364 passengers on the maiden trip of the *California* to San Francisco, fourteen were women. That other women made the trip on other vessels is clear from both men's and women's diaries. Jane McDougal is notable in that she is one of the few women who kept a journal or at least whose journal has found its way into print. Little is known of her background or education. She was born in Indiana, and her diary reveals a well-bred and well-educated young woman of social position. Her husband, John McDougal, was a veteran of the Mexican War and, according to his fellow passengers on the *California*, "his extensive knowledge of Mexico and her people, and his familiarity with the Spanish language, together with a peculiarly free and easy way of communicating with strangers . . . made him an exceedingly useful and agreeable traveling companion."[16] In 1848, John decided to join his brother, George, who had become a successful merchant in Sacramento. He engaged passage on the steamer *Falcon* out of New Orleans for himself, his wife, Jane, and their four-year-old daughter, Sue. By the time the McDougals reached New Orleans, news of the gold strikes in California had spread throughout the nation, and hundreds of anxious gold seekers were clamoring to book passage on the first available ship. The *Falcon*, which had left New York with only thirty or forty passengers, was filled to capacity with eager argonauts. At Chagres, the California-bound throng crossed the Isthmus and

---

[13]Cleland, *Apron Full of Gold*, 11; Pomfret, *Gold Rush Voyages*, 223.

[14]Dunbar, *Romance of the Age*, 61–62.

[15]Lewis, *Sea Routes*, 35.

[16]Society of First Steamship Pioneers, *First Steamship Pioneers*, edited by a Committee of the Association (San Francisco: H. S. Crocker & Co., 1874), 242.

arrived in Panama City where their number was increased by new arrivals from other vessels. It was several weeks before the first steamer on the Pacific route put into port. When the *California* dropped anchor, pandemonium broke loose. Most of the New York and New Orleans passengers did not have tickets to San Francisco, and demands for space brought about a near riot. The *California*, which had left New York long before the news of the gold discoveries reached the east coast, had embarked seventy South American passengers in Peru, and angry Anglos demanded that these passengers be thrown off to make room for U.S. citizens. John McDougal was one of a delegation of *Falcon* passengers who confronted the steamship's agents with demands for space. Finally, on February 1, the *California* left for San Francisco with an overflow crowd of nearly 400 passengers. The captain and the company had not anticipated the rush, and space, food, and fuel were in short supply. According to those who made the voyage, conditions were less than satisfactory.[17]

The *California* arrived at San Francisco on February 28, 1849. Due to the desertion of her crew to the gold fields and difficulty in procuring a new one, it was two months later before the steamer could begin her return trip to Panama. In the meantime, John McDougal had been unsuccessful in the gold fields and had turned to managing his brother's store at Sutterville. Mrs. McDougal, disillusioned with the new country and compelled by "personal and unforeseen circumstances" to return to Indiana, booked passage on the *California* to Panama and with her brother-in-law, George, her young daughter, Sue, and a servant named Turner set out on May 1, 1849, to make the return trip. It was on this journey that she kept the diary which follows.

In California, John McDougal was a failure as a merchant but had modest success as a politician. In 1850, he was elected lieutenant governor of the newly-created state and, in 1851, when Governor Peter Burnet stepped down from office, McDougal became governor and served from 1851 to 1852. Thereafter, he held various state and Democratic party offices until his death in 1866. According to those who

---

[17]The two best accounts of the voyage are *First Steamship Pioneers* and Victor M. Berthold, *The Pioneer Steamer* California, *1848-1849* (Boston: Houghton Mifflin, 1932).

knew the couple, McDougal seems to have been a "hail fellow well met" who had a fondness for drink. Jane, according to the same informants, "held in check what might otherwise have been an undesirable degree of boldness and push" and "really toned the creative down and toned the moral up."[18] In 1852, if not before, Mrs. McDougal returned to California over the Nicaragua route and was shipwrecked when the *North Star* ran aground fifty miles south of Acapulco. According to one witness, the passengers suffered severely before they reached safety.[19]

McDougal was not a particularly popular governor. He had a tendency to play the buffoon and his enemies charged that he made a mockery of his office. After he left the governor's office, the McDougals retired from public life. In 1862 Jane died giving birth to a premature child, Elizabeth. John's mind began to slip, and he made several attempts to commit suicide. He died of a stroke in 1866.[20]

Jane McDougal's diary is an interesting one for she obviously was on close terms with many of the men and women prominent in early California history. Her diary, in contrast to those of other forty-niners on the Panamanian route, takes little note of illness or the dangers of the crossing. She does give longer, although still inadequate, descriptions of the Pacific ports of call in Mexico and California than do many of her fellow travelers. She had both the time and ability to comment on events on board ship and on the land journey, and she was a perceptive and lively observer. McDougal's diary is an interesting and somewhat singular journal of a woman's experiences during the gold-rush years. Although previously published in part in the *Overland Monthly*[21] this is, so far as can be ascertained, the first time the complete journal has appeared in print.

[18]*First Steamship Pioneers*, 242–43.

[19]Bancroft, *California*, 214.

[20]Karen Pickett, "John McDougal," ms., California State Library Sacramento; Theodore H. Hittell, *History of California*, 4 vols. (San Francisco: N. J. Stone & Co., 1898), IV: 60–65; H. H. Bancroft, *History of California*, 7 vols. (San Francisco: History Publishing Company, 1888), VI: 258.

[21]"A Woman's Log of 1849, From the Diary of Mrs. John MacDougall [sic]," William H. McDougall, ed., *Overland Monthly*, 2nd series 16 (September 1890): 273–80. McDougal's name is frequently misspelled. This has led to a great deal of confusion between Jane McDougal's husband, the second governor of California, and the attorney-general of the state, James McDougall. See: H. Brett Melendy, "Who was John McDougal?" *Pacific Historical Review* 29 (August 1960): 231–43.

A Diary
Kept by Mrs. Jane McDougal

when returning from San Francisco
to her home in Indianapolis
in May, 1849, on the steamer California

May 1st. Tuesday morning.

This is the day we are to bid adieu to San Francisco. With the exception of leaving my husband & three or four friends I confess I leave it without regret. The morning is very gloomy & unpleasant. We left Mr. Bowdin's house at half past nine o'clock. Mr. Lambden walked down to the point with me. John Stephenson and Dr. Parker overtook us in the wagon. Mr. & Mrs. Wheeler, Mrs. Goodwin, Capt. Folsom, Mr. & Mrs. Grimes came down to the steamer soon afterwards.[1] We sat and talked some time. Made merry, or tried to, over several bottles of ale; but many were the sad hearts that even ale could not enliven. Friends were parting, perhaps forever, some with a long & dangerous journey before them & others [going] where comforts cannot be procured, even for gold.

Mr. & Mrs. Bowdin, Col. Stephenson, Dr. Parker & myself embarked in a whale boat for the steamer at 10½ o'clock. Found the California as cold & cheerless as ever, though much cleaner than on her trip up.[2] At 2 o'clock we left San Francisco for Sausilita where we have lain ever since getting on water. Had a very poor dinner of roast beef & yams about three o'clock.

---

[1]Only a few of the people mentioned by Mrs. McDougal can be identified. Colonel Stevenson was Jonathan D. Stevenson, colonel of the 1st Regular New York Volunteers; Dr. William C. Parker was with the United States Navy at Santa Cruz; Wheeler was the Reverend O. C. Wheeler, a missionary and later a Southern Pacific railroad official; Captain Joseph L. Folsom was quartermaster of the 1st Regular New York Volunteers. See McDougall, "A Woman's Log of 1849," 273–80.

[2]The *California*, the first steamer in service on the Pacific mail route, was a wooden side-wheeler of 1,057 tons built by William H. Webb of New York for the Pacific Mail Steamship Company. Launched in May, 1848, the *California* arrived in San Fran-

Mrs. Bowdin felt very badly at parting with her husband & she retired before dark. Indeed I regretted very much myself leaving Mr. B., the Col. & the Dr., who have shown me great kindness since I have been in C[alifornia]. The two latter insisted on having a kiss each from Mrs. B. & I & what may seem strange for married ladies, we gave it. They seem more like brothers than anything else & it was a sisterly kiss on our parts.

Sausilita is a little cove in among the hills, indeed completely surrounded by them, in a very picturesque place, although the hills are barren of trees. Very fine water here & easy of access for vessels.[3]

8 o'clock. We are just done tea & being tired, cold & low spirited, I am determined to go to bed, hoping to waken tomorrow morning in the bay of Montrey [sic].

May 2nd. Wednesday.

Was quite sick last night, the effect of change of water. But after taking a little brandy & water & eating my breakfast I felt able to go on deck & take a look at Montrey. It is one of the most beautiful situations I ever saw on the sides of several hills which sloping back from the bay are partially covered with dark pines & partly with nothing but green grass. It has the appearance of beautiful green meadows or

---

cisco via Valparaiso and Panama on February 28, 1849. She operated regular service between San Francisco and Panama until 1854. The log kept by Mrs. McDougal corresponds in almost exact detail with that kept by her commander, Captain Cleveland Forbes. McDougal was one of thirty-five cabin passengers on the trip from San Francisco to Panama. She undoubtedly occupied one of the first-class staterooms which "usually contained three berths, one above another, together with a cushioned locker which could accommodate another passenger; each room had a mirror, a toilet stand, washbowl, water bottle and glasses." Kemble, *The Panama Route*, 218; 122. For detailed descriptions of the *California* see: Berthold, *The Pioneer Steamer* California, and *First Steamship Pioneers*. Forbes's journal is in Pomfret, *Gold Rush Voyages*, 233–43.

[3]Sausilita was named for the Rancho Saucelito which, despite Mrs. McDougal's comments, takes its name from the hillside spring surrounded by sausal or willow trees. The waterfront had been used as an anchorage and supply station since Spanish times and was one of the busiest points in the San Francisco area. Mildred Brooke Hoover, H. E. Rench and Ethel Rench, *Historic Spots in California*, 3rd ed. (Stanford: Stanford University Press, 1966), 179.

rolling praires. It is certainly a lovely place at this season of the year, but I am told it is all parched up later in the year.[4]

We arrived here about 10 o'clock. Major Canby & Mr. Willey came on board. They seem like old friends as we came out from New Orleans together. Mrs. Canby sent me a package of letters, a most beautiful bouquet, some eggs & dried apples by Col. Mason, all very acceptable presents as we have a hard time to get anything to eat on the steamer.[5]

At 12 o'clock we hoisted anchor & went out to sea, but had not been out more than an hour before all the ladies had disappeared one after the other to their rooms. All were sick. The sea is always very rough passing Point Conception & it is particularly so this time.[6] Too sick to write.

May 3. Thursday morning.

We were awakened last night at 12 o'clock by the most alarming of all sounds at sea, "the ship is on fire." Great was the excitement. The women & children were screaming, gentlemen just roused from sleep running out half dressed to inquire what was the matter while others

---

[4]The usual ports of call for Panama-San Francisco steamers were Acapulco, San Blas, Mazatlán, San Diego, and Monterey. Monterey, once the capital of Spanish California, was considered one of the lovliest towns and bays along the coast. Richard Henry Dana noted the town's "very pretty appearance," as did other travelers. Bayard Taylor found the town very picturesque and noted "it is larger than I expected, and from the water has the air of a large New England village, barring the adobe houses. . . ." Bancroft, like McDougal, was struck by the surrounding countryside: "Rising behind a town of 500 inhabitants, of spacious well built tiled adobes is an amphitheatre of wooded hills glowing like an illuminated panorama. . . ." Hoover, *Historic Spots*, 216–18; Taylor, *Eldorado*, I:51; Bancroft, *California*, 35:222.

[5]Mason boarded the *California* at Monterey. Canby was General E.R.S. Canby, then a major in the Tenth Infantry, and Willey was the Reverend S. H. Willey, a popular missionary and preacher. McDougall, "A Woman's Log," 273, and Pomfret, *Gold Rush Voyages,* 234.

[6]Point Concepción, along with Point Argüello, forms the "corners of California,"where the coastline turns from a north-south to an east-west line. The winds and seas in this area are often rough and a number of wrecks occurred off the points. The cape was sometimes known as "the Cape Horn of California" and was usually, as Taylor commented, "true to its character, we had a cold, dense fog, and violent headwinds; the coast was shrouded from sight." Hoover, *Historic Spots*, 415; Taylor, *Eldorado*, 46.

were running with water. It was some time before the ladies could be assured there was no danger. The fire, as it was supposed to be, proved to be only the frictions of the wheel where it went into a motion. I believe there would have been danger if it had not been discovered in time.

The sea is still very rough & neglecting to have our port holes closed, both George & I had our staterooms filled with water & he had a fine salt showerbath, as we shipped heavy seas in at the port holes. I was the only lady at the breakfast table this morning, the rest being rather sleepy, I suppose, after their fright.

At 1½ o'clock we dropped anchor off the port of Santa Barbara, a very pretty place situated on an inclined plane that ascends gradually from the beach. About midway to the top of the hill is a mission with a very fine church, fine gardens, orchards, etc. attached to it.[7] With Yankee enterprise it might be made one of the garden spots of the earth as all kinds of fruits & flowers grow here almost spontaneously & there are a great many cattle, poultry, etc. here. But the people are so indolent that we could get no supplies for the ship, not even milk, though we could see from the ship hundreds of cows grazing on the hills.[8] The harbour is very bad for ships as the celp [sic], a kind of sea weed, grows so thick & long in the water that it is almost impossible to get a ship through it. It grows twenty feet long & is as strong as a cable.

In coming to Santa Barbara we passed an island about sixty miles from the coast on which there is a lone woman living. The Russians

---

[7]Santa Barbara was not a regular stop for San Francisco-bound ships, and most of the Pacific travelers do not comment on the town. The mission described by McDougal did not suffer the neglect of many other ecclesiastical properties after secularization. In 1842 it became the bishop's residence and later a hospice and center for the education of Franciscan candidates for the priesthood. However, confirming McDougal's comments, Forbes notes that Santa Barbara was "a mean place . . . where a white man would starve in short order. I could not get an ounce of fresh provision in the poor, deserted place." Hoover, *Historic Spots*, 418; Pomfret, *Gold Rush Voyages*, 234.

[8]Anglos were often amazed by the number of cattle and lack of milk in California. What easterners like Jane McDougal failed to realize was that cattle were raised for hides, and meat and dairy herds were rare. Bancroft also noted the numerous "herds of cattle and horses running over hills brown and dry in summer. . . ." Bancroft, *California*, 22.

some years ago had a party there catching otters. A storm came up & they were obliged to put out to sea leaving some of their party on shore. They afterward returned & got them all off but this woman who has lived there alone ever since. Some three years ago they caught her, but she was perfectly wild & had lost her speech so they left her.[9]

At 2 o'clock we hoisted anchor & left Santa Barbara. Sea rough, sea sick.

May 4th. Friday.

Was awakened this morning by Turner who brought me in a cup of tea & some nice toast which was very acceptable as we do not breakfast until after 9 o'clock & I am always sea sick if I do not eat anything before. After breakfast we went on deck to take a look at the mission of St. John's situated in a small valley surrounded with hills which at this season of the year are covered with most beautiful flowers.[10] If it could always be spring in California it would be a beautiful country, but nine months of the year it is parched & barren for the want of rain. They have no lightning or thunder here.

Between three & four o'clock P.M. of today we entered the harbour of San Diego, the entrance to which is very narrow & sometimes hazardous. After you are in it you are completely surrounded with hills covered with grass & flowers but not a tree to be seen. We anchored near the shore on which were three or four small huts. A few graves of foreigners [are] on the side of the hill with a white railing around. Far from home & friends they died & their names are unknown to the traveller, but their graves are in full view to remind us of what may be our destiny ere we reach home. Heaven grant it may not be my lot to make my last resting place in such a barren waste as this.[11]

---

[9]The so-called "wild woman" of San Nicholás Island was Juana Maria, an Indian woman reputed to have lived eighteen years on San Nicolás Island in the Santa Barbara channel. She was rescued and brought to Santa Barbara by Captain George Nidever and is reported to have been buried in the garden at Santa Barbara Mission. Hoover, *Historic Spots*, 417.

[10]Evidently a reference to San Juan Capistrano Mission some three miles inland from the coast. It was considered one of the most beautiful of all the California missions.

[11]Contrary to McDougal's comment, the bay at San Diego was considered to be an excellent harbor, although Forbes described the town as "the meanest place of

The ship Edith was in the harbour landing government troops, for the line of the United States possessions is only four or five miles below the entrance to the harbour.[12] The town of San Diego we saw in the distance some three or four miles around the bay, but it looked barren and desolate. After remaining about an hour we set off again & got out of the harbour a short time before dark. Sewed some after tea.

May 5th. Saturday.

We have no stoppages to make today but having a smooth sea & fair wind we have run very well all day & last night. Did not go on deck all day but sewed pretty steadily. Felt very unwell after dinner & retired before tea. It being a fine evening, Mrs. Bowdin & George walked some time on deck.

Still felt very unwell & did not get up this morning until I heard Capt. Forbes ask Capt. Thomas if they should have religious service on deck or in the cabin. Concluded I would get up to attend them. Capt. Thomas read the service of the Episcopal church (in the cabin). Most of the lady passengers responded. It is the first time I ever heard it at sea & it reminded me of home. After service called on the St. Clairs, Mrs. Grimes, & Mr. Hope. Returned to my stateroom where Turner provided lunch. Did not eat any but felt so unwell I laid down & am now writing in my berth. Have been reading "The Inheritance" by Miss Ferrier.[13] It is not worth much but serves to while away the time which passes heavily at sea.

Went up on deck just about sunset & walked the deck by moonlight. Had a long talk with Capt. Forbes until tea time. After ten

---

all." Taylor noted that "The old hide-houses are built at the foot of the hills just inside the bay, and a fine road along the shore leads to the town . . . three miles distant and barely visible from the anchorage. Above the houses, on a little eminence, several tents were planted and a short distance further were several recent graves surrounded by paling." Pomfret, *Gold Rush Voyages*, 234; Taylor, *Eldorado*, 45. See also, Bancroft, *California*, 217.

[12]The *U.S.S. Edith* was wrecked off Point Argüello shortly after this. According to local legend, sailors deliberately ran the ship aground in order to be free to join the gold seekers. Hoover, *Historic Spots*, 415.

[13]The reference is to a book by a popular novelist of the period, Susan Edmonstone Ferrier. *The Inheritance* was originally published in 1824, but a new edition was issued in 1847 and is probably the one referred to by McDougal.

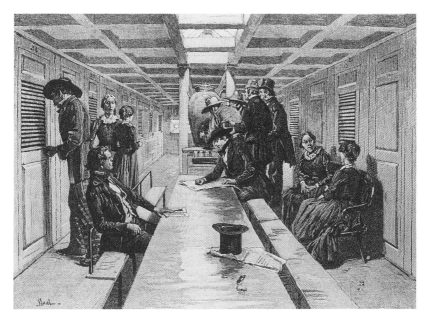

" 'Tween Decks on an Early Panama Steamer"

Capt. Forbes & Mrs. Ogden gave us some sacred music on the accordian & with their voices. I retired early as I did not feel very well. We run 251 miles in the last twenty-four hours.

May 7th. Monday.

George had a very severe chill this morning & a very violent headache all day. I watched him & sewed. Did not go on deck all day although it is a very beautiful one. Great excitement last night about a man that was missing & supposed to be overboard. Of course all his faults were buried in the deep with him & he was eulogized as the best, finest, most honest, industrious, capable man on the ship & his loss was deeply felt. About breakfast time this morning, however, he was discovered in the carpenter's room enjoying a very comfortable, undisturbed sleep.

One poor Spaniard today lost seven pounds of gold dust overboard. All, it is said, the poor fellow had. Passed a large school of porpoises this evening. We run 231 miles in the last twenty-four hours.

May 8th. Tuesday.

Doubled Cape St. Lucas about 12 o'clock last night.[14] George had another chill today & a fever after it. I have felt sick all day, owing to want of proper food, as we have very little but mutton. Anchored some eight or ten miles off the port of Mazatlan about ten o'clock tonight. The motion of the ship with the swell of the sea makes me very sick. Run 235 miles in the last twenty-four hours.

May 9th. Wednesday.

Early this morning we came into the bay & anchored about two miles & a half from the town. After breakfast Mrs. Bowdin, Mrs. Grimes, Mrs. Ogden, Mrs. Smith, Messers. Garr, Thomas, Murphy, Brown, & Col. Mason went ashore together in one of the ship's boats. We went to Capt. Mott's house, found it very cool & pleasant & the ladies very agreeable. Saw a little girl with curly hair that looked the very picture of Mary Horn, made me think of home. The Talbotts had gone to an English man of war for a large boat to take all the ladies on shore from the steamer & Mr. Mott's carriage was to have been at the levee to receive us, but we were too soon for them. Mr. Talbott went with Mrs. Bowdin, Mrs. Grimes & myself to some of the stores. Bought a few articles & returned to the Motts where we had a very fine lunch of fruit, melons, etc. Bade them goodbye & took a walk down one of the principal streets to the beach. Went into Mr. Kelly's house. Found it quite a palace, handsomely furnished, with a great many birds & flowers. Mr., Mrs., & Miss Kelly were very agreeable, & we had a delightful call. Took some wine with them & left. Walked down to the beach. Mr. Talbott got one of the custom house boats & came off with us to the ship. We spent a very pleasant day. Were delighted with Mazatlan but felt very glad to get back to the ship, for home, be it ever so humble, is still home & we consider the ship as such until we leave her at Panama.[15]

---

[14]Cape San Lucas lies at the southern tip of Baja California. Poet Bayard Taylor described it as "a bold bluff of native granite broken into isolated rocks at its points, which present the appearance of three distant and perfectly formed pyramids. The white, glistening rock is pierced at its base by hollow caverns and arches, some of which are fifteen or twenty feet high. . . ." Taylor, *Eldorado*, 43.

[15]Most Americans felt that Mazatlán was more "progressive" than other Mexican ports. "Mazatlán is the most important Mexican sea port on the Pacific," reported

The Capt. says we will positively leave here for San Blas at seven o'clock this evening so as to get there in the morning. Must write to John to go back from here, so I had better be at it. Mr. Forbes, the English consul, gets off there & returns to San Francisco by the Oregon on her return.[16]

May 10th. Thursday.

We left Mazatlan last evening about 8 o'clock & entered the port of San Blas about 9 o'clock this morning. Mrs. Bowdin's birthday today. She treated the ladies to some champaigne & cake & Turner brought us a very nice lunch. We had a very cozy little time in our rooms, as there is a door between we can throw them both into one.

The site of San Blas is very romantic, hills & valleys overlooking a bay dotted with islands, most of them though of barren rocks. The town itself is a poor miserable village with thatched houses.[17] A large party of Americans arrived here today from across the country on their way to California. May their golden dream be realized as their ideas of comfort never can be. We are to leave here this evening. Some part of the engine being out of order has detained us here all day. Very warm.

May 11th. Friday.

A very beautiful morning but rather warm in the afternoon. The passengers, most of them, very much frightened by the steamer stop-

---

Bancroft. "[It] displays unmistakable evidence of commercial activity and thrift. The population is 12,000 to 15,000, the climate healthy, the houses substantial . . . and the streets clean." Bancroft, *California*, 215–16.

McDougal and her friends were guests of the owners of an English firm, Mott, Talbot & Company. Talbot was also the British consul at Mazatlán. *First Steamship Pioneers*, 52.

[16]The *Oregon*, a 1052 ton, wooden side-wheeler, was a sister ship to the *California*. She was launched in August, 1848, and entered service on the Panama-San Francisco line in April, 1849. Kemble, *The Panama Route*, 239–40. The Mr. Forbes referred to is James A. Forbes, the English consul at San Francisco who was on a business trip to Tepic. See A. P. Nasatir, "International Rivalry for California and the Establishment of the British Consulate," *California Historical Society Quarterly* 46 (March 1967): 68.

[17]San Blas, an old Spanish naval base, was a regular fuel port for the Pacific steamers, and most comment, as did McDougal, on its beautiful setting and "miserable" appearance. Most travelers described it as "a collection of cane huts with a few stone houses." Taylor, *Eldorado*, 38. See also: Bancroft, *California*, 215; Osbun, *To California and the South Seas*, 22–23 for other descriptions.

ping suddenly, & with a great jar, about 4 o'clock this afternoon. Some of the machinery about the engine was out of order & soon rectified. In a few moments we were again under way. Have run 240 miles in the last twenty-four hours.[18]

Have been sewing and reading all day. Finished two dresses I was making, one for Sue. Mrs. Bowdin has not been to the table today. Must go to her to get out.

May 12th. Saturday.

Excessively warm today so that it has been almost impossible to stay in our rooms. Made Sue a bonnet & myself a cap today. Pretty well for ship board & warm weather. Run 230 miles last night but as we had to double a cape, we made only 150 miles on our way. Nothing occured today of note.

May 13th. Sunday.

And what a Sunday it is. We are in the port of Acapulco. The passengers have most of them gone on shore & the natives are flocking on board by dozens, running fore & aft, up & down stairs, chattering away in Spanish, keeping such a noise it is impossible to read & besides the day is excessively warm. The bay is entirely shut in with hills & there is no breeze. This is probably the best protected harbour in the world. George has been ashore ever since we anchored at 11 o'clock. The ladies went on shore in the evening & Capt. Dyer took Sue along. I did not feel disposed to go.[19]

---

[18]Except for this entry and the one for May 12, McDougal's comments on the distance run correspond exactly with the entries in the log of Captain Cleveland Forbes. Why the discrepancy for just these two days is not clear. (Forbes gives 103 miles for May 11 and 196 for May 12.) See Pomfret, *Gold Rush Voyages*, 23.

[19]Acapulco was a favorite port for passengers on the Pacific steamers. Like Mrs. McDougal, most commented on the protected harbor and the many natives selling fruits and other items. "The bay and harbor of Acapulco must certainly be one of the finest in the world," wrote Albert Osbun, ". . . it winds around like a horseshoe so that it becomes entirely surrounded by high mountain. [sic]" Bancroft noted that "the city that once boasted a busy population of fifteen thousand is now reduced to a lifeless inert town of three thousand. The population is heterogeneous but the business is mostly in the hands of Americans and Europeans. . . ." He also commented on the natives whose "canoes laden with fruit . . . come swarming from various parts of the shore and naked swimmers ready to begin their aquatic gymnastics for a consideration." Osbun, *To California*, 22; Bancroft, *California*, 211.

We hear at this place of two ships that are out at sea without a drop of water. Some of the passengers came off here in a small boat, procured water & went off in search of their ship but could not find her. Several other attempts have been made to find the ship & save them but as yet without success. Three or four beacon fires are lighted on the different hills tonight. Heaven grant they may see them & be enabled to reach this port, for to die of thirst must be horrible. The Captain of our steamer is taking on a larger supply of water in the hope that we may fall in with them tomorrow.[20]

It is said here that four men came from Panama here in a whale boat, alternately sailed & rowed in eighteen days, a distance of thirteen hundred miles. It seems almost incredible & that such a small boat could stand the sea is almost a miracle. The men certainly deserve great credit for their courage & perserveriance [sic].

May 14th. Monday.

We left Acapulco this morning about 9 o'clock. We are again in the open sea not to leave it again until we arrive at Panama, if we meet with no misfortune. I have made Sue a loose slip today. The sun is very warm but there has been a nice breeze all day which makes it very pleasant. Have not seen anything of the ships that are in distress.

About three o'clock this afternoon we came in sight of a sail. The Capt., thinking it might be one of the ships, came along side of her & on hailing her and asking if she wanted anything they cried out "*water.*" They had been eighty days out from Valparaiso & had been on short allowance of water for forty days. The Capt. sent them two large casks of water & some fruit & melons for which they seemed very grateful & sent in return four nice large hams & a box of champaigne over which we had a very merry dinner indeed. I have not seen so much enjoyment & good feeling among the passengers since we left.

Went up on deck after dinner & had a long & very interesting conversation with Mr. Johnson. He had lost a little girl named Mary Lee & as he describes her she must have looked very much like my little Mary Lane that is in Heaven. The way he spoke of his little girl & my

---

[20]Forbes also mentiones the beleagured ship, the Brig *Orion*, eighty-seven days out of Valparaiso, and the consequent "rescue" described below by McDougal. Pomfret, *Gold Rush Voyages*, 238.

mentioning mine made me feel sad & still I wanted to talk more about her. He is a very pleasant gentlemanly man & I like his sentiments on many subjects.

May 15th. Tuesday.

Nothing worth noticing happened today. We entered the gulf of Tehuantepec & had a pretty rough sea. The day excessively warm. Run 228 miles & lost some time where we stopped yesterday.[21]

May 16th. Wednesday.

Today I am 25 years old. A birthday on the Pacific, more than I had ever expected & may I be off of it before I am a week older. Day very warm. Run 240 miles since twelve o'clock yesterday.

May 17th. Thursday.

We are very short of coal & as we have to sail part of the way & there is a pretty fair wind today, the engine is stopped & all sails set & we are going at the rate of four or five miles an hour. [This is] slow traveling for us & long, loud & deep are the curses against the Captain who kept us a day at San Blas where there was plenty of coal & did not get any. He is certainly to be blamed for not supplying the ship better, but Mr. Hobbs, Mr. Garr, Mrs. Bowdin & Mrs. Grimes can grumble enough for the whole ship, so I take it easy as grumbling will not help us along any faster.[22]

I have been sewing all day & the time passes as pleasantly as it is

---

[21]The Gulf of Tehuantepec was considered the hottest part of the trip. "The heat during this part of the voyage was intolerable . . . attended by an enervating langour such as I never before experienced," recalled Taylor. Bancroft expressed similar sentiments using almost identical words. Taylor, *Eldorado*, 34; Bancroft, *California*, 209. Stowell, however, recalled this as a particularly scenic place. "Volcanoes in numbers, smoking at the craters, their sides covered with lava out of Tehuantepec Bay. Mountain upon mountain piled." Stowell, "Bound for the Land of Canaan," 39.

[22]Why Forbes did not take on additional fuel is not clear. Certainly he was concerned. As the ship left San Blas, he noted in his log that "We have consumed 153 tons, 500 bbs of coal." It may be that, contrary to Mrs. McDougal's opinion, no fuel was available. See Pomfret, *Gold Rush Voyages*, 237. Steamships of the middle-nineteenth century were fitted with sails "as a matter of course" and these proved useful in getting into port should the engines or coal supply fail. Kemble, *Panama Route*, 121.

possible under all the circumstances. Went on deck after tea, walked
awhile with Mrs. Bowdin. Capt. Thomas sung us "The Bride" & the
"Rose of Allandale." Afterward Capt. Forbes got out his accordian &
played while he & Capt. Thomas accompanied with their voices. We
are over seven hundred miles from Panama yet. Weather a little cooler
than it has been for several days.

May 18th. Friday.

Last night one of the sailors was heard to say something to one of
his companions that sounded very much like mutiny & was construed
as such by Mr. Johnson who heard it. He reported it to the Captain &
it spread like wildfire through the ship. Very great excitement prevailed, for all expected, before morning, that blood would be shed.
Measures were instantly taken to resist an attack. All the gentlemen
passengers were singled out & put on watch, eight at a time, for four
hours. The muskets & arms were all brought out of the hold & put in
order and every part of the ship was watched as it was supposed to be
the intention of the sailors, twenty-four in number, to kill all the passengers when they were asleep & then rob the ship as there is a large
amount of gold on board. Very little sleeping was done by any one on
board last night & the watch was kept up all night until after breakfast.[23] But it proved a jolly morning, for Mr. Hobbs, who can make
fun out of anything, got some person to prefer charges against several
of those on watch & had a mock court. Mr. Oregon (as he is called)
was drest up with a chapau & sword & made orderly sergeant to bring
up the criminals, who after some funny remarks & questions were
fined six bottles of champaigne which was brought out & drunk in
great glee. Withal we had a very jolly morning, but before dinner they
all got impatient at the slow rate we were going (only from half a mile
to two miles an hour). After some debate a few questions were written down & signed & sent in to the Captain as to how much coal he
had on board & when he was going to use it. He answered very satis-
factorily to them & they were in better spirits by tea time, but the
Capt. seems very much depressed. We have a fine wind, however, and
are going along finely now.

---

[23]McDougal's report of the suspected mutiny conforms closely to that of Captain
Forbes. Pomfret, *Gold Rush Voyages*, 237–38.

I had a severe headache this morning from loss of sleep, but have been sewing all day. The watch is going to be kept up tonight again, as it is thought to be safer. Heaven grant we may all get safely home.

May 19th. Saturday.

Another court martial this morning has served to while away the tedious hours when we are only making, part of the time, from a half mile to a mile & a half an hour. But the men were busy all day fixing the wheels & about 3 o'clock we were off again with the steam. The day has been very warm. The Captain & cook had some fuss this morning & the cook has been in irons all day.[24]

May 20th. Sunday.

A lovely morning. Had two very refreshing showers before 11 o'clock at which time we assembled on deck & with a very calm sea below us & a bright sky above, Capt. Thomas read the Episcopal service to us. It was very solemn & impressive & will long be remembered by me. We are way out at sea, a mere handful of us, as it were, shut out from the world. It seems as though we were nearer our Creator amidst the vast ocean than we are at home & the prayers & hymns seem as if addressed to him in person.[25]

At dinner the Capt. furnished champaigne & it circulated pretty freely. The Capt. gave us a toast, the wish that we might all have a safe & pleasant journey across the Isthmas. Mr. Hobbs & Mr. Warren drank my health & hoped I might find all my friends well at home & soon hear from John. Wrote to John today. This evening Mrs. Ogden, Mrs. Bowdin, Capt. Thomas, Mr. Johnson, & Mr. "Oregon" have been singing some sacred music on deck. It was really very sweet but made me sad for thoughts of home & how long before I get there would intrude. Another very fine shower this evening. I hope my last Sabbath on the Pacific.

May 21st. Monday.

Passed today some beautiful islands, among them the islands of

---

[24]According to Forbes, the cook "threatened to run a sword through me." Ibid., 240.

[25]Many sea voyagers, men as well as women, reported similar sentiments about the impressiveness of church services at sea. See, for example, Bancroft, *California*, 150.

Montroso & Quibo.[26] The latter [is] very pretty, just one mountain standing alone in the ocean & it can be seen with the naked eye forty miles. Have run 218 miles in the last twenty-four hours, most of the time with wood instead of coal. The latter is almost gone & the Capt. is trying to save enough to take us into Panama on tomorrow. Had several hard showers of rain today which makes it very pleasant. Have been trying to pack a little today so that I can tell where my things are. Made Sue a little sack. News again tonight that the coal is out. Mrs. Grimes, Smith, & Bowdin have the fidgets & keep the whole ship in an uproar with their scolding. The Captain is burning up everything that can be spared.

May 22. Tuesday.

Passed early this morning a large school of black fish & porpoises. Rained very hard part of the day & been cloudy & cold all day. Passed four ships, two large ones & two small ones. Have been cutting the ship to pieces for fuel. Burned all the second deck, chicken coops, settees, & everything that could be turned into wood & still very uncertain about reaching the island of Taboga as the wind & tide are very much against us & very scarce of fuel. Have burned several thousand dollars worth of good timber yesterday & today.[27] Mrs. Bowdin, Mrs. Grimes, George, & Mr. St. Clair have been playing whist all the evening. I have been sewing some & trying to pack up my clothes in hopes we would get to Panama tonight.

May 23. Wednesday.

Last night, about ten o'clock, we dropped anchor four miles from the island of Taboga.[28] Directly after the awning caught fire & there

---

[26] These islands, at the Panamanian entrance of the Gulf of Tehuantepec, were occasionally noted by travelers. "The day after leaving Panama," wrote Taylor, "we were in sight of the promontory of Veraguas and the island of Quibo, off Central America. It is a grand coast, with mountain ranges piercing the clouds." Taylor, *Eldorado*, 33.

[27] Forbes estimated the loss at $4,000. Pomfret, *Gold Rush Voyages*, 240.

[28] The island of Taboga, twelve miles from the Panamanian coast, was the coal and supply base for ships landing at Panama. It was also considered a garden spot. Both Bancroft and Taylor comment that Taboga was "to Panama what Capri is to Naples, but more beautiful." Many passengers waiting for California-bound ships preferred to stay on the island rather than in the city where there was a great deal of congestion

was another cause of alarm for the ladies, but it was soon extinguished & no harm done. Early this morning Capt. Forbes took a boat and went to the island for coal to take us in to Panama. He did not return until almost two o'clock when we got up steam & came into port where we arrived about 5 o'clock & anchored very near the Oregon. George went on board of her & found John T. Hughs there. I wrote to John & to Dr. Parker, for George, & sent on board of her. About ten o'clock tonight she put out for San Francisco. The rainy season has commenced here & everything looks very green & beautiful, particularly the islands in the bay. This is my last night on the Pacific.

May 24th. Thursday.

George rose early & went ashore to make arrangements for us to go. Mr. Farand promised to get us rooms. He came back to the ship & about 9 o'clock we bid adieu, forever I hope, to the steamship California. The tide was so low we had to walk a long way on the rough rocks.

When we got to Mr. Farand's we were very tired. Found his house very cool & pleasant & he was very kind to us & tried to get us a house, but not succeeding we came to the American Hotel, where Mrs. Bowdin, Mrs. Grimes & myself got one room between us. As our fare was very good & we had but a few days to stay, we concluded to put up with it. Have had a great deal of company, most all of the gentleman passengers of the California have been to see us. I found Mr. Coombs here & heard that Mrs. Winslow was married. Went out shopping & bought three large shawls.

May 25th. Friday.

Mrs. Grimes, Mrs. Bowdin went out early to walk & stopped at a jewellers & bought four gold chains with a beautiful pearl brooch attached. George made me a present of one. They returned too late for breakfast & we had a very nice private breakfast. Have had company all

---

and fear of cholera and other disease. Bancroft, *California*, 194; Taylor, *Eldorado*, 31. Also see: Dunbar, *The Romance of the Age*, 68–70 and Cleland, *Apron Full of Gold*, 13–14.

day, our room seems the centre of attraction for all the gentlemen. Mrs. Bowdin heard of two English ladies who are here in distress & went with Capt. Thomas & Mr. Larrentree to see them & they took a long walk, did not return until after dark. Mrs. Grimes & Mrs. Hoyer also went out walking & Turner took the children so I was alone. Sewed all day & in the evening packed up all the trunks. Mr. Hobbs & Mr. Warren took supper with us. Mr. Larrentree brought us some tea from his stores & Mrs. Grimes made it. Had a very cozy time.

May 26th. Saturday.

Roused this morning very early thinking the baggage was going off early, but it did not get off until nearly noon. Company all day today again & we are passing our time as pleasantly as could be expected. The two English ladies that were in distress were here this evening with Capt. Thomas. [They] seemed very agreeable & I pity them. Mr. Farand & a Mr. Luck, besides four or five other gentlemen, were here. The men that were to take us over to Cruces has been here this evening and wants to charge for three or four mules that did not go with the baggage at all. As George will not submit to be humbugged, we have determined not to go until Monday. The people are firing thousands of fire crackers tonight. It almost deafens us.[29]

May 27th. Sunday.

At home, but it would puzzle a lawyer to find any Sabbath in Panama. Shops are all open, all kinds of labor going on as usual, & in addition, there is a circus & cockfight. Mr. St. Clair breakfasted with us &

---

[29]Most visitors to Panama described it as an old, decaying city. Cleveland Forbes thought the houses were "miserable and going to decay & the churches are crumbling as the Roman Empire must do before civilization & Religion." Mary Jane Megquier declared that cats, dogs, and rats ran through the holes in the walls of her rooming house. Some thought that American enterprise would improve the city. "The business and general appearance of the city have undergone quite a change since the emigration to California commenced," noted William McCollum. Many of the American visitors commented on the frequent fiestas, cockfights, and other amusements. Pomfret, *Gold Rush Voyages,* 223; Cleland, *Apron Full of Gold,* 11; McCollum, *California As I Saw It,* 101. See also: Bancroft, *California,* 180–81; Taylor, *Eldorado,* 28–29; Osbun, *To California,* 17–18.

Mrs. Bowdin went with him & staid until dinnertime when he & his wife returned with her & dined with us. Mr. Coombs was here several times. Once [he] brought me a large box of guava jelly. Packed up in the evening & got all ready to start in the morning for Cruces.

May 28th. Monday.

Awakened this morning at three o'clock by our muliteer who, a great wonder for New Granada, was punctual to his appointment but the men that were to carry me did not come until nearly six o'clock. At that time we set out, Sue on a native's back & I suspended in a hammock between two men with six others following to rest them. Four of the advance guard was kept ahead of most of the party until we got out about 8 miles where we all stopped on the bank of a stream & ate our breakfast. Quite a picnic & all seemed highly delighted so far, but they changed their minds soon after, for the road were very bad. Mrs. Hoyer was thrown from her horse into the mud. My men gave out & just at dark we met Turner on a fresh mule. I got on the mule astride as it was very dangerous for me to ride over that road any other way. One man headed the mule & one on each side of me while George walked on behind. Thus we went on through the narrow mountain passes in the dark & mud & got to Cruces about eight o'clock. We saw Mr. Haws, the crazy man, about two miles from town with his mule

View of Chagres

fastened & he lying down on the ground. Sue & Frank got in about half an hour after we went to bed. Very thankful that we were safe.[30]

May 29th. Tuesday.

The alcalde charged us 20(?) dollars for our poor miserable room & three naked cots for one night. At eight this morning, Mrs. Bowdin, Grimes, Hoyer, Mr. Hobbs, George & myself started down the river in a whale boat that Mr. Hobbs had engaged for us. We were all nearly used up & Mrs. Hoyer had the sick headache but without meeting with accident, other than getting very wet (for it rained in torrents), & being frightened at two parties of tigers & panthers, we arrived

---

[30]Travelers from Panama to Chagres could go by way of Gongora or Cruces. The Cruces road was considered the best, however, particularly during the rainy season, and one guide admonished, "make them take you to Cruces." Ware, *Emigrant's Guide*, 56. The mule trip, which took one day, varied in cost depending on the demand. It usually cost twelve to fifteen dollars; baggage was transported separately at forty-four dollars for 180 pounds. Kemble, *Panama Route*, 172. Like McDougal, most women rode astride over the rough and muddy road. It was reported that "this custom was begun by Mesdames Whitney and Wheeler" who were friends of McDougal. Another female traveler recalled, "There was great frolicking and laughing with the ladies while fixing away on the mules. . . . I shall never forget *my* feelings when I found myself seated astride my mule, arrayed in boots and pants, with my feet firmly planted in the stirrups, ready for any emergency." *First Steamboat Pioneers*, 86; Bates, *Incidents on Land and Water*, 291.

safely at nine o'clock at Chagres.[31] I went on board of the "Orus," a miserable dirty boat.[32]

May 30th. Wednesday.

Mrs. Bowdin left us this morning to go on board of the English steamer & the Orus got up steam. Went down to Limon Bay & docked, but some of the passengers, being discontented, wanted to go on the English steamer & got around George & would not give him a moment's peace until he agreed to go with them. Gave the Capt. 50 dollars if he would put them on board of the English steamer, which he did, & at six o'clock we were all safe on her but being tired & sick retired soon after tea. About ten o'clock we got underway.

May 31st. Thursday.

Have had a rough sea all day. I have been so seasick as not to be able to be up. The rest of our party are no better off & even Sue is sick enough to go to sleep.

June 1st. Friday.

About twelve o'clock today we came in sight of the old town of Cartagena which is decidedly the prettiest one I have seen since I left the States. There is a fort just at the entrance of the harbour & another built out in the bay entirely surrounded by water. On the top of a high hill is the ruins of a monestary & the town presents an appearance of a magnificent but ruinous city. A great many pearl shells & coral here. Left at 5 o'clock.[33]

---

[31]From Cruces to Chagres the trip was by canoe or "bungo" boat poled by natives. Chagres, on the Atlantic side of the Isthmus, was an unprepossessing town "of about seven hundred native inhabitants, dwelling in some fifty windowless, bamboo huts, with thatched, palm-leaf roofs. . . ." The climate was considered very unhealthy and "passengers were accustomed to stay no longer than sufficed to engage boats. . . ." Bancroft, *California*, 158. See also: McCollum, *California*, 88; Taylor, *Eldorado*, 9; Dunbar, *Romance of the Age*, 56–57.

[32]The *Orus* was a small wooden side-wheeler of 247 tons built in 1842. She operated between New York and the Red Bank until 1848 when she was purchased by Howard and Aspinwall for service on the Chagres River. However, she proved too large for this and was used as a tender and tug for steamers until she was purchased by Vanderbilt for service in Nicaragua. Kemble, *Panama Route*, 241.

[33]Most steamers and sailing vessels on the American Atlantic lines did not call at Cartagena. Thus, Mrs. McDougal's description of the town is somewhat unique in gold rush literature.

June 2d. Saturday.

A rough sea again today & I begin to feel that "a life on the ocean wave" has no charms for me. The individual must be very strong that ever gets me out of the U. States again if I live to reach them this time. But our ship is very clean & nice. She is called the Tay and belongs to the Royal Mail Steamship Company. Everything is in perfect order & the only fault we any of us find is the bad arrangements of the staterooms.[34]

June 3d. Sunday.

Sea sick still today. The officers & sailors of the ship were all drest in full uniform & called up on deck to hear the Episcopal service read. The day has been a very fine one & will probably be our last on board this ship as the Capt. says we will be off the port of Kingston at 12 o'clock tonight.

June 4th. Monday.

Six months ago today I left home & this morning at 6 o'clock we cast anchor in the port of Kingston, Jamaica. At 9 o'clock we left the steamer & got into a hack & rode to Mrs. Ferron's (a Creole lady's) where we had rooms engaged. We found them very pleasant. Mrs. Grimes, Messrs. Warren, Hobbs, Tree, Perry, George & myself are all at this house. We dined at 5 o'clock, then got a hack & drove all around the town. I must say it is the most lovely spot I ever saw. Never did I so much wish to live any place as here. Such beautiful roads & fine country seats & everything in fact to make one happy. Saw Santa Anna's residence. It is rather plain in appearance being a red brick house, large but not fitted up with the same taste that most of the residences are.[35]

---

[34]The Royal Mail Steam Packet Company, chartered in 1842, operated between England, the West Indies, and Panama. Kemble, *Panama Route*, 3.

[35]Santa Anna moved to Kingston in March, 1848, following his exile from Mexico at the end of the war with the United States. He lived there until March or April of 1850 when he and his family moved to Caracas. Another 1849 traveler to California stopped at Kingston and he and his party went to call on the famous general. "Santa Anna was then living in the city of Kingston," Oscar Crosby recalled. "He received us very kindly; chatted familiarly; entertained us with refreshments, wished us a pleasant voyage and success in our new adventures. . . ." Charles A. Barker, ed., *Memoirs of Elisha Oscar Crosby* (San Marino, Huntington Library, 1945), 11.

June 5th. Tuesday.

Rose at 6 & at ½ after got into a hack & rode for an hour or two around the town. The more I see of Kingston, the more am I delighted with it. After breakfast George went down after Mrs. Bowdin. She came & staid all day. Dined at 4 o'clock, then rode until dark. Went about six miles in the country & saw an old fort & where the women were all washing in a stream together. I have never seen the poor class of society so happy anywhere as here. Returned by a garden & got some beautiful flowers.[36]

Mrs. Grimes was quite ill after we returned. Mrs. B. is going to stay all night. Mrs. Farron & her son came in & set a long while with us. She is a very pleasant, intelligent lady.

June 6th. Wednesday.

Rose at 5 o'clock, had a nice cup of coffee, rode out to Mrs. Ferron's place to bathe. Got some beautiful flowers & returned by the barracks on a beautiful open plain, perfectly clean & neat. Mrs. Hoyer came over & spent the day & after dinner we rode out a new road lined on either side with beautiful residences. Rained a little.

June 7th. Thursday.

I did not ride this morning because I felt too unwell. Had a severe headache all day. Mrs. Bowdin & Mrs. Grimes dined with Mrs. Hoyer & the Capt. of the Brig Ida dined with Mr. Warren, George & myself. Rode out after dinner & saw the troops parading in their grounds. They are well trained & although black must be good soldiers. Mr. Hobbs has been very ill today. This is a holiday with the natives in commemoration of a great storm.

June 8th. Friday.

Rode out this morning & returned by the stores & did some shopping. I had the toothache all night & part of today so I did not ride out

---

[36]Several other travelers commented on the city of Kingston and the surrounding countryside. Bancroft was favorably impressed with the city and Crosby recalled the warm hospitality of the people who greeted his party "very kindly." Bancroft, *California*, 153; Barker, *Crosby Memoirs*, 12.

after dinner. Been busy trying to get ready to go on board the ship tomorrow. Went to bed late.

June 9th. Saturday.

Rode down to the wharf this morning & George went on board the steamer with Mrs. Bowdin. We then went shopping, returned home, packed up & after dinner rode down to the wharf & went on board the Brig Ida, bound for Philadelphia. Were very much pleased with the Brig.[37]

June 10th. Sunday.

This morning at daylight bid adieu to Kingston & were on our way home. The Mate fell overboard just as we started, but was saved. Sue is five years old today. I have been very seasick all day, confined to my bed.

June 11th. Monday.

Had a very rough night & I did not sleep. We get along very finely. Past Point Morrow & left Jamaica far behind us. Have had head winds all the time & a squall last night, but still get on fast. Capt. Foulkes gave us some music on the accordian & several of the other gentlemen sang. Did not go on deck today.

June 12th. Tuesday.

A dead calm all day. Did not go a mile an hour scarcely. Three vessels in sight, all becalmed. I felt very unwell all day & did not go on deck until after tea. A little wind in the evening carried a little way toward home.

June 13th. Wednesday.

Some more wind today than yesterday. [We] go about four knots an hour. Have been sewing today to pass away the time. Capt. Foulkes gave us some more music this evening & it sounds very sweetly when

---

[37]Why the McDougal party decided to complete their journey by sailing vessel rather than the faster steamers is not clear. Steamers on the New York-Chagres line regularly called at Kingston which was a regular stop for coal and provisions.

we are so far out to sea & everything so calm & still. Staid on deck until about 8 o'clock, then retired. A little more wind.

June 14th. Thursday.

Still calm and we do not get along at all. The Capt. caught a shark this morning & we all watched it die for the sake of having something to do. Mr. Warren went up into the rigging to win a half dozen of brandy. In the evening there was quite a wind & we go along finely. Quite seasick.

June 15th. Friday.

Very rough sea all night & this morning we are far past Cuba & going at a fine rate until just as we sat down to dinner. The wind died away in an instant & we are in a dangerous place in the midst of islands and shoals. The Capt. caught a dolphin today, the most beautiful fish I ever saw & when it was dying it changed color every instant. Have a very dangerous night tonight in among small islands & the Hogsty reefe. The Capt. is very uneasy & will not go to bed tonight.

June 16th. Saturday.

Still a dead calm though we had breeze enough to bend through that passage. We have another pass for tonight & when that is over we will be clear of the West Indian Islands & in the broad Atlantic. Had a present of a book & a clean towel from Mr. Warren today. Both very scarce articles on board of this boat. What few newspapers we have have been read through & through. Quite a breeze this evening & some rain so we all had to congregate in the cabin.

June 17th. Sunday.

We are past all the islands but have a heavy sea & fair wind & the ship tosses in every direction. Kept my berth all day. Most of the passengers are sea sick & besides it has been raining hard & we had to have the cabin all closed & all had to crowd into it. A very dull Sabbath but cheered by the thought that we will be in the states next Sunday.

After tea I got up, took a nice salt water bath & sat up for an hour or two in the cabin. The Capt. came in & as soon as he saw me cried out "sail ho" as it was my first appearance.

June 18th. Monday.

Fine day & a very fair sound, all hands getting better & the ship seems a cheerful place again. After dinner the Capt. made punch in the cabin & burnt the brandy much to the amusement of the children. After tea Capt. Hoyer drest up in Mrs. Grimes dress & bonnet & went on deck & with his funny speeches made some of them laugh until they cried. Passed a large ship today.

June 19th. Tuesday.

Run 167 miles since yesterday noon. Fair wind & we go along finely. Been sick & sewing all day today. This is bean day at sea.

June 20th. Wednesday.

Had a fine wind all night but the vessel rolled so that it was with the greatest difficulty that we could keep in our berthes. But we are all so anxious to get home that we say let her roll. So she rolls ahead. Spoke today to a whale ship, Chanticler, from Provincetown, three days out & had 20 barrels of oil. She had caught a whale about four hours before we spoke her & all hands were busy cutting it up.

The rest of the diary, of which this is the last page, is so blurred that it cannot be read.

The California Trail, 1850–1859

It was a grand spectacle when we came, for the first time, in view of the vast emigration, slowly winding its way westward over the broad plain. The country was so level we could see the long trains of white-topped wagons for many miles. . . . It seemed to me I had never seen so many human beings before in all my life.

Margaret Frink, *Journal*

It is strange and almost incomprehensible to see so many of all ages and conditions, from the grey haired man of seventy to the smiling infant of a few weeks; and some, even, whose eyes have first beheld the light in this lone wilderness. . . . Can it be the love of gold or adventure, or the ever restless spirit of man which prompts to all this toil and fatigue?

Harriet Ward, *Prairie Schooner Lady*

ONE of the best publicized and most popular routes to the Golden West was the great overland trail along the Platte and across the Rockies to Utah. There the road split. The Oregon Trail turned north toward the Columbia River and the Cascade Range while the California Trail turned south along the Humboldt and across the Sierra Nevada. During the 1830s and 40s, land-hungry Americans began the long trek to the Oregon Territory. In the late 1840s, thousands of Mormons traveled along the Platte route to the new promised land in the Salt Lake Valley. But the Oregon and Utah migrations were only a prelude to the Great Migration of the 1850s. Beginning with the gold rush of 1849, hundreds of thousands of Americans hurried to California to seek their fortunes in the newly acquired territory. Merrill Mattes estimates that between 1850 and 1860 more than 200,000 people followed the Platte route westward.[1] Despite the dangers and difficulties of the trip, it was an exciting journey, and it was undoubtedly one of the best documented mass movements in American history. Men, women, and children recorded their experiences in journals, diaries, and letters or in later years wrote

---

[1]Mattes, *Platte River Road*, 23.

their reminiscences at the request of their children and grandchildren or local historical societies. Mattes lists over 700 known accounts of the trip along the Platte route, and there are undoubtedly others still hidden in trunks and attics or buried in obscure and long-forgotten publications.[2]

Most writers have pictured the California migration as predominately a male enterprise, yet the number of women, particularly after 1850, is surprisingly high. Mattes estimates that in 1849 only two percent of California-bound emigrants were female, but by 1855 the percentage had risen substantially and by 1857, in some trains, women made up fifty percent of the travelers.[3] Like the men, women kept diaries and journals or prepared reminiscences. About ten percent of the accounts listed by Mattes are by women, a healthy percentage in relation to their numbers. Nor were these women the sunbonnet saints of the traditional literature or the exploited drudges of the new feminist studies. Women's lives on the trail, and their impressions of the journey, like those of men, varied with the circumstances of their backgrounds, family, education, and the problems and pleasures encountered on the trip. Their accounts, like those of the men, range from the literate, detailed descriptions of women like Helen Carpenter and Lucy Cooke to the often unimaginative notations of Martha Morgan and Angeline Jackson.[4]

As noted in the introduction, there is no such thing as a "typical" overland journal. Each writer had different experiences, each observed different things along the route, each started with different preconceptions of the trip, and each changed these ideas along the way. However, there is a *pattern* to the journals, whether written by men or

---

[2]Ibid., 26.

[3]Ibid., 62. In June, 1852, Mary Bailey noted that the Fort Kearny register listed 20,000 men and 6,000 women on the trail, and in 1857 William Maxwell's company had eleven men, ten women, and sixteen minors. Mary Bailey, "Journal"; William A. Maxwell, *Crossing the Plains, Days of '57* (San Francisco: Sunset Publishing House, 1915), 1.

[4]Men's journals are as diverse as those of women. The best, like Edwin Bryant's *What I Saw in California* (London: Richard Bently, 1849) have become frontier classics while others, like James Akin, "The Journal of James Akin," Dale Morgan, ed., *University of Oklahoma Bulletin* (1919) are little more than a record of weather and trail conditions.

women. Most describe the preparations for the journey, the sorrows of parting from family and friends, the excitement of the "start." Each records at least some of the "firsts" along the way — the first night of camping out, the first Indians encountered, the first prairie dog town, the first buffalo, the first wolves, the first graves. Then come the comments on the scenic wonders, Courthouse Rock, Chimney Rock, Ash Hollow, Independence Rock, Devil's Gate, City of Rocks. Depending on whether they traveled north or south of the Platte, there are descriptions of Fort Kearny and Fort Laramie and, if the party took the Salt Lake road, discussions of the City of the Saints and its Mormon inhabitants. All writers document something of the pleasures and hardships of the trip; some find it exciting and generally pleasant while others see it as a grueling and difficult journey with few pleasantries or diversions. Merrill Mattes has done a masterful job of analyzing and summarizing the overland journey in his *Great Platte River Road*, and there is no need to repeat what he has done. But there are some aspects of the journey Mattes does not cover, and there are a few which deserve further comment.[5]

Contrary to the picture painted by popular novels and hundreds of Hollywood thrillers, the overland trail was not one long series of hardships, accidents, and Indian raids. In fact, the overwhelming sentiment expressed by most travelers is boredom. The trip took from four to six months of slow travel (ten to twenty miles a day by wagon — less than thirty minutes on today's highways). Most of the way the scenery was flat and dreary and any occurrence which broke the monotonous daily pace furnished occasion for a comment, or even a paragraph, in the emigrants' journals. Descriptions of the flowers, rocks, weather, condition of the road, availability of grass and water are all common. Harriet Ward's daughter, Frankie, remarked after a horse had fallen down, "there is some little excitement in all those accidents which lend diversity to the monotony of our way."[6] Lucy Cooke yearned for "amusement as I ride along," and Frizzell mourned, " . . . it is seldom

---

[5]Mattes, *Platte River Road*, 3–102, includes excellent descriptions of the organization and equipping of companies, traveling conditions, emigrant society and character, and some of the dangers and hardships of the journey.

[6]Harriet S. Ward, *Prairie Schooner Lady: The Journal of Harriet Sherrill Ward*, Ward G. and Florence Dewitt, eds. (Los Angeles: Westernlore Press, 1959), 57.

that you meet with anything for merriment on this journey."[7] Even the most vivacious diarists include many entries such as "Another day of bad roads," "Warm and dusty still," "Nothing of note occurred today." It is true that there was some spectacular scenery from time to time, but one suspects that part of the reputation of places like Courthouse and Jail Rocks, Chimney Rock, Scott's Bluff, and Devil's Gate came less from the beauty of these natural wonders than from the relief from the monotony of the journey and the sameness of the landscape which they offered the weary traveler.

Crossing the plains was a long, difficult, and often dangerous venture, not undertaken lightly. Disease, accidents, loss of supplies, violent weather, and Indian threats, real or imagined, were always cause for concern. Still, for many, the trip was an adventure, the experience of a lifetime. "I do not get tired of the journey, on the contrary, I like it better every day," wrote Angeline Ashley. Others, mostly the young people, called the journey "a lark with riding, fishing, walks."[8] Some found beauty in the many wild flowers and strange new plants and animals of the plains, in the spectacular sunsets and in the clear fresh air which followed the sudden storms. A few even prolonged the journey by making brief side trips to see special places. Mary Bailey thought the Rockies a good substitute for a visit to Switzerland. Harriet Ward, at Devil's Gate, Wyoming, wrote, "No one will regret spending half an hour in admiring this grandeur, even enroute to California," and Francis Sawyer regretted the decision

---

[7]Lucy Cooke, *Crossing the Plains in 1852* (Modesto, California, n.p., 1923), 66; Lodisa Frizzell, *Across the Plains to California in 1852* (New York: New York Public Library, 1915), 18. Most of the male journalists recount similar instances of tedium and boredom. See, for example, David Potter, ed., *Trail to California: The Overland Journal of Vincent Geiger and Wakeman Bryarly* (New Haven: Yale University Press, 1945), 102; Gilbert L. Coles, *In the Early Days Along the Overland Trail in Nebraska Territory in 1852* (Kansas City: Franklin Hudson Publishing Company, 1905), 21; William Clark, "A Trip Across the Plains in 1857," *Iowa Journal of History and Politics* 22 (April 1922): 172.

[8]Angeline Jackson Ashley, "Crossing the Plains in 1852," typescript, Huntington Library; Sarah R. Herndon, *Days on the Road: Crossing the Plains in 1865* (New York: Burr Printing House, 1902), 41. Most other women also found at least portions of the trip pleasurable. For typical comments see Mary E. Ackley, *Crossing the Plains and Early Days in California* (San Francisco: privately printed, 1928), 20; Ward, *Prairie Schooner Lady*, 132; Bailey, "Journal."

not to go by way of Salt Lake City, for, "We are all anxious to see the Mormon City."[9]

Whether pleasurable or miserable, the trip was not a lonely one. With thousands of people on the trail, trains traveled close together and there was a good deal of visiting back and forth. Some even complained that there were too many people! At a camping place on Deer Creek, Bailey fumed, "Too many here already & have been." Margaret Frink was sure "none of the population had been left behind."[10]

Nor, after 1849, was there much danger of getting lost. By 1850 the trail was well marked and guidebooks or instructions from friends and relatives who had made the trip directed the travelers to wood, grass, water, and "cut-offs." Messages about the condition of the road, camp trails, and other items of interest were posted in prominent places or written on the many bones of dead animals that lined the trail. Guides, who had made the trip before, were helpful — not in finding the trail but in their experience in locating good grass and water and in the advice they could furnish to ease the rigors of the crossing.

Contrary to the traditional picture, there were relatively few Indian attacks. There were occasional, and well publicized, "massacres," but usually only the lone wagon or a small party, like that described by Helen Carpenter, had trouble. Even then it was more likely the type of harassment Carpenter records than the full-scale attack with flaming arrows, whooping Indians, and terrified emigrants common to the silver screen. The greatest danger from Indians was in their begging, petty thievery, and running off of stock. Thus emigrants were concerned about the Indians and kept a careful guard over horses and cattle, but there was also a good deal of friendly contact. Indians visited the trains, begged food, and occasionally tried to swap ponies for some of the more attractive girls. Travelers visited the Indian camps, traded with the inhabitants, and described their dress, dances, and customs. Prior to 1855, the Sioux, the so-called scourge of the plains, were

---

[9]Ward, *Prairie Schooner Lady*, 91; Francis H. Sawyer, "Overland to California, Notes from a Journal . . . May 9 to August 17, 1852," typescript, Newberry Library, 10.

[10]Bailey, "Journal"; Margaret A. Frink, *A Journal . . . of a Party of California Gold Seekers* (Oakland: n.p., 1897), 35.

peaceful and were generally admired as "real" Indians, "tall, strongly made, firm features, light copper color, cleanly in appearance, quite well dressed."[11] Generally the Pawnee, Potawatomi,and other peoples along the eastern end of the trail were dismissed as "dirty and indolent," but they caused little trouble and their visits to the camps often furnished amusement to the emigrants. The "Diggers" of the Great Basin, on the other hand, were regarded as the most troublesome and were universally feared and loathed.[12]

Indians were so little a threat at most times that Harriet Ward could report to her son, "You would be surprised to see me writing so quietly in the wagon alone . . . with a great, wild looking Indian leaning on his elbow on the wagon beside me, but I have not a single fear except that they may frighten the horses."[13] Lavinia Porter and her husband became disgusted with the group of "outlaws" with whom they traveled and struck out alone. "It truly seemed to us in our long journey traveling alone that the Indians watched over us. . . . In our ignorant fearlessness we came through the many hostile tribes un-molested and unhurt."[14]

In many emigrant diaries Mormons and Missourians come in for more criticism than the Indians. "Many of the Mormons were to be dreaded more than the Indians," recalled Allene Dunham.[15] Most of the journalists were suspicious of Brigham Young's followers and

---

[11]Frizzell, *Across the Plains*, 18. Other descriptions of the Sioux include Lyman S. Tyler, *The Montana Gold Rush Diary of Kate Dunlap* (Denver: Old West Publishing Company, 1969), B-20; Lavinia Porter, *By Ox Team to California: A Narrative Crossing the Plains in 1860* (Oakland: Oakland Enquirer Office, 1910), 34; Maxwell, *Crossing the Plains*, 13–14; Potter, *Trail to California*, 97; Dale Morgan, ed., *The Overland Diary of James A. Pritchard from Kentucky to California in 1849* (Denver: Old West Publishing Company, 1945), 73.

[12]Good descriptions of the Missouri and Kansas Indians include Frizzell, *Across the Plains*, 10, 13; Sawyer, "Overland to California," 11; Lydia M. Waters, "Account of a Trip Across the Plains in 1855," *Quarterly of the Society of California Pioneers* 6 (March 1929): 61–62; Morgan, *Pritchard Diary*, 37–38; Cole, *In the Early Days*, 54. On the "Diggers" see: Cooke, *Crossing the Plains*, 65; Sawyer, "Overland to California," 13; Potter, *Trail to California*, 175 and note 21 for typical comments.

[13]Ward, *Prairie Schooner Lady*, 77.

[14]Porter, *By Ox Team*, 70.

[15]E. Allene Taylor Dunham, *Across the Plains in a Covered Wagon* (n.p., n.d.), 11.

some, like the Carpenter party, deliberately avoided Salt Lake City. Mormons were frequently suspected of stealing horses, joining the Indians in harassing emigrant trains, and kidnapping unsuspecting women and children. Anti-Mormon feeling reached its peak in the aftermath of the Mountain Meadows Massacre and the subsequent Utah expedition, but some prejudice against Mormons is apparent in the diaries for any given year. No tale was too far fetched, no reported crime too heinous to be believed and repeated. Men and women were equally prejudiced in regard to Mormons just as they were about equally cautiously curious about Indians.[16]

"Missourians," or at least people of a certain cultural background typified by the term Missourian or "Piker," had almost as bad a reputation as the Mormons. They were characterized by the journalists as generally being "of a 'backwoods' class," profane, hard drinking, rude, and occasionally dangerous. Lavinia Porter found them "perfectly lawless, fighting and quarreling among themselves," and many travelers had one or more complaints to lodge against these fellow emigrants.[17]

With so many people on the trail, there were bound to be a certain number of "bad characters." Tempers ran short after long days of difficult travel, and quarrels, fights, and other disagreements were common. Fortunately it was easy to leave one train and find another with more desirable companions. Many emigrants traveled in three or four different trains before reaching their goal. Some women felt there was more danger from their own men's inexperience and foolhardiness than from the Indians. Maria Shrode, traveling along the southern route, recorded in disgust, ". . . we killed a beef. The boys shot at it about 50 times before they got it. I think the Indians would be in great danger if they should attack us."[18] A few of the men even admitted to

[16]Compare, for example, Cooke, *Crossing the Plains*, 37–60; Virginia Ivins, *Pen Pictures of Early Western Days* (n.p., 1908), 17–19; Cornelius Conway, *The Utah Expedition Containing a General Account of the Mormon Campaign* (Cincinnati: Safety Fund Reporter Office, 1858); and William Chandless, *A Visit to Salt Lake . . . and a Residence in the Mormon Settlements at Utah* (London: Smith Elder and Company, 1857), 137–288.

[17]Porter, *By Ox Team*, 78; Maxwell, *Crossing the Plains*, 76–77.

[18]Mrs. Maria Shrode, "Journal," ms., Huntington Library. Also see Maxwell, *Crossing the Plains*, 16, 127, for a man's comments on their lack of expertise with firearms.

their "lack of experience" with firearms, and accidental shootings were common.

Indeed mishaps with firearms and other accidents took a far heavier toll than the Indians. Children, and occasionally adults, fell from wagons and were seriously injured and sometimes killed beneath the heavy wheels. Wagons turned over, animals stampeded, equipment failed, and injury usually resulted. Mattes notes that the most common accidents, "in descending order of magnitude," were shootings, drownings, wagon mishaps, and "injuries resulting from handling domestic animals."[19]

The most frequent cause of death on the trail was disease. Cholera, smallpox, intestinal disorders, and scurvy were common. Yet despite the heavy death toll, carefully recorded by the diarists, both male and female, many considered the trip healthful. Fifty-year-old Harriet Ward was delighted with her improving health. "I shall soon think I can bear the winds and rains as well as the youngest of our party."[20] Some doctors recommended the overland trip as a cure for "consumption," and some people actually embarked on the trip for the sole purpose of improving their health.[21] One woman, at least, believed that the presence of women and children added to the health of the companies. ". . . they exerted a good influence, as the men did not take such risks, were more alert about the teams and seldom had accidents, more attention was paid to cleanliness and sanitation and . . . the meals were more regular and better cooked thus preventing much sickness. . . ."[22]

Despite the bad reputation of the "Missourians" and occasional reports of hard-up families without adequate food and clothing, among the journalists, at least, the California trip was basically a middle class migration. Although less expensive for families than the sea routes,

---

[19]Mattes, *Platte River Road*, 90. John Unruh in *The Plains Across: the Overland Immigrants and the Trans-Mississippi West* (Urbana: University of Illinois, 1979) estimates that no more than four percent of immigrant deaths were attributable to Indians, p. 408.

[20]Ward, *Prairie Schooner Lady*, 33. Also see her comments on her improving health on page 91.

[21] Catherine Haun, "A Woman's Trip Across the Plains in 1849," ms., Huntington Library, 1; Sawyer, "Overland to California," 1.

[22]Haun, "A Woman's Trip," 18.

equipment and supplies for an overland trek were not cheap. Most of the guides estimated that animals, wagons, tools, and provisions cost between six and seven hundred dollars for four people, and many families took more than one wagon and more than four people.[23] Thus initial outfitting was more than the very poor could afford and there were additional expenses en route. Tolls for bridges and ferries, wagon repairs, additional clothing and food, new animals to replace lost or sick stock had to be taken into account. Some young men traveled with minimum provisions and others hired themselves out for passage. There are reports of poor people in desperate circumstances, but most of the emigrants were well equipped, at least at the start of the journey, and had sufficient funds to see them through.

There are many misconceptions about women's lives on the overland trail. Women's roles, at least as they are documented by the fairly well educated who recorded their experiences, were varied and often equal to those of men. There were certain sex-related chores. Men usually tended to the stock and wagons, selected roads and camp grounds, provided game, and were responsible for the safety of the train. Women's duties included cooking, washing, caring for the children, and general responsibility for health and sanitation. But on the trail, camp duties were often shared and roles were occasionally reversed. "Everyone lent a helping hand," recalled Catherine Haun, and a helping hand was "very indefinite and might mean anything from building campfires and washing dishes to fighting Indians, holding back a loaded wagon on a down grade or lifting over boulders when climbing a mountain."[24] Men frequently helped with the "household" chores. "Men and women and children all went to washing," wrote Shrode during a stop on the Pecos River, and Esther Hanna's husband regularly assisted her with the family wash.[25] Carpenter records the story of an old man and his sons who did the

[23]Joseph Ware, *The Emigrant's Guide to California*, reprint ed. (Los Angeles: 1946), 7, and O. B. Gunn, *New Map and Handbook of Kansas and the Gold Mines* (Pittsburgh: W. A. Haven, 1859), 44, both give similar estimates of the cost of overland travel. Other guide books list supplies and equipment but rarely give cost estimates.

[24]Haun, "A Woman's Trip," 3.

[25]Shrode, "Journal,"; Esther B. Hanna, "Diary of Overland Journey From Pittsburg to Oregon . . . in 1852," typescript, Huntington Library, 8.

cooking so as to relieve "Ma." Some companies, particularly those with a number of hired hands, usually had a paid cook. Some of the women did not know how to cook. Haun recorded that she was a southern lady and "had never made even my first cup of coffee." Lavinia Porter had a similar problem.[26] Lucy Cooke, on the other hand, had a hired cook but she and her mother-in-law preferred to prepare the meals themselves.[27] Women's work, then, was not necessarily any more difficult, and perhaps less so, than it was at home.[28]

Some women learned new skills on the trail and assisted with "men's" work. Although some may have resented it, others were obviously proud of their newly acquired talents. Lydia Waters drove the loose stock and boasted of her recently acquired ability to drive the heavy wagon.[29] Carpenter's aunt and cousin also assisted with the wagon and loose stock but from choice rather than necessity. Other women recorded occasional incidents in which they temporarily took over male duties. In one party, the women stood guard while the men enjoyed a Fourth of July feast. Lavinia Porter absolutely refused to stay at a pre-selected campground and insisted on finding a better and cleaner spot, which she promptly did. In the Sierras, recalled Lucy Cooke, the women and children went ahead of the wagons to "scout" the trail and point out the best route around the rocks and boulders.[30] In most of these cases, the women seem to have enjoyed their work; it gave them something to do besides sit in a wagon and watch the monotonous scenery.

The diaries which follow reflect most aspects of life on the overland trail. Yet the two women's experiences offer some interesting contrasts. Little is known of Mary Bailey's background, but from her

---

[26]Haun, "A Woman's Trip," 7; Porter, By Ox Team, 9. Virginia Ivins also wrote that she was not able to cook well and had to have another woman show her how to make bread. Ivins, Pen Pictures, 68–69.

[27]Cooke, Crossing the Plains, 15.

[28]This view is contrary to that presented by John M. Faragher in Women and Men on the Overland Trail (New Haven: Yale University Press, 1979), 66–87. However it is similar to Riley's findings as reported in The Frontierswoman: Iowa as a Case Study (University of Iowa: in press).

[29]Waters, "Account of a Trip," 66, 77.

[30]Dunham, Across the Plains, 10; Porter, By Ox Team, 82; Cooke, Crossing the Plains, 70.

carefully penned diary and her frequent literary allusions, it is clear she was a well-educated and a rather sophisticated woman. She was born in Vermont in 1830. In 1846, she married Dr. Frederick E. Bailey, ten years her senior, and moved to Sylvania, Ohio, where her daughter, Harriet, was born and died.[31] The Baileys were a fairly well-to-do couple. Their Ohio household included a servant girl, Lydia Harwood, and they had funds to "vacation" for three weeks in Saint Louis before starting west. They also made frequent purchases of equipment and supplies along the way and finally hired their passage with a large train near the end of the trip. The Baileys hoped to improve their fortunes in California, but Mary was not at all sure that the decision to move west was a wise one and she was not optimistic about the final result. But, despite her misgivings and poor health, she was a born tourist, enjoyed the scenery, and made many friends.

In contrast, Helen Carpenter was a young bride of nineteen traveling with her husband and a large family including an uncle, aunt, and several cousins in addition to her father, mother, brother, and two sisters. Carpenter's father, Thomas McCowen, was a not-too-successful homeopathic physician, and the family moved frequently, from Ohio to Indiana and finally to Kansas. Despite their itinerant life, Helen received a good education at a Quaker high school near Bloomington, Indiana, and taught at least one term of school in Kansas.[32] The Carpenters were not as prosperous as the Baileys, but they had sufficient provisions for the trip and funds for tolls and occasional purchases. Helen was happy to leave Kansas and looked forward to the trip. Her diary reflects a joie de vivre and an optimism which Bailey's lacks.

The two journals describe different sections of the California Trail. The Baileys traveled across the mid-west and began their journey at

---

[31] Federal Census, Lucas County, Ohio, 1850. Copy with the Bailey journal, Huntington Library.

[32] Emily McCowen Horton, *Our Family: With a Glimpse of Their Pioneer Life* (n.p., 1922), 1–13. The McCowens were a rather remarkable family. Of the five children, three kept diaries or published reminiscences of the overland trip. Parts of George's 1854 diary are appended to Helen's 1857 journal and Emily published her recollections in 1922. The other two children were too young to have clear memories of the journey.

Saint Joseph, one of the traditional "jumping-off" points. They traveled along the Platte to South Pass and then turned south to Salt Lake City and rejoined the main California Road near City of Rocks. After moving down the Humboldt, the Baileys took the Carson Road over Emigrant Gap to Amador County, California. The Carpenters' starting point was Kansas, and they joined the emigrant road in the valley of the Little Blue. From Fort Kearny to South Pass, their route parallels the Baileys, but the Carpenters' train bypassed Salt Lake City and went via the main California Road north to the Raft River and then south to the Humboldt Sink. There they opted for the Truckee River route and entered California over the Henness Pass to Sierra County.

Although many aspects of the two women's journeys are the same, there were differences in trail conditions. In 1852, when Bailey went west, the Plains tribes, particularly the Sioux, were peaceful; and the Mormons, although regarded with suspicion, were generally hospitable to emigrants. By 1857 these conditions had changed. The Gratten massacre near Fort Laramie inaugurated two decades of intermittent warfare with the Plains tribes, and although the Sioux had been temporarily subdued by the Harney campaign of 1855, the Cheyenne were troublesome. The growing hostility between the United States government and the Mormons just prior to the Mountain Meadows affair in the fall of 1857 and Mrs. Carpenter's Quaker schooling may account, in part, for her strong anti-Mormon bias in contrast to Bailey's more tolerant attitude. In 1852 the Indians along the Humboldt were troublesome, but by 1857 they had acquired guns and horses. As recorded in Mrs. Carpenter's diary, 1857 was one of the worst years for hostilities along that section of the route.

Although both Mrs. Bailey and Mrs. Carpenter had chores such as washing and cooking, neither could be described as "drudges." Their husbands were considerate and helpful and obviously much of the work was shared. Both women had time to record both the pleasures and difficulties of the journey and to comment on the scenery, gather wild flowers, and visit from wagon to wagon. In both parties there were family disagreements. Mary Bailey did not get along with her brother-in-law, and the Carpenters and McCowens were often disgusted with Uncle Sam McWhinney and his brood. Once they arrived in California the two women's stories diverge. The Baileys had no family to welcome them. Frederick lost his instruments and clothing in a fire in Sacramento, Mary became seriously ill and longed to return home. Finally they settled near their trail friends, the McGrews, at Prairie City where a daughter, Emma McGrew Bailey, was born. The doctor had difficulty in successfully establishing himself. Finally, after making several changes, they went to Santa Cruz in 1858 where they finally established a permanent residence.[33] The Carpenters met their brother and cousins at Grass Valley where they purchased a small ranch. Here Helen's daughter, Mary, was born in the spring of 1858. Shortly thereafter the Carpenters and Helen's brother, George, went to join the rest of the family in Mendocino County. The trip from Grass Valley to Potter Valley was more difficult than their trip across the Plains. They were forced to abandon their wagons, many of their supplies were ruined by continual rain and snow, and they feared they might not survive the journey. "In all the long journey across the Plains," Helen recalled, "nothing had happened to compare to this." Helen taught school in Potter Valley until the birth of her twins, Grace and Grant, in 1865. Shortly thereafter the family moved to Ukiah where Reel had newspaper and photography interests. Helen busied herself with her family and wrote several articles for *Overland Monthly* and *Cosmopolitan* and "a number of books of ceremonies" for lodges in the United States, Canada, and Australia. Perhaps she planned to publish a portion of her overland journal because she did type the manuscript and fill in missing portions from her brother's diary. However, her journal remained unpublished at the time of her death in 1917.[34]

---

[33]Susan B. Hicks, Fort Worth, Texas, typescript note filed with the Bailey Mss, Huntington Library. Dr. Bailey died in 1888; Mary in 1899.

[34]The Carpenter's daughter, Grace Hudson, was a well-known artist and many of the details of the Carpenters' later life can be found in a biography by Searles R. Boynton, *The Painter Lady: Grace Carpenter Hudson* (Eureka: Interface California Corp., 1978). Helen's articles can be found in *Cosmopolitan*, October 1900 and *Overland Monthly*, April 1893 and August 1899.

H. A. Preston, "Introduction" in the Newberry Library copy of the Helen Carpenter diary. This copy also includes a note that "This diary was kept by Helen M. Carpenter in 1857 and copied on the typewritter by the same in 1911."

Wed 29th Have got over the first mountain. We are not killed any of us. We now encamped on the margin of the mountain Lake — The scenery today has been truly sublime. Mountains rising to the skies, covered with snow the fine old pines — in every direction a great variety of evergreens: It seems quite like snow. cold & chilly how I wish we had a home to live in now — If it were not for hope the heart would break — Thursday 30th Rising the second summit — not so difficult as the first — Are now in the region of perpetual snow very cold & chilly camped in a valley — Friday Oct 1st Had a very rough road descending most of the way camped in a deep ravine, awoke in the morning the ground covered with snow — Sat 2nd Cold have not traveled but 5 miles. get some grass here — the animals have got weak. quite so — We some expect to go to Stockton — I feel rather disappointed in not going the Hangtown road: Sunday 3rd Had considerable of a Snow storm yesterday. but it has disappeared this morning & is very pleasant — Are going towards Stockton — Monday 4th The Dr has gone to meet his Brother & has not returned yet are getting on very well but slowly the oxen are very weak driving such large wagons over the rough Mountains Tuesday 5th 8 miles of Volcano a mining town Mr Patterson went out yesterday to meet untill we came up — They went into Town after flour & Potatoes which they brought out today — The climate is very much improved it is very pleasant now rained a very little last night Tuesday 5th in the evening Mr Withington arrived we had indeed a happy meeting — I felt to rejoice with Mrs W — Wed 6th We arrived in the first Mining town in Cal took dinner there had a variety of vegetables. The

Page from the diary of Mary Stuart Bailey (see page 87)

A Journal of Mary Stuart Bailey

Wife of Dr. Fred Bailey
from Ohio to California, April–October 1852

Wednesday, April 13, 1852

Left our hitherto happy home in Sylvania amid the tears and parting kisses of dear friends, many of whom were endeared to me by their kindness shown to me when I was a stranger in a strange land, when sickness and death visited our small family & removed our darling, our only child in a moment, as it were.[1] Such kindness I can never forget. The sympathy I received from all was truly consoling & while life lasts will never be forgotten.

We took the cars to Chicago. Owing to my illness, it was rather a hard day's ride. We passed through some beautiful & highly cultivated country. Laport is a fine place.[2] We were obliged to leave the cars & take the stage for 12 miles to Michigan City, quite a large city, but low & wet.[3] Some very romantic looking hills in the background. A good many evergreens looked very natural to me. When we got on the cars, my satchel was lost containing all my medicines & writing box. We put up at the City Garden House. It was so late that we could not get any tea, and all I had taken through the day was coffee. Rested very well.

Early in the morning to the canal boat for Peru. A good many passengers bound for California. At night we found there was a break

---

[1]Mrs. Bailey is referring to the death of her daughter, Harriet, who died December 27, 1850, shortly before her first birthday. Cemetery Records, Lucas County, Sylvania, Ohio. Copy in the Huntington Library, San Marino, California.

[2]Laport, Indiana, was founded in 1830 on the old Michigan Road between Lake Michigan and the Ohio River. It was a major commercial center for central and southern Indiana. Federal Writers' Program, *Indiana: A Guide to the Hoosier State* (New York: Oxford, 1941), 443.

[3]Michigan City, on Lake Michigan, was founded in 1832 at the terminus of the old Michigan Road. In the 1840s and 50s, it was a larger lake port than Chicago. Ibid., 294.

in the canal, and about 12:00 at night we had to leave the boat & take another, and inferior one, but succeeded in getting beds. Although they were not very nice, we were glad of them.[4]

Friday, 15th.

We passed the Rock River in an aqueduct after which we passed some bold projecting rocks. Although the face of the country seemed level & monotonous, we are now passing the Starved Rock, the seat of the Black Hawk War, 150 feet high. Tradition says that 300 Indians starved to death there.[5] Rocks & evergreens look strange to the eyes of the Wolverine & Buckeye. Expect to take the steamer soon.

Arrived at LaSalle about noon, in the rain. [It is] a new town built on a high high hill.[6] Stopped at a good house for dinner & tea, [then] took the Beaver for St. Louis. They said they would be in by Saturday night. Pleasant company, seems quite like home.

Saturday, 16th.

Passed Peoria, the prettiest place I have ever seen in the West.[7] It is

---

[4]The Illinois and Michigan Canal, on which the Baileys traveled, was begun in 1836, and was completed in 1848. The canal originated on the south bank of the Chicago River and followed the Des Plaines and Illinois rivers to Peru where the canal joined the Illinois River. By 1851, travel was so heavy that it already showed signs of outgrowing the canal, and it was necessary to order boats restricted to those with a draught not over four and a half feet. Leslie Swanson, *Canals of Mid America* (Moline, Illinois: n.p., 1964), 36. See also: J. W. Putnam, *The Illinois and Michigan Canal, A Study in Economic History* (Chicago: University of Chicago Press, 1918). Arthur Cunynghame had a less pleasant trip down the canal. See Arthur Cunynghame, "Travel on the Illinois and Michigan Canal" in Paul M. Angle, ed., *Prairie State, Impressions of Illinois, 1673-1967, By Traders and Other Observers* (Chicago: University of Chicago Press, 1968), 203-204.

[5]Starved Rock is on the old Illinois and Michigan Canal near Ottawa, Illinois. According to legend, the Rock derives its name from a band of Illinois Indians who met a tragic death here. It was not the site of a major battle during the Black Hawk War, as Bailey infers. Federal Writers' Project, *Illinois: A Descriptive and Historical Guide* (Chicago: A. C. McClurg and Company, 1939), 31, 637-38.

[6]LaSalle, Illinois, founded in 1827, was named for the famous French explorer. When the Illinois and Michigan Canal opened in 1848, it "pumped money and prosperity into LaSalle for a decade" and made it a large and important community. Ibid., 442-43.

[7]Peoria was built on one of the earliest French-occupied sites in Illinois and several trading posts occupied the site. In 1813, the United States government built Fort Clark there, and in 1825 the settlement became the county seat of Peoria County and

situated on a high bluff on the west side of the river. The river generally looks very broad, overflowing its streams.

Sunday, 17th.

Came into the Mississippi at Alton which is a very fine place.[8] Saw the first green grass & leaves here showing that we were in another climate. Arrived at St. Louis about 12 o'clock and stopped at the American. Our friend Allen called on me & invited us to his house. Mrs. Allen & her mother called also, so we were cordially welcomed to the city. We remained until morning & then left. Mrs. Wordsworth's people from Monroe left for St. Jo this evening.

Monday, 18th.

Went to Mr. Allen's to stop a few days & stopped 3 weeks. Spent our time traveling about the City, visiting gardens, riding the omnibus, making calls, shopping & also attended a course of lectures at Wyman's Hall from Dr. Lord on the Refformation [sic] with which I was very much interested. Attended church 2 Sabaths. The singing was very fine indeed. Good preaching. It was a feast to hear it.

Monday, 10th of May.

Bade farewell to the busy City of St. Louis & our dear friends there. Started for St. Joseph on the Steamer Alton. Passed a fleet of steamboats on dock. No vessels to be seen but steamboats. Passed the shot tower, the mound one of the largest I ever saw. It is flat on top and large enough to set a good sized house upon, 20 feet high perhaps. We could not see Hyde Park (a handsome place we had visited at the north of the city) on account of the darkness.[9]

---

the governmental center for most of northern Illinois. Due to the available water transportation, by 1850 the population exceeded 2,000, and the town had a number of factories for the manufacture of farm implements. Ibid., 257-61.

[8]Like Peoria, Alton, "just above the confluence of the Mississippi and Missouri and just below that of the Illinois and Mississippi" was the site of a French and Indian trading post. The first white settlers arrived in the area in 1783, and by the early nineteenth century, Alton rivaled St. Louis as a river port. Ibid., 148-51. For another, and more detailed, description of the trip from Peoria to Alton see Eliza R. Steele, "By Packet from Peoria to Alton, and the Towns Along the Way," in Angle, *Prairie State*, 185-94.

[9]St. Louis, in 1852, was a bustling and exciting city. The population had reached nearly 75,000, and the city was known for its lovely parks and gardens and imposing

Tuesday, 11th.

Good company. We enjoy ourselves well. One very agreeable family from Kentucky, McGrew. Father, Mother (a lady), daughter, one son & brother-in-law. Well educated. Oldest sister, Emma. Bound for Sacramento, California.

Wednesday, 12th.

Got acquainted with 5 fine young gents from Skenectecy, New York, Oregon bound & full of life & spirits, some of whom the storms of adversity have never wounded their hearts. Found them good company.

Thursday, 13th.

Going up the Missouri last night, we struck a sandbar. It gave some of the passengers quite a shock. I was asleep & did not know it. We also struck a snag which is very dangerous. It was said that one man jumped overboard. Our life is rather monotonous — sleeping, eating & chatting & once in a while we get a run on shore.

Friday, 14th.

Did not progress much on account of sandbars. We are aground several times. The Missouri is a bad river to navigate. We stopped at Lexington which is a fine little town situated on a high hill.[10] We saw

---

public buildings. Hyde Park, which Bailey mentions, was a four-block area enclosed "with a substantial stone and iron fence." A favorite picnic and party spot, it was sometimes called "the people's garden of North St. Louis." The shot tower, also mentioned by Bailey, was begun in 1844 and reached an elevation of 170 feet before it collapsed destroying several buildings. It was rebuilt on a new site in 1847 on a "solid stone of immense size," evidently the mound to which Bailey refers. It was used for the manufacture of lead shot. Nathan Parker, *Stranger's Guide to St. Louis* (St. Louis: G. B. Wintle, 1867), 12–13; J. A. Dacus and James W. Buel, *A Tour of St. Louis or the Inside Life of a Great City* (St. Louis: Western Publishing Company, 1878), 336–38.

[10]Lexington, Missouri, was a thriving river port and a prosperous commercial center for the overland trade. In the 1850s, it had a busy but genteel air. Large profits from hemp, cattle, and tobacco kept the town prosperous, and it was known for its attractive homes and educational institutions. James A. Pritchard, who visited Lexington in 1849, wrote that it was a "handsome town" and "the lands around this place cannot be surpassed either in beauty or fertility." Federal Writers' Program, *Missouri: A Guide to the "Show Me" State* (New York: Duell, Sloan and Pearce, 1941), 373; Morgan, *Pritchard Diary*, 53.

some most beautiful flower gardens. On the shore was the wreck of the illfated Saluda. 200 lives were lost in a moment as it were. Nothing but the bare hull remained. Heavy articles were thrown up nearly half a mile from shore. They said eyes, fingers & toes of the poor unfortunate sufferers were found on the shore & quite a distance.[11]

Saturday, 15th, 1852

Did not get on much last night on account of the fog. Stopped at Wayne City, had a fine run on the hill. Some very romantic spots resembling more Walter Scot's descriptions of Ben Vanait in his Lady of the Lake. We are now stopping at Kansas' Independence Landing.[12] The first California tents saluted our view. Here we saw Santa Fe traders with their heavy wagons, long whips, dirty clothes. Here we saw any quantities of buffalo robes & everything for immigrants. We met with a Mr. Caso, formerly from Lyman, N.H. He is traveling agent for the Fairbankses & a very interesting, intelligent man. Had a good visit with him.

Sunday, 16th.

Did not arrive at St. Joseph as we expected. Passed Weston, a

---

[11]The Saluda disaster is well documented. On April 9, 1852, while the captain was trying to get up steam against a strong current, the boilers exploded, "blew the boat into splinters, and scattered them far and wide." Most of the crew and over 100 of the passengers were killed and some bodies were never found. See Hiram M. Chittenden, *History of Early Steamboat Navigation on the Missouri River*, 2 vols. (New York: Francis P. Harper, 1903), 1: 124. Other travelers along the Missouri in the spring of 1852 also mentioned the ill-fated side-wheeler. See, for example, Frizzell, *Across the Plains*, 8, and Louise Berry, ed., "Overland to the Gold Fields of California in 1852: The Journal of John Hawkins Clark," *Kansas Historical Quarterly* 11 (August 1942): 281.

[12]Independence Landing, Kansas, was one of the earliest "jumping off spots" on the overland trail. Although frequented by Santa Fe traders and Oregon-bound emigrants during the 1840s, by late 1849 the town had become "a bedlam in the center of a vast ring of encampments" as gold seekers hurried to start for California. Independence itself was several miles from the river and was served by various landings including "Old Independence Landing and a new excrescence of shacks by the gloried name of Wayne City." Mattes, *Platte River Road*, 107. The bustle and excitement of these starting points is well described in Walker D. Wyman, "The Outfitting Posts," in John W. Caughey, ed., *Rushing for Gold* (Berkeley: University of California Press, 1949), 14–23.

flourishing place, early in the morning.[13] Mr. Stone of Monroe was buried here several years ago. Arrived at St. Joseph at evening. We did not like to leave the boat on Sunday, but the Captain did not let us stay on board. We went to the City Hotel, were indifferently accomodated. Mr. Bailey was encamped 3 miles out of town.[14]

Monday, 17th.

Mr. Bailey came for us. We bade goodby to our acquaintances. We had become quite attached on the boat. Went into the woods & slept out on the ground for the first time. It seemed as though it would kill us to sleep outdoors without anything but a canvas to protect us from the dews of Heaven, but it did not make any of us sick.

Tuesday, 18th.

Were up early to make a tent. It seemed hard to sit on the ground to sew. We would take a trunk or sack for a chair. Was very tired that night.

Wednesday, 19th.

Started on our long journey today. We are too heavily loaded I know.

Thursday, 20th.

The bustle of starting is over. We are now riding over a pleasant & sparsely settled country. Do not intend to start across the river. Left camp early. Passed New York. Now indeed surrounded by a beautiful

---

[13]Weston, Missouri, was a flourishing river town with a population of about 5,000 in 1850. It, too, was one of the starting places for the overland trail. For a description of Weston in the 1850s, see Bertha Bless, *Weston, Queen of the Platte Purchase* (Weston, Mo.: The Weston Chronicle, 1969), 20.

[14]St. Joseph, situated north of the great bend of the Missouri, was about eight miles closer to the Platte than the other "jumping off" spots and was therefore one of the most popular. By 1850, the town had 3,000 people and all kinds of establishments to serve emigrants. See Wyman, "The Outfitting Posts," 18–21, and Eleazer S. Ingalls, *Journal of a Trip to California By the Overland Route Across the Plains in 1850–51* (Waukegan: Tobey & Company, 1852) for excellent descriptions.

country. 10:00 Forded a stream for the first time, 50cts for each wagon. Very hilly.

Friday, 21st.

Rained last night. Slept in the tent for the first time. I was Yankee enough to protect myself by pinning up blankets over my head. I am quite at home in my tent.

12:00 Have traveled in the rain all day & we are stuck in the mud. I sit in the wagon writing while the men are at work doubling the teams to draw us out.

Saturday, 22nd.

Camped in the woods last night. Started in the rain, rode over some fine rolling prairie. Stopped in some bushes beside a stream to spend the Sabbath.

Sunday, 23rd.

Walked to the top of the hill where I could be quiet & commune with nature & nature's God. This afternoon I was annoyed by something very unpleasant & shed many tears & felt very unhappy.

Monday, 24th.

Exchanged our spring wagon for it did not do well with all the load we had on. Passed some of the most singular looking bluffs I ever saw. They looked more like boulders, large & small, piled up. Seemed to be composed entirely of sand. The wind had blown away all that was gone.

Tuesday, 25th.

Expect to cross the Missouri today. Were nearly all day crossing. Our men had to do all the work & we had to pay $10 besides. Camped on a high prairie without wood near for the first time.[15]

---

[15]Because of the great crush of emigrants at the ferries at St. Jo, many emigrant trains drove up the Missouri and crossed at one of the other ferrying points. Just where the Bailey train crossed is not clear from the diary although they probably used one of the six "middle ferries" between St. Jo and old Fort Kearny (Nebraska City). For a description of these crossings see Mattes, *Platte River Road*, 116–17.

Wednesday, 26th.

Saw *Wolves*. Fine roads & good weather. Some splendid scenery.

Thursday, 27th.

Mr. Holt & Cockren are not very well. The wolves are about the size of brown dogs. By going out of the way we found a good camp, wood & water. Boys better.

Friday, 28th.

Found a stream where the horses can drink. At times it seems to run very swiftly. 12:00 Very warm but a fine breeze. I am lying under the wagon with my head on the saddle & the Dr's head on my lap. We have taken our lunch & are resting ourselves. The feed for the horses is as good as need be. All as need be except Sarah Withington who is very miserable. Her mother is suffering much on her account.

Passed 3 graves made 2 years ago. How gloomy to think of one's friends buried alone in a strange land. Found a good place to camp on Salt Creek with a company from Michigan. We think that we made about 20 miles today.

Sunday, 30th.

A day of rest. It does not seem much like keeping the Sabbath. The men are all airing their bed clothes. Many wash, bake & do all their work. I have not washed yet nor do I intend to on the Sabbath. We received a visit from an Indian early in the morning. He brought a paper stating that the tribe were in a very destitute condition. This one was nearly naked. At night 2 others came & slept under the wagons.

Monday, 31st.

Feel quite refreshed after resting one day. We past [sic] any quantities of Indians, some dressed in robes & others not dressed at all scarcely. All wanted to eat, eat. They wanted to swap mogisins [sic] for corn or anything to eat. They do not want money as they have no use for it. One of our men exchanged a blanket for a robe, a good one. He was so well pleased that they all wanted to get blankets, but we did not stop to trade with them much as we wanted to keep provisions enough for ourselves. We might have given them all we had & they would want more.

Tuesday, 1st of June.

We had very fine roads. Did not know where we would find camping ground & as we had what water our horses wanted to drink, we did not stop until when it came time to stop we did not find either wood or water. We drove until it was too late to go any farther & lay down to sleep with nothing but dry crackers & cheese & meat. We fought miskeetoos [sic] all night and early in the morning, we started to find a place to cook some breakfast & water our horses. We soon found a good place.

Tuesday, 2nd.

Fine prairie roads. Passed a deserted Indian village. Met what we thought was a Soix [sic] which did not appear very friendly. Wanted to see if we were armed. Found we were. He said 30 more of his men were coming to kill the Pawnees. He was dressed in good style & his horse had a nice blanket also.

Wednesday, 3rd.

Had a hard drive. Weather very warm. Good feed. Saw a shower coming so we hurried to pitch our tent. Some things occured that were not very pleasant. We got our beds made in our tent when the lightening flashed & the thunder roared. I think I never witnessed a more terrific shower. It was as much as we could do to keep our tent from blowing over for some time. Were very glad to get a drink of tea & go to bed if not to sleep.

Thursday, 4th.

Very cold this morning after the shower. Quite a change since yesterday when it was uncomfortably warm. Now it is cold enough to wear overcoats. 12:00 We stopped on the banks of the Platte to take dinner. I am sitting on the banks of the Platte with my feet almost in the water. Have been writing to my Mother. How I wish some of my own relations could be with me.

We passed a place where we saw 63 horse skulls all laid in a circle, their noses toward the center. Suppose it to be the grave of some warrior who had killed the horses. They are very whitened indeed & present the appearance of a flowerbed from the road.

Friday, 4th.

Drove rather late to overtake some other teams as we were somewhat afraid that we might be molested by the Indians. Set a double guard to protect ourselves, but were not disturbed. Met a lone Indian. He did not appear friendly. He was dressed better than any we had seen in blankets of white striped with blue, putees (?) of the same, a rich warrior equipped for the chase or fight. Wanted to know what firearms we had. Took his horse off quite a distance & covered it with a blanket. We supposed that it might have been stolen.

Saturday, 5th.

We are glad that we are so near a day of rest & that our lives have been preserved. This morning we came into the road that came from St. Joseph.[16] Saw any quantity of teams, horses & oxen, mules, men, women & children. All pass through Fort Kearney. We left letter there. It is a military post & quite a stirring place the government built up. The residences of the officers are very fine, some small framed buildings, others built of sod or turf laid up like brick, with windows & doors. [There is] a blacksmith shop where our people paid $1.00 per pound for horse nails. Some other things were not so dear, but almost everything was so. We went into the register office & looked over the names of those who had passed before us. Some 20,000 men, 6,000 women, besides cattle & horses, mules & sheep to almost any amount. We saw a great many new made graves. There had been a good deal of sickness on the St. Jo's road, almost every company had had one or more. We encamped 4 miles beyond the Fort to spend the Sabbath.[17]

---

[16]The Bailey train traveled along the old Fort Kearny or Nebraska City road which met the St. Jo-Independence road about fifteen miles east of Fort Kearny. See Mattes, *Platte River Road*, 164–66, and P. L. Platt and N. Slater, *Traveler's Guide Across the Plains Upon the Overland Route to California*, reprinted from the 1852 edition with introduction by Dale L. Morgan (San Francisco: John Howell, 1963), 1–4, for descriptions of the two routes.

[17]"New" Fort Kearny (or Kearney) was estblished in the summer of 1848 on the

Sunday, 6th.

The Dr. had a hard chill & was quite ill all day. We made him as comfortable as possible in our tent. Most of the company spent a good part of the day writing letters to their friends at home. Went & carried them to the office as it was the last chance until we get to Laramie. Towards evening, the Dr. had one of the men take our rig & go to town. As we were both sick, we retired early with the expectation of arousing early. After we had been asleep we heard the sound of a horn & an outcry. The man Ben has not come in. He is lost or something. They all got horses & guns & all started for him & he was coming.

Monday, 7th.

Started early, went by everything, a great many oxteams. It does not seem as though we are out of the world to see so many people. More stir than you would see in a goodly city. Eliza is not well today. We are traveling up the Platte River. No good water but river water that is muddy.[18]

Tuesday, 8th.

Eliza is quite sick & the Dr. has had a hard chill. I am sick, too. It seems rather hard. We did not drive more than 10 miles & stopped to get rested by a frog pond. In the night a French man was watching the horses and heard something which also frightened the horses. He

---

South Platte at the head of Grand Island. Here five major travel routes converged to form what Mattes has dubbed "The Great Platte River Road." By 1852 the post, in addition to quarters for the troops and officers, had a hospital, workshops, storehouses, a blacksmith shop, post office, and a store where emigrants could purchase essential supplies. Usually trains camped here for a few days in order to make repairs, post letters, redistribute and sometimes discard supplies and equipment, and to reorganize their trains. For descriptions of the post see: Lilian M. Willman, "The History of Fort Kearney," *Nebraska State Historical Society Collections* 21(1930): 211–318; Lyle E. Mantor, "Fort Kearny and the Westward Movement," *Nebraska History* 29 (September 1948):175–207; Albert Watkins, "History of Fort Kearny," *Nebraska Historical Society Publications* 16 (1911):227–67; and especially Mattes, *Platte River Road*, 192–216.

[18]Most emigrants complained about the poor quality of the Platte water. One guide book recommended settling the mud by "sprinkling a handful of corn meal slowly into a pan of the water, and stirring at the same time. It will," the guide assured, "shortly become quite clear, palatable and wholesome." Platt, *Traveler's Guide*, 5.

began to holler, Ben, Ben, the horses are all gone. An Indian or something had driven off the horses. We were all very much frightened. I was so nervous that I thought I would fly away.

Wednesday, 9th.

Eliza is better today. Some of our men went out to see if they could kill Buffalo but without success. After we started we saw 3 coming down to the river. Some of the men took horse & again started off. We did not see anything of them until noon, when we saw them coming on the horses. We thought they were making believe they had got meat. When they came near, we saw the blood on their hands. They had killed one & brought as much as they could. I never saw men more excited. Had some of it cooked so that night they had jokes to crack & stories of hunters life. They say that the next time they hunt buffalo I shall take the revolver & take Nig & go with them.

What cause of gratitude we have that so many of us are well & are all spared while we pass so many new graves everyday. Still we have not seen a dead person.

Thursday, 10th.

Started in good season. Found several ox teams had passed us, also a flock of sheep. We have passed them as often as twice a day for several days since we left Fort Kearney. Have noticed a substance on the surface of the earth resembling salt. The cattle lick it up. We see buffalo trails everyday where they go to the river to drink. It makes the road rough.

Friday, 11th.

Very warm. We are coming near the South Crossing of the Platte. Have been traveling over the bluffs. Very warm & dry, dusty. Nothing green to be seen excepting on the banks of the river. Fortunately for us, it is not very windy.

[There are] a great many wolves prowling about seeking what they may devour. Nothing dangerous. Antelope are plenty but seldom caught. Camped at noon near 10 large wagons filled with buffalo robes for the states. Do not feel well today. It is rather hard for me to ride in a wagon & I feel the want of a chair when we stop. I like my sleeping room very well, that is the tent.

Saturday, 12th.

Called on Mr. Miner's people. They had lost their Mother after they left St. Jo. A very interesting family. We got acquainted with them coming down the Illinois River. They crossed the Platte at South Crossing & wanted us to go with them. Stopped at noon to wash & attend to other matters. Frank Farewell is quite sick, has not been well for several days. It was really amusing to see the men stand in the river to wash. They all acted so awkward.

Sunday, 13th.

How thankful we ought to be for the Sabbath. None but an Infinite Being could have foreseen the absolute necessity of one day in seven for rest to man & beast. I never realized that good of a Sunday so much before.[19]

Monday, 14th.

We are on the south side of the Platte or Nebraska. The wind is perfectly sultry. [indecipherable] We have our own mess. That is, Dr., John Leonardson, Ben Farewell, Mrs. Withington, Sarah & myself. We enjoy ourselves much better. It rained all the afternoon. Frank Farewell rode with us as he is quite sick. We feel quite independent as we can get what we want to eat & eat it without jumping.

Tuesday, 15th.

Our men were up, ambitious to get started. We get milk often, it seems good to have it for coffee. A drover came along & saw some hogwort (?) drying. The Dr. called me out to tell them how it was made. I told him & he offered me some mutton & called one of the boys & sent me a sheep. We went on until we came to the end of the road where we had to cross the Platte River. Had to raise the bed of our wagons, but got over safely but were somewhat frightened when

---

[19]Most trains tried to stop on Sunday. The reasons were not entirely religious. Most spent the day in doing necessary chores and mending equipment. One guide advised, ''Never travel on the Sabbath; we will guarantee that if you lay by on the Sabbath, and rest yourselves and teams, that you will get to California 20 days sooner than those who travel seven days in the week.'' Of course trail conditions often prevented companies from stopping on Sunday, but most did try to take one day of rest each week. Ware, *Emigrant's Guide*, 10.

River Crossing

we saw them go into the water. The Dr. was thrown from his horse. We were very much frightened but were very thankful to get over safely. We got everything ready for supper for the men when they got the goods all over.[20]

Wednesday, 16th.

Traveled between the forks of the Platte, some of the most romantic scenery I ever saw. One mass of rocks all worn into every fantastic shape. In the deep ravines were large trees. I noticed a stone that resembled a bust of an old lady sitting alone. She looked as though she

---

[20]There were three main crossings on the South Platte. Evidently the Baileys used the Upper or California Crossing. Travelers dreaded the Platte crossing, and many had narrow escapes. Mattes details some of their experiences in *Platte River Road*, 266–69.

felt lonely. We came to Ash Hollow, a good spring & plenty of wood. It seemed good to see trees once more.[21]

Thursday, 17th.

Crossed Ash Creek. Never saw sand so deep, it seemed so hard for the horses. I walked some distance in the deep sand, very fatiguing. At noon we overtook Mr. Patterson with a long train bound for Salt Lake. The Dr. stopped & prescribed for them. We have seen them often for 2 weeks passed [sic] although they drive oxen with heavy load & we have horses.

Friday, 18th.

Very heavy sandy roads. Made up our mind to dispose of everything we can spare to make our freight less. I am writing to my dear parents for I well know how anxious they are on our account.

Saturday, 19th.

Left our trunks. Passed Courthouse Bluff.[22] It looks like a large public building of stone but the fact is it is mostly composed of earth, the surrounding soil having been washed away leaves them in almost

---

[21]Ash Hollow, a "picturesque wooded canyon" about four miles long and 250 feet deep was an important landmark on the trail. Mattes notes, "In a country otherwise devoid of noteworthy features, Ash Hollow, with its high white cliffs . . . and beneficent clear springs is an outright marvel." Ibid., 282.

Although Bailey does not mention the steep descent into the canyon commented on by most travelers, her description of the surrounding countryside corresponds closely to the Platt and Slater guidebook which also mentions the sand. "You now travel up the . . . Platte over small ridges of deep sand (the deepest found on the road from the States to Fort Laramie) which makes heavy wheeling." Platt, *Traveler's Guide*, 6–7.

[22]Courthouse Rock, a famous landmark in the North Platte Valley, is located at the east end of a low rolling ridge which gradually rises and broadens to the west. Other famous sites in the ridge include Jail Rock, Chimney Rock, Castle Rocks, and Scott's Bluff. Courthouse Rock was near several overland and stage routes and was frequently mentioned by travelers along these routes. For a detailed history of the site and a number of comparative descriptions by travelers, see: Earl R. Harris, "Courthouse and Jail Rocks: Landmarks on the Oregon Trail," *Nebraska History* 43 (March 1962): 29–51 and Mattes, *Platte River Road*, 339–77.

any shape. Are in sight of Chimney Rock. It looks very like the shot towers (in St. Louis).[23]

Sunday, 20th.

We have camped near Chimney Rock. Weather fine, grass good some little distance from the Platte River. Towards evening we rode up to the rock. Left our horses at the base & walked, or rather climbed, up about 100 of the 300 feet. The material of which it is composed is so soft that names that could not be numbered have been left there. It was so late before we left we had some difficulty finding our way back.

Monday, 21st.

Crossed Scotts Bluffs & some of the most romantic scenery I ever *saw*. It would not require very great imagination, however, to think it some ancient city with high walls, great towers & every prerequisite to it. Why I could not compare it to anything else. Would like to have spent days there. What a theme for the novelist. Our road passed between the bluffs, crooked, rough, but still hard, no sand. You could not see the road unless for some small cedars at the summit & in the ravines. Camped on the river bank.[24]

Tuesday, 22nd.

Passed a Frenchman's blacksmith shop. His wife is a squaw of the

---

[23]Many emigrants described "this great natural curiosity" and like Mrs. Bailey, commented on the "soft material" and the many names inscribed there. Several of the writers noted the resemblance of the rock to a shot tower. For other descriptions see Merrill J. Mattes, "Chimney Rock on the Oregon Trail," *Nebraska History* 35 (March 1955): 1-26 and Mattes, *Platte River Road,* 378-420.

[24]"Courthouse Rock and Chimney Rock were the appetizers," wrote Mattes, "Scotts Bluff was the grand climax." The Bluffs, a long range of hills at present day Scottsbluff, Nebraska, were supposedly named for a fur company trader, Hiram Scott, who died on or near the bluffs. Like the other Platte landmarks, the Bluffs elicited comments from many travelers. The area was also a favorite subject for artists, and the Bluffs were sketched and painted by a number of well-known artists including Alfred Jacob Miller and William H. Jackson. For a detailed history and comparative descriptions see Merrill J. Mattes, *Scott's Bluff National Monument, Nebraska,* National Park Service Historical Handbook Series, #28 (Washington, D.C.: National Park Service, 1958).

Siox tribe. She sat at the door of their log hut, well drest, robed in a scarlet blanket. She looked rather sober but well. Another squaw on horse back chasing a drove of horses & mules, half dressed.[25] We are still on the Platte. Cattle, cattle, it really seems as though the whole country is alive with men, women, horses, mules, cattle & sheep with a smart sprinkling of children.

Wednesday, 23rd.

We are near Fort Laramie. More droves. All well. It has been a very cold evening. Passed some trees, the first for some days. Our men go back to the bluffs to get cedars to burn [although] buffalo chips answer a good purpose. More stone. The country is hilly, looks like Vermont. Crossed the Laramie River on a very rough bridge for $2.50 a wagon.

11:00 At Laramie at last. It is a fort established by the government to trade with the Indians & white man, too, if his necessity compells him to give 50 ct a pound for sugar, raisins, $5 for salartus, 50 cts for a paper of tacks, etc. etc.[26]

We traveled 10 miles to Warm Springs which are out of the rock & warm enough to wash. The horses drank it well as 10 miles has been the longest time they have been without water.[27]

---

[25]This is undoubtedly a reference to a famous trading post and blacksmith shop operated by a French mountainman named Robidoux. A detailed description of the post and its owner is in Mattes, *Platte River Road*, 438–53. From Bailey's description it is not clear which road the train took through the Bluffs, the older, northern Ribidoux route or the newer, southern Mitchell Pass. Mattes thinks they took the Mitchell route. Ibid., 433. Also see: Merrill J. Mattes, ''Robidoux's Trading Post at 'Scott's Bluffs,' and the California Gold Rush,'' *Nebraska History* 30 (June 1949): 95–138.

[26]Fort Laramie was the second of the posts established along the Platte road. Originally the site of a fur trading post, the land and buildings were purchased by the United States government in June, 1851, and garrisoned by a company of mounted riflemen and Company G, Sixth Infantry. Like Kearny, the post eventually boasted a store, blacksmith shop, and post office in addition to the military buildings. This was the last opportunity to purchase essentials and send mail back to the states until travelers reached Salt Lake City. For an excellent history of the post, see LeRoy R. Hafen, *Fort Laramie and the Pageant of the West, 1834–1890* (Glendale: Arthur H. Clark, 1938), especially pp. 197–220. See also Merrill Mattes, *Fort Laramie and the Forty-niners* (Estes Park, Colorado: Rocky Mountain Nature Association, 1949).

[27]At Fort Laramie travelers had a choice of two principal routes. The river road kept to the banks of the Platte to the mouth of Warm Springs Canyon and then proceeded up the canyon to the Springs. The ''hill'' route, a shorter, albeit rougher,

Thursday, 24th.

The scenery is ever varied as we pass over the Black Hills as they are called from the dark pines with which they are covered. Have not seen scenery to compare with them since I left St. Jo.[28] We enjoy ourselves better as we get used to this way of traveling & living out of doors. We have good appetites and plenty to eat although we sit down & eat like Indians.

Friday, 25th.

Passed an Indian village. They have a great many horses & also some cattle & mules. A Frenchman lives with them, too. They were well dressed with blankets trimmed. They were all out running after sheep & took not the least notice of us. Are still on our winding way over the hills and far away out of any civilized community where everyone "doeth that which is right in his own eyes." It has been well said that on this road the bad passions of men show themselves.

Saturday, 26th.

Are on the Black Hills yet & such scenery is not to be seen many times in a man's lifetime. I had almost said it was well worth the journey. Descend the hills to the Bouton Creek where we find a large Indian village.[29]

Sunday, 27th.

Spent the day in camp as we have done every Sabbath. Very pleasant surroundings with trees. I would be relieved did not so many others share it with us. About noon Dr. Gilfithing's (?) company from

---

road went directly west from Fort Laramie to the Springs. The Baileys appear to have taken the second, or shorter, route. See: Morgan, *Pritchard Diary*, 152, *n* 38 and Robert H. Becker, ed., *Thomas Christy's Road Across the Plains, A Guide to the Route . . . to the City of Sacramento, California* (Denver: Old West Publishing Company, 1969), maps 30–32 and p. 8.

[28]The Black Hills, not to be confused with the more famous Dakota range, was an early name for the Laramie Mountains. As Bailey notes, they were named "for their dark growth of pine and juniper. . . ." Becker, *Christy's Road*, 8.

[29]Evidently LaBonte Creek, a smaller stream which is mentioned in many emigrant journals. See Platt, *Traveler's Guide*, 10, and Becker, *Christy's Road*, map 32.

Pontiac Michigan came in. They had buried him on the plains where we left them. O how sad & what sad tidings to send his poor wife at home.

Toward evening we rode over to see our neighbors the Indians. It was really a great curiosity to see so many at home. They are very indolent but healthy looking, hardy & capable of enduring fatigue. I would think there were 200, from an old blind woman to a little baby not more than 4 days old, all sorts & sizes. A trader lives with them. He will not let them sell a pony without his consent. One old man had been to Washington. They all wear rings on their wrists & on every finger. Some of the children were white enough to belong to any white family. My heart aches to think of their extreme ignorance & as many white men & Christians as pass them without thinking of doing them good. Our government officers are very strict in regard to selling them ardent spirits.

Monday, 28th.

Traveled over the red hills. The dust looked like pounded bricks. Some are pyramids. Red & white chalk abounded.

Tuesday, 29th.

Started from the banks of the LaPrell. Made a short drive, crossed Deer Creek & stopped [within] 3 miles of it to stay a day or two. Too many are here already & have been.[30]

Wednesday, 30th.

Stayed in camp all day, pleasant. [We have been] shoeing horses, baking, getting rested — all but the rest. We want to be going. "Forward is my motto" on this trip. We have a new horse, price $75. The Dr. bought him of an emigrant who got him of an Indian. We call him Siox.

---

[30]Deer Creek, about 55 miles from the Platte, was considered a good camping spot. According to the Platt and Slater guide, "Trains often go up this stream from 6 to 12 miles and tarry a number of days to recruit their animals." The Baileys seem to have taken this advice. Platt, *Traveler's Guide*, 10.

Thursday, July 1st.

Started in good season. I rode on horseback most of the morning with the Dr. Very pleasant, could keep out of the way of the dust. Saw a good many stones that resembled old brick blocks. I am now sitting on a rock on a high one, some 50 feet high, composed of sandstone, quite soft but still hard enough to stand & walk on. Some bushes on the top. They are high enough to give a good shade & I am reminded of "the shadow great rock in a weary land." The country is barren & the crickets are as large as the end of your fingers. It looks like a city here. The streets, to be sure, are rather irregular but the rocks resemble dwellings, large & small, courthouses & other edifices. It is really a curiosity to know how they are formed. They evidently show the action of water.[31] We are near the river but sand piles are to be seen all through the country. One of our men found a mockingbird's nest & took 2 of the young ones.

Friday, July 2nd.

Crossed the North Fork of the Platte in safety. The horses had to swim. We were somewhat frightened, as usual, but thankful no accident occurred.[32] Met a Dane who seemed to be very intelligent. He is living on the plains for the present. He frankly told us that he had an Indian wife. He bought her while he staid here for a pony & two blankets. I was somewhat shocked to think of such a loose state of morals. He said it is nothing more than Yankee men do.

After passing over a high hill, sandy & hard, we encamped on the sand. Had to take the horses 1½ miles to grass.

---

[31]Mrs. Bailey's comments are in interesting contrast to those of Lodisa Frizzell at a similar spot in the same area. "What has caused the earth to be to its center shook? Sin! the very rocks seemed to reverberate. . . . Viewing these symbols of divine wrath, I felt humbled; I took a small stone & wrote upon a flat rock beside me, Remember me in mercy O lord." Frizzell, *Across the Plains*, 24.

[32]There were two main fords on the North Platte, the Lower Ferry and the Mormon or Upper Ferry. Most travelers preferred the latter because of the lower tolls ($4.00 per wagon as compared to $5.00 at the Lower Ferry). The crossing was followed, as Bailey notes, by a long drive without water. Platt, *Traveler's Guide*, 11. On the tolls at the ferries see, Austin E. Hutcheson, "Overland in 1852: The McQuirk Diary," *Pacific Historical Review* 13 (December 1944): 428 *n* 14.

Saturday, July 3rd.

Started on a long hard drive, 26 miles, without grass or water. It seemed hard to drive so far. We took water in our casks for the horses. At noon we gave them some but they did not have anything to eat until dark. We camped on the sand beside the water & had to go a great ways to get a little grass. We did not get any sleep. Such a noise I never saw.

Sunday, 4th.

Started at 3 o'clock to find feed or know where it was. Had to go 4 or 5 miles off the road. Found water & good grass. Camped on the sand with sage roots for fuel. It is wintery, cold & somewhat inclined to rain, not pleasant. Rather a dreary Independence Day. We speak of our friends at home. We think they are thinking of us. "Home Sweet Home." I dare not think of it while so far away from the hundreds of dear friends so dear to me from whom I have been a long, long time separated. They now find very easy access & grateful admission into my heart. It is sad to think that everyday takes me farther from them.

Monday, 5th.

We are stopping in camp today. The sand blows so fast I can scarcely write. I have to blow my paper every minute to write. The men are fixing the wagon, the horses eating good grass. We start on 12 miles this afternoon. Camped without water but had grass. Very sandy. I am tired of camping on sand.

Tuesday, 6th.

Started early. Came to Independence Rock about noon. We had intended to be there on the 4th but were behind our time on account of lying by to recruit. It is a massive rock entirely naked. Very many names inscribed on it. We did not stop being as we were in a hurry to get to the Sweetwater, a lovely stream of fine water which was truly refreshing to our horses. We drove through it & as the grass was not inviting continued to drive. Passed Devil's Gate as a deep cut through which the river runs is called. It is a great curiosity resembling the hotel of the White Mountains excepting for the road does not run through it but leaves it at the left & is on level ground comparatively.

It is said to be 400 feet high. The report of pistols echoed & reached most inforcingly.[33]

A company passed us from Cold Water, Michigan. We left them 3 days ago. A lady with them was so sick that she could not travel. The Dr. visited her & she came on 30 miles to overtake us but did not. The ladies left her at Willow Spring to die. O how sad, they could have found us in 2 or 3 miles of them where we stopped part of two days.

Wednesday, 7th.

Had a good camping ground on the grass last night. Very cold this morning. We can keep warm with difficulty. Good road, some grand mountain scenery. At noon we dined beside the Sweetwater. On the opposite side is one of a long range of the Rattlesnake Mountains composed entirely of naked rocks. A very few trees are striking in the fistures of the rocks. The mountains 500 feet high, some of them are in grotesque shapes. Noticed one crowned with a coronet. Have had a mountain squall with rain & hail.

Thursday, 8th.

Camped without much grass. Crossed the Sweetwater 3 times, traveled 10 miles, found grass in a marsh, alkali. Saw the Wind River Mountains covered with snow. Very handsome. Roads sandy & hard.

---

[33]Independence Rock and Devil's Gate were considered the two outstanding landmarks on the Sweetwater. Independence Rock, an isolated granite outcropping 1,552 yards in circumference and almost 200 feet high, was covered with the names of emigrants. According to Dale Morgan, the rock was named by William L. Sublette's party when they stopped at the site to celebrate the Fourth of July in 1829. Federal Writer's Program, *Wyoming: A Guide to Its History, Highways and People* (New York: Oxford University Press, 1941), 387; Morgan, *Pritchard Diary,* 154 n 43. An interesting description of the Rock and the surrounding country is Maurine Carley, "Oregon Trail Trek No. Four," *Annals of Wyoming* 29 (April 1957): 78–82.

Five miles west of Independence Rock is Devil's Gate, an "extraordinary chasm" over three hundred feet deep through which the Sweetwater River rushes and falls. Most of the travelers went a bit out of their way to see this natural phenomenom which Robert Becker notes "was a curiosity worthy of the traveler's notice, and indeed it still is." Lucy Cooke thought it "a grand sight! Surely worth the whole distance of travel." Federal Writer's Program, *Wyoming,* 387; Becker, *Christy's Road,* 8; Lucy R. Cooke, *Crossing the Plains in 1852,* 34.

Very many high rocky bluff barrens. We will have to go 14 miles to the river. Camped late without much grass.

Friday, 9th.

Feel very tired. Such long drives are hard for man & beast. Started in the morning intending to drive until we come to grass. At noon stopped at the roadside to rest. Had to drive on the Rocky Mountains 7 miles to find feed. We intend to lay over Saturday & Sunday to rest our horses.

Saturday, 10th.

This morning found our dark horse had a lame shoulder so that he could not walk. He is one of our best horses. Do not know what we shall do without him.

Sunday, 11th.

Are camped on the Rocky Mountains near an ice cold spring. Dug out a spring; it is just like a permanent spring. We are in sight of the snow capped mountains. Very beautiful scenery. It is very cold & windy. Our horse is not much better. I am afraid we will have to leave him. Remained by a good cold spring of water & enjoyed a day of rest although it is some trouble to take care of the horse.

Monday, 12th.

Stayed in camp another day to get our horse better. He is much improved. It is cold enough. Washed in the morning & had the sick headache in the afternoon.

Tuesday, 13th.

Started this morning. Very pleasant indeed. We are able to get the horse along by leading. The horses begin to fail. It looks discouraging as [we are] not half way through yet. Crossed the Sweetwater for the last time. Saw snow banks on the bank of the stream. It looks odd enough. The mountains are covered with snow & the evergreens look most beautifully.

Wednesday, 14th.

Our man that looks for feed missed us & staid out all night. We drove until dark, stopped beside the road, tired enough to be sure. Very pleasant morning. We shall cross the South Pass today. We have had fine roads & generally level although we are crossing the Rocky Mountains.[34]

Thursday, 15th.

Traveled only about 7 or 8 miles. Stopped only until night. Let our horses eat through the day & at night we started to travel 20 miles without water. Took some in our casks. Rode all night. It seemed rather hard but I slept. It was hard for the men to drive & ride & lead a horse that was sick.

Friday, 16th.

Last night camped on Little Sandy. Crossed the Big Sandy & have 17 miles of desert to go over. Arrived at 3:00, found good company although Mr. Bailey's people went by & missed us.

Saturday, 17th.

Drove up the Big Sandy & crossed the desert to Green River, 10 miles. Good roads. When we got to the ferry we did not see Mr. Bailey's train. About 20 or 30 wagons stood along, one after the other.

---

[34]South Pass, 290 miles from Laramie and 921 miles from St. Joseph, was an important milepost on the long road to California. Here the emigrants crossed the Continental Divide and began the last half of their trip towards the Pacific. There were several routes from South Pass. Those bypassing Salt Lake City could take the Greenwood or Sublette Cut-Off and go by Fort Hall or the Hudspeth Cut-Off, rejoining the road from Salt Lake City on the upper Humboldt. A second possibility was to go to Fort Bridger and then swing north to Fort Hall, a longer route than the Sublette, but easier on the stock. Another road followed the old Mormon Trail through Fort Bridger to Salt Lake City and then by one of the several routes to the main California road from Fort Hall. The route followed by the Baileys is not clear from the diary. They may have taken the Sublette and then turned south to join the Salt Lake City road or used one of the other roads, Kinney's or Lander's, in the area. Their route sounds similar to that described in Hutcheson, ''Overland in 1852,'' 429 and n 16. On the various routes see, Platt, *Traveler's Guide*, 14; George R. Stewart, *The California Trail* (New York: McGraw Hill, 1962), 245, and the following diary, n 28.

We drove out to one side. While [we were] standing the Dr. was out of the wagon & our teamster was sick on the bed. He heard a noise. Some of the ox teams were frightened & started to run. It started the rest & they all began to run. The Dr. jumped in & drove our horse out of the road. We just escaped being run over. A wagon struck the horse that was tied behind but did not hurt him. Be assured that there was screaming among the women & the men looked pretty pale. What was most strange was no one was hurt excepting a black woman. The wagon she was in was thrown over & pretty badly broken but she was not hurt as bad as she thought. She was a slave of an old man who is traveling alone.

Drove 2 miles to the ford & camped for the Sabbath. Found Frank Farewell very sick. His brother was taken the night before, mountain fever I suppose. Took them into our tent & took care of them both.

Sunday, July 18th.

We are 160 miles from Salt Lake. Good grass, that is what we depend upon most to accomplish our journey. The Farewells are both very sick. Frank has been sick a good deal & I am afraid it will go hard with him.

Monday, 19th.

Remained in camp all day as the Dr. did not think it best for Frank to try to travel. Our horses get a good rest, our sick one is much better. Today I feel as though I wanted very much to hear from our many friends in the east. Not one word have we heard since we left St. Louis. It is 2 months since we left St. Joseph. It seems a good while not to hear from anyone. We are just halfway after we cross this river.

Tuesday, 20th.

Forded the Green River. Had to raise our wagons but did not get into the water although we were somewhat frightened. Do not know as there was much danger, but the men say the women must always be frightened. Drove some 20 miles. The miles seem long as the country is entirely barren excepting on the streams. Camped early & had good grass on Ham's Fork.

Wednesday, 21st.

Fine weather. Country barren as usual. Nothing is to be seen but the wild sage & that rather stinted [sic]. In all this region the country in many places has the appearance of being the bed of a vast lake or stream. In many places the earth mingled with rocks are left in shapes of buildings or cupulows [sic]. At a distance, they resemble a large town.

Thursday, 22nd.

I was not well & had a long drive over stoney roads & steep hills. Camped on Muddy Creek.

Friday, 23rd.

Traveled over high hills, down ravines. Did not find much water until we came to a branch of the Bear River [where we found] a cold spring. After descending some very steep hills, we came to Bear River, one of the swiftest streams we have seen. Good cold water, very swift.

Saturday, 24th.

Drove 20 miles. Roads steep, ravines bad to cross. Stopped late by a good cold spring rather tinctured with iron.

Sunday morning, July 25th.

It seems that we are going to be cheated out of our day of rest. The Capt. thinks that we can find a better place if we go on a half day's drive. They have started & I suppose we shall go although we do not approve of it.

Traveled 20 miles over the worst roads & ravines which were very steep to drive into. Crossed one creek some 17 times. Camped on the bank of the Red Fork of Weber River, a good place. Plenty of service berries and fine spotted trout.[35] We had a present of some from Mrs. Scott, a lady from Virginia we had met before. We had a sight of more rocks & mountains than we have ever seen before.

---

[35]From the Red Fork of the Weber River there were two roads to Salt Lake City, each about fifty miles long. Both are described in Platt, *Traveler's Guide*, 48–49.

Serviceberries are the rather acid fruit of the serviceberry bush. Many of the emigrants, hungry for fresh fruit, gathered the berries for pies or compotes. See, for example, Cooke, *Crossing the Plains*, 42.

Monday, 26th.

Drove 16 miles through passes such as we saw yesterday. Perpendicular rocks from 500 to 1000 feet high. In some places there was hardly room enough for road & the creek. We think it is not worthwhile for anyone to go to Switzerland to see mountains. We see many covered with perpetual snow.

Tuesday, 27th.

Drove over a rough road, crossing ravines as usual. Camped on Canon Creek which we will cross 13 times. Passed a Mormon there with some things to sell.

Wednesday, 28th.

Crossed another very high hill today, steeper & more difficult than the one we crossed yesterday. Some of the finest views of mountain scenery that was ever seen by mortals. Peak upon peak, the highest covered by perpetual snow. About noon came in sight of Salt Lake Valley. It was really beautiful to look upon. It extended beneath high mountains entirely shut in by hills & mountains. We were not allowed to go into the City & camp because it is said the smallpox is on the road. We turned to the left, traveled 3 miles into a deep valley beside a swift stream & encamped entirely out of sight. Mountains reach 500 or 600 feet into the clear blue sky with snow with occasionally a shrub.

Thursday, 29th.

Are in camp resting. We are all so completely tired out that we hardly know what to do. 2 days of hard road & hills so steep that we did not dare to ride down & again so steep we would not ride up. It has kept us jumping out & climbing in again. For two days past I have rode on horseback or led the horse up & down the hills. Our folks have gone to town to get some vegetables & see the City. It is said here that Governor Brigham Young was out with 73 wives last Saturday at a celebration. I will not vouch for the truth of the thing.

Friday, 30th.

Are yet in camps. We get wheat for our horses at $1.00 per bushel. Had some green pease [sic], beans & potatoes. They tasted good. We do not find butter, lard & such things very plenty. They got quite a City here for 6 years growth. Very many are here from various parts of Europe. Strange that such delusions should spread so far.

Saturday, 31st.

Think of moving beyond the City tomorrow. Started for the city in the morning. Drove through the valley which is really pleasant. Buildings generally small but comfortable. Vegetables plenty although imported & very high. Sugar 40 cts, coffee the same. Not one yard of calico for sale in town. A good many goods coming in. We are camped in a farming neighborhood near the City. It seems strange to hear the cock crow it has been so long since we have been among civilized people.

Sunday, August 1st.

It does not seem as though it could be so late in the season. I cannot realize that our summer is so far spent. Went to the Tabernacal [sic] in the afternoon with Mrs. Scott to hear some of the *Saints*, as they call themselves, exhort. They related dreams, visions & etc. Their singing was very good, two violins. Gov. Young rose & said that he had to correct a mistake that some of the bretheren & Elders were laboring under that no one but Mormons ever got to heaven & that John Wesley & St. Paul went straight to hell when they died. But he said if anyone did the best they could, the Lord would not send them to the Devil & finally closed by saying God bless you Brethern & Sisters. The people seem to be poor but very well disposed.[36]

Monday, 2nd.

Are in camp yet. Mr. Scott started today. Patterson has arrived

---

[36]At this time, Salt Lake City had a population of about 6,000. As the guidebook noted, "Salt Lake City contains 1,440 lots . . . laid out in blocks . . . and contains about three square miles or something less than 2000 acres of land. . . . The buildings are generally small. A part of them are built of logs; the rest with adobes or sun dried brick." An interesting comparison with Mrs. Bailey's description of the city is that of Lucy Cooke who spent the winter of 1852 there. See Cooke, *Crossing the Plains*, 37–60.

Some travelers avoided Salt Lake because of their hatred or fear of the Mormons, "Many . . . were to be dreaded more than the Indians." E. Allene Dunham, *Across the Plains*, 11. The following diary, by Helen Carpenter, also gives an anti-Mormon view.

today with 12 wagons loaded with merchandise. We think some of going on with him at $11.00 per hundred.

Tuesday, 3rd.

Are yet in camp. Get plenty of vegetables to eat & milk & eggs. We were getting on very well until Mr. Bailey came up & said that 3 of our best horses, one of Mrs. Withington's, & 2 of his own were missing. We think they must be stolen.

Wednesday, 4th.

Have not found the horses but think they have heard from them but may be disappointed. Mrs. Withington feels very badly indeed. I do not wonder for she was taking a span of fine horses to her husband in California. The weather is very fine, a little rain every day or night. Since we left the mountains have rain or snow every day.

Thursday, 5th.

Our men were employed all day yesterday & today searching in vain for our horses. They traced them some distance, but think they have gone south to Utah. Saw very unexpectedly some of our acquaintances we traveled with from St. Louis & St. Joseph.

Friday, 6th.

Met Mr. McGrew's people. They were all well & had enjoyed themselves well. O how glad we were to see them all. It did really seem as though we had seen some of our own folks.

Saturday morning, 7th.

Started in Mr. Patterson's train. We have hired our passage with him. The Dr. has sold his horses, 3 of them, for oxen, 2 yoke. His brother has them to drive. We feel as though we should get through in safety now.

Sunday, 8th.

Staid in camp all day. It did not seem much like Sabbath for everyone was doing something, fixing wagons, doing something that was work.

Monday, 9th.

Started onward today. The day we left the City we passed the warm springs, also the hot springs. We could not bear our hands in the water. It will boil eggs in the water. But put an egg in fresh water & that in a tin bucket in the hot water & it will cook.[37] Wrote to Mother a line today & sent it back to the states.

Tuesday, 10th.

Took an early start this morning almost as soon as light. Took a hasty breakfast or merely a cup of coffee. Drove until nearly noon & stopped for the day. Crossed Weber River. The boys tipped Mr. Bailey's wagon over in a mud hole & spoiled a bag of crackers for us. He himself has returned to the City to see if he cannot find the horses.

Wednesday, 11th.

Did not make a very long drive. Saw our acquaintances ahead of us.

Thursday, 12th.

Very warm. Slept until we stopped to take breakfast. Mr. Patterson starts as soon as light & stops in the heat of the day to rest the animals. We stop late at night. We do not have much time to do anything except 4 or 5 hours in the middle of the day.

Friday, 13th.

Very warm today. Have left the settlements altogether. We are stopping near some hot & cold springs. The water tastes like a strong brine & is so hot you cannot bear your hand in it. Some of the springs are very cold & boil up out of the ground beautifully. Others are very hot. Different mineral waters mingle in a stream which is so hot that the cattle cannot drink it.[38]

---

[37]From Salt Lake City, the road turned north around the lake and rejoined the California road west of Cathedral Rock about 167 miles from Salt Lake City. The springs mentioned by Bailey are described in detail in Platt, *Traveler's Guide*, 51.

[38]These springs, about fifty-one miles from the previous group, are also described in Platt who estimated the temperature of the hot spring at "about 136 degrees." Ibid., 51.

Saturday, 14th.

Morning cold, as usual here, & hot in the middle of the day. Very dusty. Indeed such clouds of dust I never saw. Sometimes there comes a whirlwind or as the boys call it, a hurricane. As we were eating our dinner our food got well peppered with dust for a few minutes. When it was over we washed our dishes & finished our meal. Expected to drive 20 miles but drove until dark. Stopped without water.

Sabbath morning, 15th.

Started early, drove until 7 o'clock. Came to a spring of salt water. The cattle relished it much. We cooked our breakfast with it, but it was not good to drink. How glad I should be to have a day of rest. When we drove our own teams we did not drive except one Sunday, but now we have hired our passage with this large train we have to go when they do. We expect to get to good water in 19 miles.

Monday, 16th, 1852

Camped with our friends the McGrews, or very near them. We received calls from them all. It seems like seeing old friends to meet them. Traveled 12 miles before breakfast. I took the occasion to sleep. It seems as though it is hard to travel everyday so late. We have to cook at noon about all we eat. We are more annoyed with dust for a few days then we have been at all.

Tuesday, 17th.

Camped very late last evening. Took our breakfast before starting this morning. Saw our friends the McGrews. We are stopping at noon near a beautiful mountain stream. Do not feel quite well.

Wednesday, 18th.

Very warm & a dusty, barren country. Very poor grass. Our horses fail without working more than they have before. Mr. Bailey returned with one recovered horse only. Was very glad to get that.

Thursday, 19th.

Saw Mr. McGrew's people. Took a ride with them. We came over some very bad hills, very steep indeed. Camped early on the banks of Goose Creek.

Friday, 20th.

Started early. Very cold indeed, frost last night. We needed all our winter clothes. Stopped on Goose Creek at noon. Hard roads, good to travel, for 18 miles.

Saturday, 21st.

Still are pressing onward. Very barren, nothing but flowering (?) artemisia covers the ground. Called on our steamboat friends & took tea. Left them expecting to see them soon. Drove late, pleasant moonlight.

Sunday, 22nd.

Drove 2 or 3 miles to water. Stopped to water only. How I wish we could have a day of rest. My eyes are getting very weak. Our faces and hands are chapped & sore. It is a long & tedious journey. Water scarce. We are in what is called a thousand spring valley but have not seen but one or two.[39]

Monday, 23rd.

Are still in the valley. Have received a call from Mr. Smith & his companion. They are before us. Erickson & Elvin called on us. They are traveling behind us. .

Tuesday, 24th.

Expect to see our old friends the McGrews today. Very pleasant. We are in sight of the Humboldt Mountains, covered with snow. We shall come to the headwaters of Mary's River soon. Grass very good. A spring of hard water, somewhat sulphery.

Wednesday, 25th.

Mr. & Mrs. McGrew made us an early call, also our steamboat friends. Erickson was very sick, staid with us until we started at 8:00.

---

[39]Thousand Spring Valley, twenty-five miles from the head of Goose Creek Valley, was named for the numerous springs in the area. There were two sub-basins, the Well Springs Valley and Hot Springs Valley. See Morgan, *Pritchard Diary*, 163 *n* 70.

Thursday, 26th.

Very dusty. It is impossible to see a road in most places. We have heard of the dust but never saw anything of it until we crossed this river. Saw Erickson. He appeared much better.

Friday, 27th.

Most of the train have lost the day of the week. Really I thought it was Thursday. Good roads, good water & the best of grass.

Saturday, 28th.

Very pleasant but dusty. We like this place well. Crossed through a high canon where there was a beautiful spring which we could scarcely see for the dust. Camped on the river bank.

Sunday, 29th.

Are in camp this morning. It seems a luxury to rest. Suppose we will move this afternoon. Saw Mrs. Grafton, a widow who has lost her husband on the road. She has 5 children. She seems to be very energetic & respected. She is from Canada.

Monday, 30th.

Very pleasant weather but dry & dusty. Nothing of importance has occurred. We see our friends that travel near us everyday. It is pleasant.

Tuesday, 31st.

Our train moves on systematically. Everything is done without any trouble. We are passing down the Mary's River.[40] It abounds with excellent trout but we do not get much time to fish.

Wednesday, September 1st.

Delightful weather, very good feed. The greatest profusion of hills & mountains. It seems as though Dame Nature was in a fantastic

---

[40]The Mary's River was one of the old names for the Humboldt. One of the upper branches retained the name Mary's River after the use of Humboldt became common. The mountains described by Bailey in the next paragraph would have been the party's first view of the Humboldt range. Ibid., 164 *n* 73; Stewart, *California Trail,* 137.

mood when she formed these hills. High mountains in the distance, hills upon hills, bluffs & everything in the shape of hills.

Thursday, 2nd.

Did not make a very long drive. Encamped on the banks of the river. Excellent grass.

Friday, 3rd.

We have now been on our journey 105 days. As we took provisions for only 100 days we should be short if we had not taken a bountiful supply. As it is we have enough excepting, perhaps, we will need to buy some flour at Carson Valley.

Saturday, 4th.

Passed over some very dry alkaline country. The mountains look very much like snow drifts in shape. It is astonishing what a growth everything attains. On the banks of this stream the rushes are at least 10 feet high & other things in proportion.

Sunday, 5th.

We are now within 100 miles of the sink of the Humboldt or to where the river looses itself. Met a Mr. Leggett looking for his wife, an old acquaintance of ours.

Monday, 6th.

Did not pass a very agreeable night. Mrs. _____ was, as some thought insane. The children staid with us. There is more sand here than anything else. The banks of the river are very steep.

Tuesday, 7th of September

It is the anniversary of our wedding day. 6 years have passed, how many changes. Our young friends Erickson & Elvin left us this morning. They are marching through. They will, if nothing prevents, be through before us. Our route lays through a very barren, desolate country. Excepting on the immediate banks of the river there is not a green thing, [just] sand & a few dry weeds. We are in very good health and have the greatest cause of gratitude to that Being who has watched over us until the present time. Whenever another year will round it is well to recall that passed and think of the future. We, for 6 years, have spent our time together & as the Dr. says have traveled pretty well towards round the world.

Wednesday, 8th, 1852

We have often heard of the sand but now we see it. No grass for the poor animals. Deep cuts in the banks through which the road goes.

Thursday, 9th.

We have today left Mr. Bailey's wagons behind. Do not know as we will travel near any more. The dust is awful.

Friday, 10th.

The weather pleasant. Today we have met many a returned Californian. Mr. Patterson has met 2 brothers. On in the morning it seemed as though we had got almost through our journey for we see so many out on horseback. Mrs. Withington is looking for her husband. Hope she may meet him.

Saturday, 11th.

We arrived late in camp last night. We had thought that some of our profane men were bad enough but the Californians are so much worse that we will not compare them. A man here that had come out to meet his wife & she was married to another man before he got here. He says he shall shoot her father before morning.

Sunday, 12th.

We are still in camp. It seems like anything but Sunday but we are getting a good rest. Plenty of good grass, no wood but willow. We will spend another day here. Mr. Patterson's brothers go with us.

Monday, 13th.

Did not start until noon. Drove to the sink. Found a great many encamped there. A relief station there had sold out everything & were about starting back.[41]

Tuesday, 14th.

Staid in camp all day preparing to cross the desert.

Wednesday, 15th.

A dreadful occurance took place. A wicked man who had whipped one of his men overheard Ben Farewell say that no man could make him run by whipping. He came into our camp, took an ax & felled him like a beef. We thought he was killed. Will not describe the excitement.

Thursday, 16th.

Ben is better. We think he will recover well. We have got across the desert. Went very soon 40 miles in 15 hours. Stopped but twice to feed. Did not see anything but bones & dead animals.[42]

---

[41]The party had now arrived at the famous sink of the Humboldt, the point where the river disappeared into a maze of sloughs and marshes. Mrs. Bailey's description of the long trip down the Humboldt to the sink, a distance of almost 400 miles, is similar to, though not as detailed as, those of other travelers along the route. See Morgan, *Pritchard Diary*, 113-23 and 164-65 *nn* 76-81; Dale L. Morgan, *The Humboldt, Highroad of the West* (New York: Farrar and Rinehart, 1943); Federal Writers' Program, *Nevada: A Guide to the Silver State* (Portland: Binfords and Mort, 1940), 11-15; and Irene Paden, *Wake of the Prairie Schooner* (New York: MacMillan, 1943), 390-414.

Many parties reached this point on the trail with teams and supplies exhausted, "victims of unavoidable delays . . . with cattle dying or dead and still two or three hundred miles to travel." Thus the relief stations were set up to provide assistance. Becker, *Christy's Road*, 11. For descriptions, see Sarah Royce, *A Frontier Lady: Recollections of the Gold Rush and Early California* (New Haven: Yale University Press, 1932), 63, and Catherine Haun, "A Woman's Trip Across the Plains in 1849," ms., Huntington Library, 39.

At the sink, the road forked. The right road led to the Truckee River and Donner Pass, the other road led almost directly south to the Carson River.

[42]This dread forty-mile desert crossing was the great "elephant" on this part of the California trail. Most parties crossed at night, but the crossing was still difficult and stories of the hardships of the crossing and the hundreds of dead cattle, mules, horses, and other livestock can be found in almost every diary. However, another traveler in 1852 noted, ". . . the desert is easier to cross this year than it has ever been

Friday, 17th.

Have been confined ever since Monday with ague in my face which is very much swollen. Have suffered very much. We are now in Carson Valley.[43] Plenty of trees but the country is very barren.

Saturday, 18th.

Very pleasant, delightful weather. Feel much better today. We are not stirring this afternoon. We have heard of a great deal of suffering, people being thrown out on the desert to die & being picked up & brought to the hospital.

Sunday, 19th.

Sunday, it has not seemed much like it. Bought beef at 25 cts per pound & flour the same.

Monday, 20th.

So late in the season and we are not in California yet. We are following Carson Creek yet. Some very fine trees & a little good land on the banks, but the hills & mountains are as destitute of vegetation as it is possible for them to be. Do not feel well yet & very much wish we were at our journey's end. Provisions are very scarce, 20 & 30 cts. for flour & beef. Mr. Patterson has got to buy all that his men eat. We will have to buy more.

Tuesday, 21st.

Very pleasant. Are still following in the Canyon. I am not well yet, feel so very weak. Do want so much to hear from home. All well in

---

before. There are seven or eight trading posts on it now, where refreshments and supplies of all kinds are kept for sale." "Overland to California, Notes from a Journal kept by Mrs. Frances H. Sawyer in a Journey Across the Plains, May 9 to August 17, 1852," typescript, Newberry Library, 16. Also see Berry, "Overland to the Gold Fields," 289; Morgan, *Pritchard Diary*, 167 *nn* 85 and 87.

[43]The thirty-mile-long Carson Valley was "the largest fertile spot on the route since leaving the head waters of Mary's river." Some trains stopped here to recruit their teams before starting the ascent over the Sierras. Platt, *Traveler's Guide*, 28. Also see Grace Dangberg, *Carson Valley, Historical Sketches of Nevada's First Settlement* (Reno: Carson Valley Historical Society, 1972) for a brief history and description of the valley. Descriptions by other travelers are cited in Hutcheson, "Overland in 1852," 431 *n* 25.

the train. This afternoon our cow we bought at Salt Lake sickened and died in an hour. We hardly know how to spare the milk, it was half our living. She was so fat & nice it seemed a pity.

Wednesday, 22nd.

Are passing through Gold Canyon, very rough indeed. The Dr. went & saw them digging. Saw 3 rude looking dwellings. Encamped at noon near a Housier tavern. Potatoes 25 cts per pound, onions 75.[44]

Thursday, 23rd.

Pleasant but very cold & wintery. I am afraid of being cold before we get across the mountains. This is truly a delightful valley. The mountains are sparcely covered with pine. The Mormons are beginning to settle this valley. Also saw several dwellings, very rude. Flour at 25 cts., bought 50 lbs.

Friday, 24th.

Passed the Mormon station at the foot of the Sierra Nevadas. It is truly a romantic spot. Saw a post office, blacksmith shop and even heard the sound of the breakfast bell for the first time since we left St. Joseph. The pine trees are growing almost down to their dwellings. Most beautifully clear streams of water. The soil is very rich. It will eventually become a fine place but it must necessarily be cut off like Salt Lake Valley from all water communication. Everything must be brought over the mountains or raised here.[45]

Saturday, 25th.

Are just going into the Canyon previous to crossing the mountains.

----

[44]Gold Canyon was the first of the great Virginia City mining strikes. Between 1848 and 1850 Mormon travelers panned gold in the canyon near the Carson River. A modest strike was made in the canyon in 1850 and a year later about 100 men from Placerville began mining in the area. By 1852, there were several hundred miners and several small camps had been established. Federal Writer's Program, *Nevada*, 271–72.

[45]Mormon Station, later Genoa, Nevada, was settled in 1849, one of the first settlements in what is now Nevada. In 1851 John Reese established a trading post on the site and by 1852 it was the thriving spot described by Bailey. Ibid., 207–208; Dangberg, *Carson Valley*, 9–11.

Such a canyon was never seen before. The scenery was delightful but the roads dreadful. Stopped for the night without getting through. Fine old pines to burn.[46]

Sunday, 26th.

Have got to climb a bad hill before we can get grass. The poor oxen had nothing to eat last night. It took 3 or 4 hours to get all the teams one half mile with 10 yokes of oxen to each wagon. Mrs. Withington is very sick with dysentary. It hurts her very much to ride. Hope it will not be much worse crossing the mountains.

Monday, 27th.

Are passing through a beautiful valley hidden among the snow capped mountains. Camped at the foot of the first ascent near Red Lake. Mrs. Withington somewhat better.

Tuesday, 28th.

Are now ascending. It is very steep & difficult. It is now afternoon & we have not made one mile. Mrs. W. is able to sit on a saddle. Mr. V. Patterson is so sick they are going to swing him between 2 mules & take him. It is so bad for the sick. Think it is hard going to California. We now feel almost worn out. Poor Mr. Carmichael that was wounded sometime since must suffer today.

Wednesday, 29th.

Have got over the first mountain & are not killed, any of us. We are now encamped on the margin of the mountain lake.[47] The scenery today has been truly sublime. Mounts rising to the skies covered with snow. Fine old pines in every direction, a great variety of evergreens.

---

[46]The guidebooks agreed with Bailey's assessment of the canyon. Platt and Slater called the road, "one of the worst pieces of road between the States and California." Many wagons and teams broke down and had to be abandoned here. Platt, *Traveler's Guide*, 29.

[47]The mountain was called First Mountain and was considered "the steepest and rather the most difficult mountain on the route." Mountain Lake was a small lake between First Mountain and the main ridge of the Sierras. From here it was about five miles to the 9,000 foot summit. Ibid., 29–30.

It seems quite like snow, cold & chilly. How I wish we had a house to live in now. If it were not for hope the heart would break.

Thursday, 30th.

Rising the second summit not so difficult as the first. Are now in the region of perpetual snow. Very cold & chilly. Camped in a valley.

Friday, October 1st.

Had a very rough road descending most of the way. Camped in a deep ravine. Awoke in the morning, the ground covered with snow.

Saturday, 2nd.

Cold. Have not traveled but 5 miles. Got some grass here. The animals have got weak, quite so. We some expect to go to Stockton. I feel rather disappointed in not going the Hangtown road.[48]

Sunday, 3rd.

Had considerable of a snow storm yesterday, but it disappeared this morning & it is very pleasant. We are going towards Stockton.

Monday, 4th.

The Dr. has gone to meet his brother & has not returned yet. We are getting on very well but slowly. The oxen are very weak drawing such large wagons over the rough mountains.

Tuesday, 5th.

We are within 3 miles of Volcano, a mining town.[49] Mr. V.

---

[48]The Hangtown, or Placerville, road was one of the main branches of the Carson Emigrant Road. Established in 1850 as the Johnson Cut-Off from Diamond Spring, the road was heavily traveled. Hoover, *Historic Spots*, 76.

[49]There were two mining camps called Volcano, one in Placer County and the other, to which Mrs. Bailey refers, in Amador County. The latter town was in a very rich hydraulic mining district where, according to one report, "a million dollars in gold was taken out of one mine" in the area. In 1852, there were already 300 houses in the town, and by the following year, Volcano had eleven stores, six hotels, three bakeries, and three bars. Ibid., 31–32; Erwin G. Gudde, *California Gold Camps: A Geographical and Historical Dictionary*, Elisabeth K. Gudde, ed. (Berkeley: University of California Press, 1975), 360–61.

Patterson went out yesterday to rest until we came up. They sent into town after flour & potatoes which they brought out today. The climate is very much improved. It is very pleasant now. Rained a little last night. In the evening Mr. Withington arrived. We had indeed a happy meeting. I felt to rejoice with Mrs. W.

Wednesday, 6th.

We arrived in the first mining town in California. Took dinner there. Had a variety of vegetables. The buildings are very rude, some of logs, others framed & covered with cloth. The village is without form & prices continue very high. Saw a good many mining. It seemed like very hard work & rather low pay but some do very well.

Thursday, 7th.

The climate is very mild here. The season of rain has not yet commenced. I am afraid it will before we get settled. This morning Mrs. W. started for her *home* with her husband. They are expecting us tomorrow evening. Mr. Patterson found good grass & we are stopping today. I do feel so uneasy to hear from home I do not know what to do.

Friday, 8th.

Very delightful weather. The air soft & balmy like early summer. It is really astonishing to think what a variety of climate we have passed through. On the, or rather in, Salt Lake Valley it was midsummer, on the Humboldt like autumn, in Carson Valley like early fall, on the Sierra Nevada hard winter, this side of the mountains spring. The grass was just beginning to spring up green. We have just heard of a train that we left behind. One negro froze to death & 20 cattle. They say that the snow is 5 feet deep.

We have just seen what is to me a curiosity, a horned frog covered with scabs. I should think something like a crockadile [sic] with a tail & sharp points all over his body. Also saw something resembling a spider covered with a thick coat of hairs.

The Dr. has been back to Volcano. Says that Mr. Bailey has moved into a house & has gone to living of which I am glad to hear. Do not know what will become of the poor emigrant that is yet in the mountains.

Saturday, 9th.

It is very pleasant yet. We are progressing slowly towards our place of destination. Camped at Hick's ranch 5 miles from Mrs. Withington's.

Sunday, 10th.

Are yet in camp. Shall go as far as Mrs. W's today. Are in camp waiting to kill a beef. How little regard is paid to the Sabbath. Started in the evening with the Dr. & went to Mr. Withington's on Dry Creek. They were very glad to see us. Expected the train but they did not get up.

Monday, 11th.

Mr. & Mrs. Patterson came up & took dinner with us. We went & gathered a fine lot of grapes equally as sweet as the Isabella. The Dr. left me with Mrs. W. & went on with the train to Stockton.

Tuesday, 12th.

Very pleasant. If I did not feel so anxious to hear from home I should feel quite happy. I want to get a home of my own again & hope to soon. Feel quite fatigued & want the rest which I am getting. Mr. & Mrs. W. are very kind to me. It is really a favor to find such friends in a strange land.

Wednesday, 13th.

Weather charming. Went out today to gather grapes to eat. Very fine. The stream on which we are is dry, rightly named Dry Creek.[50]

Thursday, 14th.

Went up the creek to where there is water & washed some of our dirty clothes. On our return we were visited by quite a number of Indians, all sizes from the old grey headed chief to the infant laced into the wicker basket. They had been gathering the grapes we intended to get. They wanted sugar but we did not give them anything.

---

[50]Dry Creek was another of the rich Amador County mining areas. Hoover, *Historic Spots*, 30; Gudde, *California Gold Camps*.

Friday, 15th.

Went to gather grapes before the Indians got them all. Gathered about a bushel and intend drying some.

Saturday, 16th.

Yet very pleasant. G. Withington started for Volcano, their market. They are hurrying to get off their hay & barley before the rainy season sets in. I wonder that the boys don't come back from Stockton. I expected them. If the Dr. did not come he may go to San Francisco before he returns.

Sunday, 17th of October

It is as pleasant as I was expecting. The nights are cold. The mosquitoes are biting me now while I am writing. O how pleasant it would be if we had a church to go to. I have sent to Sacramento for some things & hope to get letters if we do not get them before.

The Dr. returned on Wednesday bringing some letters but none from Mother. One from my sister and another from Mrs. Deland. I feel very thankful that I was not doomed to hear any very bad news. My friends at home think now they can only hear from me as it is out of the question for me to visit them. I do not feel so if we are prosperous, & I see no reason why we shall not be, I can go home yet & intend to do so.

Tuesday, November 8th.

Sacramento City has been nearly consumed. The Dr. has had all his instruments & a good deal of clothing burned, loss not exceeding $300. It really seems as though it was not right for us to come to California & lose so much. I do not think that we shall be as well off as at home.[51]

---

[51]Sacramento suffered several devastating fires during the 1850s. The one which occurred on November 4, 1852, destroyed most of the city. Damage was estimated at six million dollars. Thor Severson, *Sacramento, An Illustrated History, 1839-1874* (Sacramento: California Historical Society, 1973), 106.

Evidently Dr. Bailey did not remain in Sacramento after the fire. His name is not listed among the medical practitioners in the city during the 1850s. See: J. Roy Jones, *Memoirs, Men and Medicine, A History of Medicine in Sacramento California* (Sacramento: Premier Publications for the Sacramento Society for Medical Improvement, 1950), 24.

Helen Carpenter

Helen Carpenter

A Trip Across the Plains in an Ox Wagon, 1857

May 26th, 1857

Ho — for California — at last we are on the way — only seven miles from home (which is to be home no longer) yet we have really started, and with good luck may some day reach the "promised land." The trip has been so long talked of, and the preparations have gone on under so many disadvantages, that to be ready at last, to start, is something of an event.

At least two trips were made down into Missouri for young cattle for the teams. Then came the "breaking" process, which was accomplished by yoking them up and putting them "in the swing" between old Smut and Snarley (leaders) and Dave and Start (wheelers). It was hard to say which way ones sympathy should turn, to the young cattle, to the old, or to the drivers — surely commiseration was due somewhere. Then there were several trips to Lawrence (15 miles) for dry goods and food supplies. I got two pairs of shoes, calico for two spencer waists, jeans for a dress skirt, needles, pins and thread and so forth. In the way of supplies there was flour, sugar, bacon and ham, tea, coffee, crackers, dried herring, a small quantity of corn starch, dried apples that we brought from Indiana, one bottle of pickles, cream of tartar and soda and that about made up the outfit. Not having fresh fruit in the Territory, we have no jam or preserves.[1] All that trouble is over with now, and we are not worrying about what is ahead of us.

It was thought best to make a short drive today, to merely pull up and start to enable us to go back for anything needed or forgotten.

---

[1]These were the usual supplies recommended by the guidebooks. When possible, a few "delicacies" were added for special occasions. The Ivins women, for example, included "wine, brandy and medicine" as well as a fruit cake to their stores. Equipment, as outlined by Carpenter on page 3, was more varied depending on the type of wagon and team. For typical lists of supplies and equipment see: Andrew Child, *Overland Route to California*, reprint ed. (Los Angeles: N. A. Kovach, 1946), vii; Ware, *Emigrant's Guide*, 7–8; Gunn, *New Map*, 44. See also Ivins, *Pen Pictures*, 63.

Tonight we are camped on the open prairie near Mr. Fullers and two miles from Centropolis — quite a name for a few pegs driven in the ground for that is all it amounts to except the hope the owner may have in it someday being a town.[2] We trust it may not be a vain hope, but it looks that way now.

Our party consists of three families, and young men as helpers. Already our places have been assigned, that is, the order in which we are to travel. Uncle Sam Mcwhinney is the Captain of the train, he having crossed the plains in '49, has experience, of which we are so much in need, and will most likely get. His spring wagon, drawn by old Suze and Arch (farm horses), is to be in the lead, and Aunt Sis is to be the driver when he is elsewhere. Following this are his two baggage wagons to be looked after by some of the boys of which there are John and Hugh, his 18 and 19 year old sons, and George Haven, Enos St. John and John Newcomb, the last named to act as helpers. The next in order is our wagon with A. O. Carpenter (my husband), myself and Henry Wilson, a 17 year old boy who, by the way, was sold to us by his father the consideration being that Henry receive six months schooling and that he, Mr. Wilson, receive $25.00. The boy was so hard working at home that he feels he has made quite an escape. Carlo, the white bull dog, completes our household.

The last in line is father's wagon. There is father (Thomas McCowen), mother, 16 year old sister Emily, 9 year old brother Hale, and three months old baby sister and father's man, John Fossett. To all the wagons except the one in the lead there are from two to three yoke of cattle. Cousin Teresa is going to ride her Indian pony and help the boys drive the cattle which bring up the rear of the procession. That is, she will help when she wishes to and when she is tired of this, she will ride in the spring wagon with her mother.

The camp tonight looks very pretty. The five wagons with white drilling covers (double thickness over the top) are looking very much dressed up as they stand in a semicircle in the waving green grass. The cattle and horses, 100 or more in all, are off to one side grazing and the camp fires within the circle are burning brightly, inviting the cooks to get to work. I am glad to have enough already cooked, for things do

---

[2]Centropolis, on the Santa Fe Trail, was located in southern Douglass County not far from the Carpenter's home near Ottawa. Gunn, *New Map*.

seem so inconvenient. Everything wanted is at the bottom. Yet our wagon gives promise of more comfort than any of the others. That, I suppose, is as it should be, for a bride should have more detail to her outfit than an ordinary emigrants, and although I have been married four months, this will be my bridal trip.

Our wagon has square bows, which makes it much more roomy than the rounded bows. Inside the cover on each side are pockets in which odds and ends may be stowed away. Then there is an "upper deck," or double floor, the supplies being packed between floors and the bed on the upper one. Henry is to sleep on the ground under the wagon. A spring seat painted bright red sits bolt upright in the front and refuses to bend or budge, regardless of size or weight, so we are not relying on this for much in the way of comfort. The greatest convenience of all, and one which none of the rest have, is a new fangled brake to check the speed in going down hill. The others have lock-chains which are a great inconvenience and take up much time to fix and undo. All have boxes at the back of the wagons for carrying the cooking utensils. In ours there is a Dutch oven, a camp kettle, frying pan, and coffee pot. These, with some tin plates, tin cups, tin spoons, knives and forks, a rolling-pin, bread pan, milk can and a smoothing iron, constitute my entire kitchen furniture. What we are to have to eat is going to be of much more importance than how it is cooked or served.

As we are about to bid farewell to Kansas, I go back in fancy over the two years spent here. First the weary journey of three weeks on a river boat between St. Louis and Westport, Missouri, with children of the party critically ill. Then the struggle to get a roof over our heads on the preemption claim with fencing and planting, for a crop was of prime importance as all supplies had to be hauled from Westport, a distance of 50 miles. Then followed long days of lonesomeness and longing for youthful companions, my late school mates and a summer school of fifteen pupils. Before the summer waned, the entire community was stricken with fever and ague (none escaped). After eight months of pioneer privation and loneliness met some young people at a Christmas party. Other such gatherings soon followed, but such pleasures were cut short by border troubles and an army of "Border Ruffians," under H. Clay Pate, who invaded the neighborhood with no regard for life or property. The mother of our little colt was taken and our only cow. At the battle of Black Jack, Reel (not then my husband) received a painful wound. A spent ball, having followed the ribs around, was cut out of the back. It is some satisfaction to know that in making Sharps rifle cartridges I helped to make Kansas a "Free State."[3]

This is certainly the most beautiful country. The grass is from one to 10 feet high, and there is a profusion of wild flowers all over the prairie. But the violent thunder storms are enough to wreck the nerves of Hercules and the rattlesnakes are as thick as the leaves on the trees, and lastly "but not leastly," the fever and ague are corded up ever ready for use. *Notwithstanding* all these *allurements*, in consideration of what we have undergone, physically and mentally, I can bid Kansas Good Bye without a regret. Still we are sorry to part with Aunt Catherine, Uncle Tom and the children. The picture they made in the old farm wagon this morning when they came to see us off will never be forgotten. Aunt Catherine looked very sad when saying she was sorry that Kansas was not good enough for us.

It was well that we came no farther today. Uncle has sent one of the boys back for something that was forgotten. We are told that it is 15 miles from here to the next timber.

27th May

There were no laggards this morning. Perhaps the beds were a trifle hard and uninviting, making it easier to obey the call, "Get up." Made an early start and nooned on the prairie in the rain. Near us was a Mexican train of 30 wagons and a great number of horses. These are on the way to Missouri for goods to take back to Santa Fe, New Mexico.

Traveled all day over beautiful broken prairie and camped on the

---

[3]The problems of Free Soil settlers, like the Carpenters and McCowens, have been well documented. A good summary which includes the career of Henry Clay Pate, is found in Jay Monaghan, *Civil War on the Western Border, 1854–1865* (Boston: Little Brown, 1950). There are a number of interesting contemporary accounts, many of them listed in Monaghan's bibliography. For a more detailed account of the McCowens' problems with the Border Ruffians, see the account by Mrs. Carpenter's sister, Emily Horton, *Our Family*, 13–21.

bank of 110 Creek where there was sufficient wood and water for our uses.[4]

28th May

Noon on the prairie where there was neither wood nor water. This, of course, precludes the idea of making tea at noon as some of the party wish to do. The cattle would certainly like a drink, but they will have to wait for some miles yet. Traveled 20 miles today and camped in a creek bottom, name of the stream not known.

At times the cattle are quite unruly and it requires the help of all who are not driving a team to keep them from breaking away. Doubtless they think they are getting too far from home.

29th May

A cold rain has made the traveling very disagreeable today. When we stopped on the prairie at noon we were glad to have wagons to sit in to keep dry while eating a hasty meal that seemed the coldest one we have had. Did some one have the hardihood to audibly express the wish that he had a "good warm meal." How indiscreet.

We came 20 or 25 miles. Rolling prairie all the way. The boys found some wood that had been left by campers which was picked up and taken along and proved useful as wood was not plentiful in the ravine where we camped. Yet we had small fires and enjoyed the warmth to the utmost. The only water was three fourths of a miles from camp (could get no closer). As there was nothing but a puddle, it served the cattle only. Father has a fire in the little sheet iron heating stove in the tent. The baby is crying with the cholic [sic] and Mother is vainly endeavoring to make her comfortable. This isn't very homelike. We will have to go to bed to keep warm.

30th May

As usual we nooned on the prairie. Found water for the cattle but none we could drink. During the afternoon passed Elm Springs where

---

[4]The party was traveling on a portion of the Santa Fe Trail. 110 Creek, between Willow Springs and Burlingame in Shawnee County, was 110 miles from the Missouri River. Gunn, *New Map*, 46.

the water kegs were refilled as it is not known where the next supply may be found.

The prairie gradually slopes from the Eastward down to a small stream which lies at the foot of a high rocky bluff that is covered with elms and gooseberry bushes. It relieves the monotony to see some running water and trees and bushes. By the roadside today were the carcasses of two cows. Our stock ran and bellowed and pawed up the earth and had a most "uproarious" time. It was difficult to make them move on. Camped in the most delightful little spot on McDowell Creek. The ground is low and almost surrounded by the creek and scrubby elm trees. Outside of these a high bluff rises which entirely surrounds the place.

The boys saw an animal feasting on a dead ox. They are not sure, but thought it a panther.

May 31

Today has been extremely disagreeable, quite cold and raining most of the time. We nooned and camped in a little valley on Humboldt Creek, four miles south of Riley City. The most of Kansas that I have seen is beautiful country and in the words of Burns, "Ther's no a place in a' the lan' that's match't to this." The bluffs are covered in cedar and are so high and steep that a mile or more would have to be traveled to reach the top. The water of Humboldt Creek is clear and green (the reflection from the cedars on the bluffs) and in places is very deep.

June 1st

One ox could not be found this morning which detained us until noon when he was brought in. After crossing the Humboldt we ascended a ridge on which we traveled for a mile or two, then went down the *longest, steepest and stoniest* hill that I ever saw traveled. The road was barely wide enough for the wagon track, and it took all hands to each wagon to keep them from upsetting and get down safely. This was very hard on both teams and men and sufficiently hard on the women to have to walk over such a rocky road. On reaching the foot of the hill we were in the Kansas River bottom. Here we missed the road and went to Smoky Hill which was three miles out of the way and above the ferry where we had to cross the river. It took a couple of hours to find the ferry. The wagons were ferried across and the cattle were made to swim. It was nearly sundown when all were safely over.

We were told that the reservation extends seven miles in each direction from Fort Riley and that we would not be permitted to camp inside the reserve. We concluded to make the attempt and halted in the timber a mile north of the Fort. Before the cattle were all unyoked a soldier came and gave us notice to leave but finally told us we could stay if the cattle were kept out of sight of the Fort. This we did, regarding it a great privilege to stop here as it was already late and everybody tired.[5]

We have a very kindly feeling for Uncle Sam's men. This is the second time that we have been befriended. In the summer of 1856, a company of U.S. Cavalry was sent from Fort Leavenworth with orders to "disband and disarm" the settlers (who were protecting their homes against the raids of the "Border ruffians" in Kansas). "They came, they saw" and were conquered. When they got in our neighborhood (Ottawa Creek), they halted at Reel's home, sat in the grass, allowing their horses to graze while they took in the situation. At the end of an hour they were so in sympathy with the settlers that they not only "*Did not find a company of armed Settlers*" but offered pecuniary assistance out of their mere pittance of $8.00 per month army pay. *Long live Uncle Sam's men.* Had they disarmed us, we would have been entirely at the mercy of the invaders who were giving their assistance to President James Buchanan to drive from the Territory those who were not in favor of making Kansas a slave state.

June 2nd.

We were very much surprised to find such nice frame and stone buildings at the Fort. Having come over so much wild country, we

---

[5]Fort Riley, Kansas, was established in 1853 on the Kansas River near the junction of the Republican and Smokey Hill rivers. In 1857 it was a large and busy post. Riley City, described by Mrs. Carpenter, was one of three small towns located across the river from the fort. Woodbury F. Pride, *The History of Fort Riley* (Fort Riley, Kansas: n.p., 1926), 88–95, 110–11. For several excellent descriptions of life at Fort Riley in the late 1850s see Percival G. Lowe, *Five Years a Dragoon ('49 to '54) and Other Adventures on the Plains* (Kansas City: F. Hudson, 1906).

were not expecting anything so nice. And then it has been so long since we saw such buildings. Without exception this is the cleanest village we ever saw and is beautifully situated on big rolling ground. On a bluff above the town is a monument that can be seen at a great distance. This is, I suppose, the Fort's cemetery.

The Fort was to our left and above the main traveled road. I left the train and went up into town to make some purchases finding that my trousseau is incomplete since we have so much cold rainy weather. The store contained but little in the way of ladies goods. The best I could do was to buy some brown and black chequered cotton pants cloth to make a jacket.

While we were taking dinner a train of nine wagons and 320 head of cattle from Missouri passed us and nooned nearby. Camped on Wild Cat Creek, 16 miles from the Fort. Plenty of wood and warm water.

June 3rd.

I had no pattern to cut the jacket by, but as I am used to cutting, I blocked it out and mother helped in the fitting. It has been too cold for sewing and the road has been so rough and uneven that I accomplished but little with the needle. If it were not for my dire necessity I would give it up as a bad job. The horses travel faster than the oxen which enables Uncle Sam to go ahead and find stopping places. There was plenty of water in a ravine where the train stopped for the nooning. During the afternoon three *horribly muddy* ditches were crossed. Father's wagon was broken in one of them, and the little stove, which was fastened on the back of the wagon, got pretty well smashed up. They have succeeded in straightening it up so it will still be of some service. After getting through the muddy ditches the road was both stony and sandy. Passed a stream of running water and then, when camping time came, had to go three fourths of a mile from the road to find water, full of wiggletails at that, almost no wood. Saw four wolves.

June 4th.

Still prairie country. Crossed a small stream that is well timbered and then on the prairie again nooning where there was no water. Camped on a small creek to the left of the road. It is of the utmost importance to know where water is to be found, and not knowing but this journal may some day be of service to someone as a guidebook, I more carefully note where there is wood and water than I otherwise would. Each day's journey measures the road off into spans, so it would not be difficult to keep track of the desirable and undesirable stopping places.

There was no train in sight of our camp so we were surprised in the dusk of the evening to hear the laughter of children as though having a big romp. The hilarity grew "fast and furious," increasing in volume and distinctness. It took a few minutes for the wiser ones to convince us that our neighbors were a pack of wolves and the assurance that there was "no danger" was received with some incredulity.

In leaving camp this morning, Aunt Sis (in the lead) called out to know which way she should go, to the right or to the left. It then developed that nearly all in camp were so turned around that they were uncertain which was the right way to go. Uncle Sam's head was considered clearest on points of this kind, so it was left to him to decide yet it was some time before we got straightened out so as to tell that we really were going right. I believe some of the boys went to where we left the main road the evening before and saw where the wagon tracks turned out before they were convinced. The oddest thing about it was that so many at the same time should lose their direction.

June 5th.

Rough road and plenty of dust. It seems odd to find dust so soon after the recent rains. The explanation is that the rain is not general but "in streaks" following the timber which lies along the streams and in the ravines.

Nooned in a ravine where there was water for the cattle only. Wood is more plentiful here. Carlo cheated us out of some fresh meat this morning by frightening away an antelope that would have otherwise fallen in our hands. This afternoon crossed a stream with such high steep banks that it was with great difficulty we got safely over. Sitting in the wagon under such circumstances is not only very unpleasant but dangerously near *frightful,* yet it is the only thing to do since these places must be crossed. When once over I feel that another bridge behind us has been burned. A couple of men who had been after horses that took the back tract [sic] stayed and helped at the crossing. One of the men had lost a thumb. While leading the horses a halter was wrapped around his thumb then pulled back and the result was a lost thumb.

June 6th.

Road today was similar to what has been gone over. Camped on a small stream supposed to be Little Blue. *Another bad* crossing.

June 7th.

"Laying by" today not because it is Sunday but to give the cattle an opportunity to feed up on the good grass which is plentiful and to give the men a chance to repair the damage done at those fearful creek crossings. The women are taking advantage of the stop to do the family washing and make light bread. Of course the cattle must be considered, but I am sorry for one day to pass without getting a little nearer to California.

June 8th.

Rained last night. The thunder was louder than we are accustomed to which is saying a good deal for we know all about Kansas thunder storms and had thought they were not to be equalled anywhere. Nooned on what they are *sure* is the Blue which is quite a stream. The crossing was not quite as bad as some we have passed.[6]

Three Pawnee Indians came while we were nooning. They asked for food, but the order was "*don't give them a thing.*" It was thought that they would follow and be a nuisance if shown any kindness. I could not eat lunch with those poor wretches watching every mouthful like hungry dogs. Mother found an opportunity to slip something to them, and they did not follow nor give any trouble. We do not coincide with all of Uncle Sam's views, but he is the "boss" of the train and as such his views must be respected. Early in the afternoon, we

---

[6]Carpenter confused the Big Blue and the Little Blue. The party, at this point, was on the Big Blue, "a fine stream, some four or five rods wide, with a swift current. . . ." Platt, *Traveler's Guide*, 2–3.

came into the "St. Jo" road which is the main line of travel for emigrants who come this side of the Platte.[7] There are trains to be seen in front and back of us. This is going to make it harder to find grass, wood and water and nice camping places. At night found water for the cattle only and no wood whatever.

June 9th.

Nooned and camped on the Blue. We are now in Nebraska. The country is more level than what we have come over, and the road is good. Met a large party of Mormons going to the States. There seemed to be twice as many women as men and twice as many children as women. All were in rags and tatters and, must I say it, scabs. They [were the] very worst lot I ever saw. All who were large enough (except the drivers) were out of the wagons holding out rusty kettles and pans begging for milk. Fortunately we all together had what made two large buckets full which was given to them very cheerfully and then went on their way rejoicing.

We are solely tried tonight with gnats and mosquitoes.

June 10th.

Rained again last night. Near camp were two graves. The wolves had taken charge of the "last sad rites" as was evidenced by the human bones scattered about. A herd of 27 buffalo was seen by some of the party, also some elk. Nooned and camped on Blue River. This is quite a large stream. It is very warm.

June 11th.

Still traveling near the Blue. Camped on a branch of it. Had sufficient wood and water but we are told that there is no more of either for 28 miles.[8]

---

[7]The Carpenter party probably joined the St. Jo road near Marysville, 140 miles from St. Joseph in Marshall County, Kansas. From this point to Fort Kearny, the next "settlement" of any size, the party had to travel some 165 miles through uninhabited country. Gunn, *New Map*, 47.

The guide books also warned emigrants about the Pawnee, "who are often troublesome." Platt, *Traveler's Guide*, 3.

[8]The party was now traveling up the Little Blue which the road followed for nearly fifty miles, several days' journey by wagon. The route along the Little Blue, including accounts by other travelers, is well traced in Mattes, *Platte River Road*, 150–61. See also: Platt, *Traveler's Guide*, 3–4; Morgan, *Pritchard Diary*, 59–61.

During the day we passed an Indian hanging cemetery which was quite a little distance from the road and we did not care to go nearer. Some 25 or 30 feet from the ground three bodies in wrapping were suspended like hammocks between rather small trees. We never before could understand why any people should adopt such a method of disposing of their dead, but since seeing the ravages of the wolves yesterday, we feel that it is the only thing for them to do.

June 12th.

The train was detained a considerable time this morning by others stopping in the road to water their cattle. It was not possible to pass as the stock would have gotten mixed and made no end of trouble. We were in sight of the Platte River most of the afternoon and made camp near it. It seems very odd to see a river with neither tree nor bush along its banks. On the other side of the river, a mile or two back, there is some timber in sight. Cooking has to be done with green willows. This need be tried but once to enable one to give an opinion on this kind of fuel. The water is full of yellow sediment and looks still thicker and less inviting than Missouri River water. After standing a while the sand is partly settled rendering it a *little* more drinkable.[9] In the river the sand keeps continually rolling up and washing about so there is constant change in the river bed and also in the depth of the water.

In the dusk of the evening, the women went a short distance down stream for a dip in the river even if the water was somewhat thick. At this point there was almost no bank, but the tall bunch grass and increasing darkness was a sufficient protection against a "Peeping Thomas" if there had been one in camp. The sensation on stepping into the stream was one never to be forgotten. When the foot touched bottom, the bottom began to fall out and there was a hasty scramble for terra firma with recollections of dreadful stories about quick-sand and its victims. It was only the most courageous, or foolhardy, of the party that dared to stay in the water and hang on to the bunch grass that was in easy reach. We made a rather queer looking swimming party as we perched along the river bank and were reminded of the old song, "Hang your clothes on a hickory limb, But don't go near the

---

[9] On the quality of the Platte River water, see the Bailey journal, note 18.

water." In the absence of bushes the clothes could not be hung, but I, for one, was ready to follow the remaining instructions.

Some people from Michigan by the name of Inmann and Taylor joined us here and want to be of our party. They have four wagons. There was a "Split up" in their train and they are looking for more congenial company. Such things are not unusual as the conditions are not favorable to patience and good temper.[10]

June 13th.

Arrived at Fort Kearny about noon. The surrounding country very much resembles the Grand Prairie of Illinois. There are three quite nice looking two story frame houses, the rest are of sod. All are on two sides of a square plot, presumably where the soldiers drill. One lone soldier was on guard and paced back and forth halting at certain points. He was very noticably oblivious of our presence, not deigning to glance at the very best looking women of the party. There is also a blacksmith shop and a store. We bought a can of peaches and one of blackberries and some cheese. The latter should have been "mustered" out long ago, it is too old to be in the service. One mere taste took the skin off the end of my tongue.[11]

Pawnee Indians are in evidence everywhere. They have no clothing but are wrapped in very unsanitary looking blankets and are adept in the management of them. Without pins or string the blankets are kept in place, and there is no undue exposure of the person. On a day like this (very hot) they would find mosquito bars more comfortable than Makinaw blankets. I think I will suggest it to them. We are told that they have just returned from a buffalo hunt and horse stealing expedition and are here at the Fort for the express purpose of disposing of their dried meat to the emigrants. They know how to charge for it too. The meat was well sold out before we knew it was to be had so

---

[10]Such split-ups were common on the trail. For several excellent references see Hutcheson, "Overland in 1852," 427 n 5 and John Reid, "Dividing the Elephant: The Separation of Mess and Joint Stock Property on the Overland Trail," *Hastings Law Journal* 28 (September 1976): 79 – 92.

[11]Carpenter's description of the fort is similar to that of Mrs. Bailey in 1852. From Fort Kearny to South Pass the Carpenter and Bailey trains followed the same road, and it is interesting to compare the two women's descriptions of the journey and the various landmarks. Annotations for the sites mentioned in both diaries are in the Bailey journal.

would have missed this rare opportunity of adding a much needed change in the bill of fare if we had not done some lively rustling. That Indian is most likely still wondering why we so suddenly became indifferent and refused to buy. I am constantly told that I am too fastideous, no doubt that is so, and that is why I objected to the fellow's *meat chest*, down which were trickling little rivulets of perspiration.

Camped a mile from town and half a mile from the river, that being the closest we could get on account of mire or quick-sand. The boys waded and swam across to an island for wood which was nothing but green willows yet rather precious after being carried so far.

June 14th.

Sunday. Passed Houks and Farmers train and several others "laying by" to dry their clothing which was drenched in the rain last night. It only sprinkled where we were, but here, five miles farther on, there was a furious storm with hail stones the size of a quail egg. Our wagon and father's are the only ones that seem to have a double thickness of cloth over the top, and they are rain proof.

The road and country over which we are passing is quite level. At all times the road follows the river as closely as the nature of the ground will permit. From the river on the right to the bluffs on the left, the distance varies from one to four or five miles and appears to be on a level. Some are speculating as to whether the river overflows this land. They think it has, at some time, even if it does not now. The bluffs are from 200 to 300 feet high and from this distance appear perpendicular, though it is known that there are places where they may be ascended and that high table lands are beyond them. Some timber is to be seen now on islands in the river.

June 15

Met another train of Mormons going to the States. One of the party said, "We have been in heaven long enough and are going to hell." The poor creatures did not look at all happy and it was a stretch of the imagination to place them anywhere with heavenly surroundings. They do not seem to fear "Going from the frying pan in the fire." One member of the party had been to Salt Lake to visit his daughter and claimed that the Mormons took $300 from him.

Found no water at noon. A herd of buffalo was seen this afternoon at a comparatively short distance away. This created general excitement and eight or ten of the company gave chase, some on foot, some on horseback, armed with muskets, revolvers and knives. The train kept right on until the usual camping time (a little before sundown), then halted by a slough. When the oxen were partly unyoked, Reel came in bringing the good news of his success in capturing a big buffalo bull. As it was two miles from camp all haste had to be made in returning with the oxen to haul it in, if they made the trip before night set in. Five yoke were taken and there should have been one or two yoke more as it turned out to be a very heavy job. Old Smut and Snarley were the only oxen that could be gotten near enough to the buffalo to hitch on. They did not like the scent of the animal nor the blood.

They estimate the animal's weight at one ton and age anywhere from 12 to 20 years. The old fellow was grazing apart from the herd when one of the hunters crept up within 60 yards and from behind a little knoll fired a load of buck-shot from his old musket. The buffalo made off and Reel, following on horseback, was soon at close range and being an excellent shot and armed with a Sharp's rifle loaded with ounce slugs, the chase was of short duration. A shot in the hip and ranging almost the entire length of the body brought down the game. Yet another was fired through anxiety to have a job well done. The buck-shot merely penetrated the skin and would have caused the animal little or no inconvenience.

This is the greatest animal show that we have seen. Hale is a large boy for nine years of age and when he stood by the shoulders (the largest part of the body) his head could not be seen from the opposite side. We would have liked a nice buffalo robe of our own capturing, but unfortunately this is the time of year when they have little or no hair having "shed off" and besides dragging it for two miles would have ruined the beauty of the skin. About the only hair is between the horns where it measures 16 inches in length.

All are busy caring for the meat of which there is plenty. Camp looks like a meat shop with "Things that niver were neighbors before." There is no wood to be had without going a mile in one way or taking a short cut through the muddy slough and then wading the river which is shoulder deep. Both ways have been tried with the result that each party wishes he had gone the other way. We brought a little wood along from the last camp and that, with some buffalo chips, answers the purpose very well.

June 16

The first to rise this morning got a good view of coyotes making an assessment on the buffalo which was right in camp. Hunger seems to have made them very venturesome. A lone footman would be fortunate if they did not overpower him. Mother got a large bucket of tenderloin this morning; the coyotes had not yet reached it.

Decided not to travel today as the meat is to be cared for. It is as tender and good as could be desired. More buffalo were seen this morning and the boys could not resist the temptation to go after them regardless of the present supply of meat. Am glad that no more was added to the larder. Three passing trains were very glad to get some of the meat. The last got little but soup bones. Tonight the wagons are decorated with slices of meat dangling from strings fastened to ropes that reach from front to back along the side of the wagons, looking very much like coarse red fringe. My string of meat is to hang inside the wagon in the day time to keep it out of the dust as much as possible.

June 17

Three buffalo were seen this morning going diagonally across the valley toward the bluffs. They were probably lost from their party and were on the back track. At this season they are migrating to a cooler climate and all others seen have been going toward the river. I hear that it is almost impossible to turn a herd from its course. Many places in the valley have well worn trails made by the animals going to the river for water. These trails are cut into dust by the many hoofs passing over them. High winds and frequent rain storms sweep away the dust leaving the trails below the level all the way from one foot to four or five feet owing to the soil and locality, the greater depth being in the approch to sags and ravines.

Reel and Hugh and one of the other boys started off in a direct line to the point the buffalo were heading for and arrived in time to get off of their horses and line up on a little knoll within 50 yards of the trail and in full view of the on coming buffalo. They did not swerve a hair's breadth to the right or to the left and when directly opposite there was a simultaneous pulling of triggers and — every gun failed. What the boys said is not herein stated. Damp powder or damp caps alone prevented us from having three more buffalo for all three of the boys are dead shots. Yet as we are not needing meat it is just as well as it is. Before the guns could be gotten in condition the buffalo had climbed the bluffs and were out of sight. The boys were too disgusted to pursue them.

Met 34 merchant wagons that have been out to Fort Laramie and are on the way back to Missouri. It has been immensely disagreeable for the drivers today for a strong northwest wind drove the dust in clouds into their faces as they walked beside their teams. Am glad that I am not an ox driver. Henry hurries up the team until the leader's heads are at the tail gate of the wagon ahead, then he steps in behind old Dave's heels and takes a seat on the wagon tongue. In this way he gets a rest from walking for a few lengths of the wagon but soon the oxen begin to lag and the driver must be alongside to apply the very necessary encouragement.

A large grey wolf kept pace with the wagons today for more than an hour. He was on the side next to the bluffs and just out of shooting distance. Whoops, yells and firing guns did not change his intention of bearing us company. We knew there was no danger yet it did get on our nerves. Reel mounted Billy and started in pursuit. There seemed no special hurry to get away; in fact, he gave us up reluctantly but as Reel gained on him the speed finally increased until he slunk into some uneven ground and was lost sight of.

June 18

Where we nooned today the road lay directly at the foot of the bluffs some two or three miles from the river. The bluffs at this place are much higher than any we have passed. A few cedars and a very little grass is all that is growing on them. They appear to be nothing but vast heaps of sand. Camped a mile from the road near a small miry branch that circles around in the prairie before reaching the river.

The men went hunting again. A small band of buffalo, some 14 or more, crossed our path on their way to the bluffs. They were so near that it caused intense excitement and there was a rush for firearms and horses. Hugh and Reel were of the party. Hugh was mounted on a small Spanish dun mule branded M.R. and said to have been the property of Major Russell from whom it was taken by the Sac and Fox Indians.[12] Later the Comanches, in a raid against these tribes, murdered the Indians and captured the mule which afterwards became the property of the Mcwhinneys. The herd was soon overtaken. Hugh exclaimed, "Golly what a whopper," and took off after a big bull intending to ride up closely and then dismount and shoot. He knew if he shot from the mule he would be quickly landed on the ground, the habit of the animal being to turn round and round under such circumstances in a way to unseat the very best rider. When close enough to have speared the buffalo, and when about to dismount to shoot, "Major Russell" (accustomed to the Indian style of hunting and warfare to strike and run) whirled end for end and in a twinkling Hugh lay sprawling on the ground on top of his gun and in the very face of the bull. In describing the occurance Hugh said, "I believe I could have poked him in the eye with my fingers. Anyway that is the way it looked to me at the time." The bull must have been as badly frightened as Hugh for after sidling around, with head lowered to the ground, he backed off to what he must have considered a safe distance and then made off at great speed.

In the meantime, Reel wounded a calf and had a good prospect of getting it when he had to give up the chase to get Hugh's mule, and by the time he was caught, the gun could not be located. Hugh remembered just where it lay near some partially dried bunch grass, yet when they came to look over the mesa there were several hundred little circles of grass with a few feet of open space between them and all looking so much alike that the boys were quite bewildered. It was a long hunt and took up the rest of the afternoon, but they finally succeeded in finding it. In the excitement of starting none of them thought of ammunition so they merely had what was in their guns

---

[12]"Major Russell" is impossible to identify from the information in the journal. The unfortunate mule may have been named for fur trader and trapper Osborne Russell, but more likely the reference is to the well-known freighter and stagecoach operator, William H. Russell. See Howard Lamar, ed., *Reader's Encyclopedia of the American West* (New York: Crowell, 1978), 1053, for a brief summary of each man's career.

and pistols. So if "Major Russell" had behaved like a white man's mule instead of an Indian's the hunt could not have lasted long.

The others of the party soon emptied their guns and went home. By the time Hugh and Reel reached the edge of the bluff, it was dark and the various campfires down in the valley twinkled like so many stars and looked about as far away. The train had traveled right along and the bluffs and level looked so much the same day after day, with no distinguishing feature that the hunters could make no approximate guess as to which particular twinkle of light was "in the window" for them. After going to three camps they gave the horses the rein (as a last hope) and were not long in reaching us. The word *tired* is quite inadequate for their physical condition, but whatever it lacked they made up for in appetite for any thing edible. We were beginning to think that they were lost so were very glad to have them safely back. Did not even regret the loss of the calf and bull.

June 19

The valley is narrowing and the bluffs are much nearer the river. Consequently the road has been more uneven than any since coming into the St. Jo road. Where we nooned the road forked, the right hand crosses the river soon and the left continues a few miles farther before crossing. Most of the travel seems to have gone to the right so, entertaining hopes of better feed on the least traveled road, we took the left hand one. Camped directly by the river. The mosquitoes have been extremely troublesome all day and are *much* worse tonight. When they are particularly troublesome in the day time a buffalo chip is lighted and placed in the wagon. This soon smokes them out. We can stand it longer than they can. By the way, these buffalo chips, when well cured, are not at all offensive and make a very good substitute for wood. The frequent heavy rains of perhaps one or two years wash away the objectionable parts and what remains is like *papier mache* and burns like punk.

There is a bride and groom in the Inmann party. The bride wears hoops. We have read of hoops being worn, but they had not reached Kansas before we left so these are the first we have seen and would not recommend them for this mode of traveling. The wearer has less personal privacy than the Pawnee in his blanket. In asides the bride is called "Miss Hoopy." Fairly good grass in camp and willows for wood.

June 20

Almost the longest day in the year and a more uncomfortable one could not be made to order. The heat has been intolerable, the bright sunshine on the white wagon covers has been blinding, the dust suffocating, and the mosquitoes painfully tormenting. Mosquitoes all day long and they are here for the night and we have nothing to protect ourselves in any way. Today we made the attempt to drive ahead of the two baggage wagons as no one rides in them and the eight yoke of cattle do stir up the dust at a great rate. But we are given to understand that we can travel behind the baggage wagons or leave the party which is slightly irritating from every point of view. I am sure to get my "peck of dirt" before this journey is half done.

The dust and wind has given everybody sore lips. The worse cases ache, swell, crack open, and bleed. The lower lip is invariably in the worst condition. Some of the boys stick a piece of paper on the lip to prevent it from being moistened by the tongue as we will otherwise *continually* have an inclination to do. The paper gave me no relief but made the burning ache just that much worse. Met another train of Mormons. In order to find a camping place, we had to drive half a mile from the road over the roughest ground I have seen and cross two muddy sloughs and then had no wood except willows and very poor grass.

June 21

Rough road, heat and mosquitoes the same as yesterday. Reached the river at five P.M. Two trains have crossed today. Uncle Sam went on horseback to learn the depth of the water and a safe course to take and at the same time strike the coming out place on the other side.

June 22

There was neither time nor inclination to write more yesterday. It was night before all were across the river and then supper had to be gotten and the damp things pulled out of the wagon, etc. etc. and everybody dead tired. The first team was an hour in making the trip, and the distance (the way we had to go) was a mile. Those who had just crossed said it would be necessary for us to double teams. This being done, only two wagons could go at the same time which made it necessary for all the drivers and oxen to cross the stream *three times*, going over and back and then recrossing.

As Uncle Sam was going to ride near one of his baggage wagons, mother and I thought that would insure a little more safety so pre-ferred that to our own. Where we went down into the water the river bank was steep and about four feet high. On our first entrance into the stream, the wagon came so near standing on end that all view of the team was cut off for a few seconds and there could be seen only the muddy water well up to the wagon bed. When the wagon was righted there was little to reassure us. The water runs very swiftly and that, together with the sand washing from under the wheels or the wheels settling down into the quicksand, caused a shaking, trembling sensation that was truly terrifying. There were four drivers to each wagon, yet it was difficult to keep the cattle moving in the right direc-tion as they bore off down stream on account of the swiftness of the water. If they halted for just a moment, they had difficulty in getting their feet out of the quicksand and the settling down of the wagon could be plainly felt. In places the water was midway of the wagon beds. In this great expanse of muddy water there was no way of telling the deep places from the shallow ones. Each team and wagon cut down into the sand which was at once washed away leaving an entirely different footing for the one following immediately after.

On the way over, it was necessary to pull onto two different sand islands and traverse them a short distance. Between the islands the cur-rent was so swift that the lead wagon cut into the sand badly and the consequent washing out left the water of such a depth that the cattle to the next wagon were forced to swim and the wagon floated. At this juncture Henry plunked off into a hole and went in all over and being unable to swim he was turned over a few times and was going down stream when Reel caught him and put him on his feet. If immediate assistance had not been given, there would have been one boy less in camp. John Fossett, on a mule, rode ahead of some of the wagons to show them which way to go. The mule went off into a hole, and they both turned a somersault. The mule then decided to go his own way, and John had to wade the rest of the way across the river. There were a good many jokes about him being such a "dandy guide." It was really too bad since he got such a wetting, and the very same might have happened to any of them as there is no way of telling where these dangerous places are. All in all we came off well. No life lost, cattle all safely across, and provisions but slightly injured by the water. Yet we had to take everything out to air and dry out the wagons. The cattle are very tired and quite a number need shoeing so we stay here for the day.

The Inmanns have been with us for ten days, yet we did not know that there was a grandmother in their party until today after the wagons were emptied when she was seen sitting in a rocking chair looking out of the back of the wagon. In answer to inquiries she said that she was large and feeble and could not get out and in without help so she just stayed in the wagon. Think of that, and we who can wait on ourselves and get out and in at pleasure have thought we were *so uncomfortable* and *complained* so *much.*

The foregoing does not sound as though we were sociable or on good terms with our fellow travelers. The plain fact of the matter is we have no time for sociability. From the time we get up in the morning until we are on the road it is hurry-scurry to get breakfast and put away the things that necessarily had to be pulled out last night. While under way there is no room in the wagon for a visitor. Nooning is barely long enough to eat a cold bite and at night all the cooking utensils and provisions are to be gotten about the camp fire and cooking enough done to last until the next night. Although there is not much to cook, the difficulty and inconvenience in doing it amounts to a great deal. So by the time one has squatted around the fire and cooked bread and bacon, made several trips to and from the wagon, washed the dishes (with no place to drain them), and gotten things ready for an early breakfast, some of the others already have their night caps on. At any rate, it is time to go to bed.

In respect to the women's work, the days are all very much the same except when we stop for a day. Then there is washing to be done and light bread to make and all kinds of odd jobs. Some women have very little help about the camp being obliged to get the wood and water (as far as possible), make camp fires, unpack at night and pack up in the morning, and if they are Missourians they have the milking to do if they are fortunate enough to have cows. I am lucky in having a Yankee for a husband, so am well waited on.

There is another crossing of the river two miles farther on that we have heard of. Two days ago two wagons turned over there. Two men were drowned and their bodies were not recovered. Their wagons and provisions were lost. Two trains are on the other side preparing to cross where we did.

The boys found a skull of a white person near the camp and regardless of my protests put it up and shot at it with their pistols. Of course there have been all kinds of surmises as to whom it belonged to and how it came to be here. If the wolves could only be interviewed, something could be learned of the matter. As there are neither stones nor timber in this section, there is no way to secure the bodies of those so unfortunate as to require interment.

No fuel here except chips and they are not at all plentiful. It is 20 miles across to North Platte and there is no water on the way so that is to be our next stopping place. Today has been the warmest day of the season. It would be more correct to say *hottest*. This evening is very cloudy and such a stiff wind that it is difficult to walk against it.

June 23rd.

The bluff we had to ascend to get on the dividing ridge between the North and South Platte was very high and *very* steep in places. The road was necessarily sandy as the whole country is little but sand. Once on the ridge the road is quite level and not at all bad. In most fertile places there is a very little grass and bunches of cactus. The cattle would not eat the grass so nooning was short.

When we got to the going down place, we certainly felt that we were "between the Devil and the deep sea." Had it been possible to avoid this, the place would have been thought impassable. In the past, the wagons were let down with ropes. The places are still plainly marked. Some more venturesome ones, or perhaps ones who had no ropes, left their tracks in the sand and like a band of sheep the rest followed. Only one yoke of cattle was left to each wagon and all four of the wheels were locked. Besides being dreadfully steep, the road was badly cut up and the dust and sand so deep that the chuck holes could not be seen (but were plainly felt) and anyway the air was so full of dust that much of the time the oxen were barely visible. "My kingdom" for a breath of fresh air.[13]

Once down this *terrible* hill we were in what is called Ash Hollow. This name I suppose because the earth and dust look like ashes. There were two miles of hard pulling through deep sand to reach the river which looks just as muddy and turbulent as the South Platte. The bluffs come down closer, leaving a narrower valley than on the other side of the divide and there are some cedars near the top. We are glad to see a tree even at a distance. The grass is very poor.

Before the teams could be unyoked, the camp was full of Sioux Indians. We are not accustomed to meeting Indians on such familiar terms and were somewhat nervous to have so many standing about in the way of the camp arrangements for the night. Uncle Sam kept charging us to keep on our guard as "nobody knows what they may be up to." They are tall, fine looking Indians. The women and men alike wear the hair in two long braids hanging down the back. From its sleek, glossy appearance it shows the care that it receives. The dress is the same as the Pawnees have, government Makinaw three point blankets. They came with moccasins to trade for something to eat. Some of the Inmanns got a pair for one biscuit. Some one else gave two biscuits while I got a pair for a quart of "soog" (sugar). They are very eager for sweetness of any description. Their moccasins are not at all pretty and not durable. They are of poorly tanned buffalo hide and are stiff and rough. A piece the shape of the foot, for the sole, is fastened to the upper with stitches half an inch long made of string. I believe such sewing is called "whanging." It doesn't keep out the dust effectively. The Indians know but little English so the bartering was

---

[13]The descent into Ash Hollow, sometimes called Windlass Hill, was very steep, crooked, and difficult. It required that "at least two wheels of the wagon be locked." Platt, *Traveler's Guide*, 6. The descent and the Hollow are described in detail, with accounts by other travelers, in Mattes, *Platte River Road*, 281–310.

Despite Mrs. Carpenter's comments below, the Hollow was named for the many ash trees in the vicinity. However, another traveler in 1857 reported, "The beautiful trees that were growing in this delightful spot when I passed it in 1850 have been all cut down. . . . and the place has quite a dreary aspect." William A. Carter, "Diary of Judge William A. Carter," *Annals of Wyoming* 11 (April 1939): 91.

done mostly by signs. It was suggested that as the Traders were principally Frenchmen that if we only spoke that language there would be no trouble in making them understand. Old gentleman Inmann said he could talk French. "Hadn't thought of it. Just stand back boys and I'll make them understand peteet, peteet, peteet (petite)." Those stupid Indians did not understand French any better than they did English. Their camp is a short distance down the rivers where there is a white man with whiskey for sale. Another skull found near camp.

June 24

It has been very hard on the cattle and drivers today. Rough road and deep sand most of the time. The sand was so soft that the wagons cut down into it from eight to ten inches. Met a train of 20 wagons. Mormons again. They say there are plenty more that would be glad to leave Salt Lake if they could only get away. These are in just such squalor as the others we met. Nooned close to the river, had very poor grass.

We passed the graves of five soldiers who were killed in Sept. 1855 in an action between the Sioux and the U.S. soldiers at Fort Kearney. The tombstones were made of cedar brought from the bluff and hewn into shape, then painted white with black lettering. This silent story brought to mind the song of Napoleon which I learned from Bertia, "He sleeps his last sleep, he has fought his last battle, No sound can awake him to glory again." This has been running through my head all day, despite my efforts to think of something else. So I have sung and hummed and sung until I never want to hear it again. In this engagement the Indians were routed. Those who took refuge in a cave in the bluffs were followed by the soldiers who tried every means to induce them to come out. Being unsuccessful, volley after volley was poured into the cave with the result that not one Indian came out alive. There were in all 18 men, women and children. A mother and infant at the breast fell at the same shot and in such a way that in death she sat clasping the child to her bosom. Those soldiers were there for the purpose of exterminating Indians. Were they disloyal to the government when they shed a few tears? If the Sioux had sent their squaws and children instead of their warriors to meet Uncle Sam's men, they would have received the blankets which the government invariably issues to them after a raid and treaty of peace, and there need have been no blood shed on either side.[14]

And as for the treaty of peace, it is not worth the paper it is written on when once an Indian begins to feel ugly and is aching for a "scrap." The foregoing was learned from one who was in the raid just spoken of. His term of enlistment expired soon after, and as he had no further desire for Indian fighting, he did not re-enlist.

Camped near the river. No wood and poor grass. Came near forgetting to say that should the services of a physician be required one may be found in one of the trains ahead. His ad, freshly written in bright red keel, was conspicuously placed on each of the cedar slabs to the memory of the soldiers, "Dr. J. Noble." The Dr. is a deep thinker for no more sightly place could have been selected to catch the eye of the entire traveling public.[15]

June 25th.

I am wondering just how hard the wind has to blow before it is called a tornado. We were visited last night by the most violent wind storm that we ever experienced. The wagon was so shaken up that one could not tell which way the vibrations were, backward, forward, side-wise or all three together. Aunt Sis was curious and putting her head outside came near going overboard and lost a fine new silk handkerchief that was doing duty as a night cap. Nothing more was seen of it.

It was the intention to make an early start this morning so as to get ahead of some of the trains that are doing their share in making feed

---

[14]This engagement occurred during Colonel William S. Harney's campaign against the Brule Sioux in the fall of 1855. In the course of the battle, eighty-five, not eighteen, Sioux and seven soldiers were killed. Robert M. Utley, *Frontiersmen in Blue: The United States Army and the Indian, 1848–1865* (New York: MacMillan, 1967), 116–17. A longer account of the battle with descriptions and comments by eye witnesses is in Mattes, *Platte River Road*, 311–29. Helen's sister, Emily, recalled that Helen wrote the line, "He sleeps his last sleep . . ." on one of the grave markers. Horton, *Our Family*, 29.

[15]There are few diaries for 1857, and none of the other writers mention the well-publicized Dr. Noble. Mattes notes that another traveler (whom he erroneously identifies as Francis Sawyer) "noted signs posted at intervals for a 'J. Morely, Physician and Surgeon.'" Mattes, *Platte River Road*, 87.

scarce. But an ox was missing and we were detained two hours in consequence. The ox was found four miles ahead in Farmer's train. Nooned at an old camping place quite a distance from the road and even then found very poor grass. We more often eat bread and milk at noon than any thing else. The milk is carried in a can swung to the wagon bows overhead. By noon (if the churn works well and it seldom fails), there is a ball of butter the size of a hickory nut and innumerable little ones like shot. If the day is hot, we have hot milk; if cold, we have cold milk, but unlike the "bean porrage" of school days, it is never "nine days old."[16]

Overtook Farmer's train this afternoon. Camped on the bank of a clear cold stream just where it empties into the river. Its individuality is soon lost in the muddy river. No wood whatever. When going into camp where there is no wood various chip gatherers may be seen, bag in hand, intent on getting enough to cook the evening meal. It would be amusing if it were not dire necessity which drives them to it. Hale made a gathering this evening and reported to mother that he got "some good fresh ones." Very poor grass on the island where the cattle were taken. Much of the road today was through deep sand. Gnats were very, very troublesome and the wind blew a gale. Nothing more was needed to make the day a disagreeable one.

June 26

Camp was astir early so made a good start. For some reason the camp road made a detour to the left before reaching the main road. The Inmanns, instead of following as usual, struck off in a direct line. Their aim seemed to be to get into the road just ahead of us. Their wagons went bumping over the sage brush at a great rate, but soon came to a standstill on account of some obstruction, and they were obliged to bump back to the road and fall in behind. We did not blame

---

[16]This method of "churning" butter was common on the trail and is recounted in many journals. One young woman was disappointed on arriving in California when she realized she would lose her mechanical churn and must return to the old hand method. See: Ackley, *Crossing the Plains*, 20; Virginia V. Root, *Following the Pot of Gold at the Rainbow's End in the Days of 1850*, Leonore Rowland, ed. (Downey, Cal.: Elena Quinn, 1960), 2–3; Maxwell, *Crossing the Plains*, 78; and Haun, "A Woman's Trip," 12, for other descriptions of this unique overland technique.

them for not wanting to stay the tail end of the train where they got so much dust but would rather they had said so and gone on earlier so as to be out of our way.

Soon after leaving camp we came in sight of Court House Rock which appeared to be but a short distance ahead. Yet it was noon before we were opposite the immense landmark. While nooning some of the party set out to go the few hundred yards away, as it appeared to be. But distances here are so deceptive that it proved to be a long way off still, so only two of the boys had the courage to keep on until the place was reached. There are three rocks, two comparatively small ones and the large one called the Court House which rises to the height of 100 feet. They stand out boldly and alone in the open prairie, no other rocks nor bluffs being near them, and look very much indeed like houses of sod. Another point of interest is Chimney Rock which is in sight.

Uncle Sam killed an antelope this evening. The meat is very fine. He is an excellent shot and traveling in advance of the wagons has had many opportunities of getting rabbits, prairie chickens and antelope. They are always very generous in dividing it if the supply will admit of it, but with a family of eight this occurs only occasionally. It has been a trifle cooler than yesterday but still was very warm and the gnats extremely troublesome. This evening it is cloudy and there is a high wind and with an occasional sprinkle. Camped by the river. Grass only moderately good. Green willows can be seen on an island, but the boys will not wade for them so we must make out with a scant supply of chips. If anything is underdone tonight it can be attributed to the wind and a lack of fuel. It is a good time to be cross if one were so inclined.

After supper Hugh and George Haven seemed to have gotten into some difficulty and first one and then another of the boys joined in. It was a surprise as we had never known of any disagreement whatever. During the shoving and pushing they got pretty close to the river. Uncle Sam sprang into the midst of it like a flash. Hugh grabbed his father and sprang into the river. We later learned that it was George's birthday and Hugh, as master of ceremonies, was trying to put him in the river. Uncle Sam thought he could get the joke on Hugh by pushing him in. Hugh, divining his purpose, gave him the most of the ducking that any one had. George, I believe, got his feet wet only.

June 27

Very cold and disagreeable with such a hard wind that we came near not getting enough cooked for breakfast and as a result everybody got as cross as a bear. Chimney Rock was in fair view of camp so mother said she would walk on and go to it as she was anxious to see it close by. I intended to go to it too, but would ride a while first. At 11 oclock we came to mother beside the road and ready to ride as the chimney did not seem much nearer than when we left camp. Some two or three of the boys went on horseback and they said that in the most direct line it was 14 miles from the road. Chimney Rock, like the Court House, stands in the open prairie which makes it look all the more beautiful and curious. Its height is estimated at from 150 to 200 feet above the level. From a distance (that is the only way we got to see it), the base appears round and gradually tapers to the chimney proper which, though only four feet across, rises 100 feet above the base. The fact that we were all day in passing this great curiosity filled us with a still greater desire to be near it, and there were many regrets that we had no time to devote to natural curiosities. To the left, rocky bluffs extend as far as the eye can reach. Cedars are growing on the more distant ones, and those intervening are rocky and square looking like houses and forts. Scott's Bluffs have been in sight all day. They are 14 miles from Chimney Rock.

Very poor grass where we nooned. A short distance before going into camp we passed a wagon and tent where Frenchmen are living with squaws. The place is called a trading post. Here the road forks, one going over the hills and the other following the river a few miles farther.[17] Took the latter and found good feed. It has been so long since we had wood that some water soaked pine or cedar, I believe it was, looked much better than we found it to be. Chips are preferable. Also tried sage brush for the first time and found it would burn well. The mosquitoes are of the largest size yet seen and just as thick as the smaller variety has been. We have heard of a place where "Many of the mosquitoes would weigh a pound." It would not take many of these.

---

[17]As noted in the Bailey diary, there were two roads through the Scott's Bluff area, the so-called "hill road" through Robidoux Pass, and the newer "river road" via Mitchell Pass. Carpenter and her family took the river road which rejoined the older Robidoux route near Horse Creek. Mattes, *Platte River Road*, 435–38.

In cutting ham for supper the knife slipped and the left fore finger was cut to the bone between the first and second joints. The Inmanns did not come into camp tonight.

June 28, Sunday

It was very cold this morning. In order to be comfortable I had to wear a sacque, jacket and shawl. The weather seems to be one extreme or the other, but the dust and mosquitoes continue about the same regardless of the temperature. The latter must have a coat of mail to be able to stand such cold weather. Soon after leaving camp we came to where the road forks, the left goes partially around the bluffs and is said to be the best road but as it has not been traveled this year we took the other which goes through the bluffs. We were really surprised to find the road as good and smooth as it was for the country is so rough and there was so much up and down hill.[18]

The bluffs are of light colored sandy clay and the road is cut down into it more or less all the way, in places to the depth of from six to eight feet with little more than room for the wagon to pass through. It looks as though this cut had been made by a great body of water rushing through making many curves and angles and at such points cutting out underneath leaving overhanging walls. Most of the way the walls are perpendicular. This is so far above the river that we cannot conceive of any other agency than a cloudburst to have caused this great curiosity. In under the over hanging places many persons had left their names, written in pencil. Some had been there for three years and were just as legible as those of more recent date. An opportunity like this is not to be overlooked so we went on record with the rest, not omitting Dr. Noble. An ox belonging to some train ahead was found at the foot of a 30 foot bluff from which he had fallen breaking one hind leg and dislocating the other. Either the owner was so inhuman as to leave him to suffer and starve or the dust was so thick that the accident was not observed.

One of the boys went out for antelope. Did not get any but found a

---

[18]The party was still on the Mitchell Pass road. For other emigrant's descriptions of the road, see ibid., 459–60.

nice cow. The owner will soon be claiming her. After passing through the narrow cut just spoke of we came out on a little mesa or semi-level landing part way up the bluffs from which there was a beautiful view of the river, valley, and Chimney Rock, etc. On the higher bluffs which are still to be passed there are cedars growing. At the foot of a perpendicular bluff which faces the mesa is a plainly marked grave that has been visited by so many that a little trail is worn. Pieces of cloth the color the soldiers wear and a bloody bone told of the despoiling wolves.

By noon we had passed through the hills and were two miles up the valley by the river. The valley is gradually narrowing and the river diminishing in size. During the halt, a grave was seen in a low, inconspicuous place near the river. It was that of a young man that had been drowned in the river, as we learned from a bit of board written on with a lead pencil. There were comments on the apparent shallowness of the grave as the little displacement of earth showed that it could not be more than one or at most two feet below the level to the body and further more, that the wolves had not molested it. Aunt Sis detected the unsanitary atmosphere and urged a hasty retreat. As she is noted in the family for her unerring olfactories, we did not tarry.

During the afternoon the road left the river and was rather level and over the very poorest country that one could imagine. The short grass was all crisped up and prickly pears everywhere. When it came camping time, we left the road and traveled half a mile before reaching the river. While in the bluffs we got some cedar roots and brought along. They burn very nicely. Chips are also plentiful and the grass is pretty good so we are quite well fixed. There is no wind tonight and after our varied experiences we feel that this is the very pleasantest night since leaving home. Soon after camping the picked up cow took the back track. Carlo is not with us tonight and we fear she got lost in the thick dust while going through the bluffs. The dust has given her sore eyes and she has had a place on the fancy red seat in the wagon much of the time of late.

By eight o'clock this morning we came to Horse Creek, a fine little stream with a nice sandy crossing. As far as the eye can reach there is not a tree nor bush of any kind near it. Here is a trading post and 17 Sioux lodges. Our oxen got frightened at the Indians and tried to run away. It is 39 miles from here to Fort Laramie.[19] Went some distance from the road to noon by a small stream of clear cold water. After using the muddy waters of the Platte so long, a cup of this is very inviting. The grass is very poor. One good thing at a time. Will they last any the longer. Prolonged the nooning to wait for one of the boys who has gone back for an ox that is missing. He may have to go eight or ten miles. While we wait the boys are catching some nice little fish.

June 30

As the man did not return with the ox, we remained at the nooning place until this morning making a late start as we did not want to get too far ahead of him. This afternoon passed a trading post kept by a Pennsylvanian with a squaw wife. He had quite an assortment of things to dispose of to the emigrants. Buffalo robes, moccasins, bows and arrows, etc. I got a very pretty pair of moccasins with a bit of scarlet broadcloth on the instep bordered with white beads. Price $1.00. We were told that they were made by the Snake Indians. Father got a large, partially worn buffalo robe for $3.00. One that was very much smaller but fresh and new with nice long hair and as white inside as unbleached muslin suited me but $10.00 was more than I would pay for it. Still I was tempted. Paid 75 cents for a pound of candy. The trader was anxious to get sugar and as we have more than we think will be required for the trip we sold some.

Where we nooned near the river the grass was very poor. It seems odd to again be among trees. Even if they are small and far apart, we enjoy the change from no trees at all for so many miles as has been the case. A cow died of alkali this morning. The cattle are so accustomed now to seeing their fellows by the way side that they have grown quite indifferent and pass by without more than a casual glance. The same may be observed of the people for the little trails leading to lonely graves are not so well worn as those seen heretofore.

We have learned that the young man who went back for the ox is in Farmer's train sick. Aunt Sis and Uncle Sam have gone back for him.

---

[19]The trading post at Horse Creek was also a collection point for buffalo skins which were sent to the East. The Platt guide lists the distance from Horse Creek to Fort Laramie as 39½ miles. Platt, *Traveler's Guide*, 8.

Had to go quite a distance from the road to reach the river where we camped. Miserable grass. Plenty of dead trees and stumps to burn and all the water the muddy Platte affords.

July 1st.

The sick man was brought into camp last night. He is not seriously ill. The road has been rough and uneven all day. Not finding water nor any good place to noon, we stopped in the road long enough to eat a bit [but did] not turn the cattle out. Near where we stopped a woman had been buried some time before beside the road where there was little more than room for the wagon to stand. A couple of holes (like squirrel holes only much larger) and bits of clothing and other remains showed who had been there. The whole front of a waist of Dolly Varden goods, made in musk-melon style and gathered into the old fashioned long pique, was the largest piece of clothing. Here was another good opportunity for "Dr. J. Noble" to advertise. Some one wrote in pencil, just below his signature in red, "Is a Jack Ass." After serious consideration, we are wondering which one we should stand most in awe of, the Dr. or the wolves. This is the third day since Carlo was lost and nothing has been heard of her so we have given up seeing her again and can imagine her, blinded by the dust, starving alone back in the bluffs. Laramie Peak is in sight, and we are within one days travel of the Fort.

July 2nd.

Fort Laramie stands near the foot of a gentle slope and but little above the prairie and river which it faces. The hills are on three sides and though a considerable distance from the buildings completely overlook the place. Laramie Creek is quite a stream and flows on the eastern side down to the river. As the Fort was quite a distance from the road and nothing was needed, we passed by without calling. Camped on the river where there was a moderate supply of wood. The river is growing smaller — only 200 yards wide at the Fort. The water is also less muddy than lower down the stream.

July 3rd.

The road today was varied but mostly rough and up and down.

". . . black clouds were seen in the West. . . . About four o'clock a terrific storm broke upon us."

During the afternoon, for some little time very black clouds were seen in the west, and from the wind and increasing darkness it was evident that we were soon to come face to face with the unwelcome visitor. About four o'clock a terrific storm broke upon us. The wind blew and it rained, hailed, thundered, lightened in a way never before seen even in the two years experience in Kansas storms. The cattle refused to

obey the drivers or face the storm and turned directly about and had to
be well guarded by all the men to keep them from running away. The
thunder crashed at our very heads and the guards said the lightning
circled around the wagon tires and ran on the log chains. The men,
although in oilcloth suits, were pretty well drenched. We moved on as
soon as the storm abated sufficiently for the cattle to be made to face it.
As the heavy clouds passed (though it continued to rain), Laramie
Peak could be seen off to our left in the distance with a halo of bright
sunshine about its head and a storm (such as had visited us) raging on
the lower slopes. We were reminded of the lines:

> As some tall cliff that lifts its mighty form
> Swells from the vale, and midway leaves the storm
> Though round its breast the rolling clouds may spread
> Eternal sunshine settles on its head

It was after dark before we got to the camping place where Uncle
Sam had a campfire awaiting us. That was the only campfire made.
Everyone was tired, some of us were cross and wet, but any kind of a
humor was excusable on such an occasion. Not until the next morning
did we see that the campfire was on a grave. But it was not moved. I
have mentioned our growing indifference and can but think that what
we are obliged to endure each day is robbing us of all sentiment. It is
to be hoped that we will not be *permanently changed.*

July 4th.

This has not seemed at all like "Independence Day" but just the
same old jolts with plenty of dust thrown in. I did succeed in finishing
my book, "Dred or The Dismal Swamp." Have been quite a while in
getting through it. It is hard to read when it is too warm and the mosquitoes bite and the wagon jolts and the dust comes in until you lose
the place. Do not think I will try to read anything else. We had a
beautiful camp beside the river. Directly opposite perpendicular bluffs
75 or 100 feet high rose from the very bank of the river making a
delightful change from the levels we have had to look at so long.

As it was the 4th Reel wanted something extra for supper. Well
what should it be? He said "Corn starch." I had never heard of that
being a 4th of July dish and further more I did not know how to cook

it. But he did "Just as Aunt Hannah used to." So I stood by and saw him burn his fingers and scorch the starch which when done was of the consistency of very thin gravy. But we ate it, for on a trip like this one must not be too particular.

July 5th.

Nothing of note until we reached a bridge where our road crosses the river. As the toll is $5.00 the ford, which is two miles and one half up the river, was investigated before crossing. The toll man said that the ford was unsafe and that two or three men and some cattle were drowned there recently. We did not know but anxiety to secure the toll made the ford more "unsafe," but they found the water too deep for the wagons so they crossed on the bridge and the loose cattle were taken to the ford and had to swim. The keeper of the bridge was a white man with a white wife. He wanted mother's baby wagon and as it had been of little use and was always in the way when anything in the wagon was wanted, she let it go for toll.[20]

The record of the next 15 days was lost when the house in Potter Valley, California, was burned. In order to cover all the ground and make the trip complete, I will quote from my brother's diary (for the 15 days) of the same trip made three years previously and will make such notes of incidents as places described may bring to mind after a lapse of 54 years. My brother reached Fort Laramie almost a month earlier in the season than we did, yet the road and conditions were practically the same, and a space of three years made little or no difference in what was encountered. After crossing the Platte on the bridge we came into the route he traveled and from there on his diary served us as guide book and was of the greatest assistance in giving distances to water and grass so that we were always able to tell what was ahead and prepare for it. On the other hand, the guide books were very unreliable.

June 16th, Friday. [George McCowen's diary]

Got a late start this morning. Were delayed by an antelope that we

---

[20]Evidently the Carpenter train used the Lower Ferry. See Bailey, note 31.

found it necessary to take care of. The country is rolling and hilly and quite barren. The roads sandy. Passed the Platte Bridge. It is made of lumber that was brought from Salt Lake. Here was a store house with a good assortment of goods for sale. The folks from the other side of the river are rolling in fast. Some that left the Fort the same day we did are among them. From what they say of the road it is better than ours has been.

This evening one of the boys complained of a "misery" in his breast. I advised a light supper. "What," said he, "you don't think eating caused it? If it did not it will do no good to quit." I had noticed the previous meal the filling of his pint cup, three times with tea of the strongest quality. "I am entirely too hungry to eat light and I won't do it while I can stand it. I would rather be in hell than do without enough to eat." His principal enjoyment is in eating. We camped four miles above the bridge near the river. Had very poor grass. Passed several alkali spots. Distance traveled, 20 miles.

June 17th, Saturday.

By starting early we left about 20 wagons behind that were before us last night. Some distance from the camp the road forked. The left hand follows the river a few miles farther and the right takes off over the hills and is a nearer route to the Sweetwater River. We took the right.[21] There was no good water during the day, and the ground was white in many places with saleratus. Crossed one or two small branches strongly impregnated with alkali. We got in company with a train and drove of cattle belonging to S. Lamont & Co. of St. Louis. Camped with them on the best grass we have had since leaving Scott's Bluff. Good spring water only slightly alkaline. The camping place was about one mile from the road to the right soon after passing rock avenue. For wood there was plenty of dead sage brush. Distance traveled, 21 miles.

[Helen Carpenter's (H.M.C.) diary: During this day's journey, which is in the Black Hills, there were so many beautiful stones along the road that we did a great deal of walking just for the pleasure of picking them up to admire for a little while. I tucked some of the prettiest ones away in the pockets of the wagon cover, but they were soon

---

[21]This was the same trail chosen by the Bailey train.

thrown away "to lighten the load." All the colors of the rainbow were represented. There was cornelian, amber, emerald, topaz, rubies, etc. and any amount of the coarser articles as gingerbread, sassafras and castile soap, &c.

The high wind which prevailed interfered very much with our locomotion and switched the dresses about leaving the pedal extremities in a precarious condition. To overcome this Aunt Sis and Emily pinned some rocks in the bottom of their skirts never dreaming of the black shins they would carry for the next week. It is needless to say that their invention was not a success and so was never patented.]

Sunday, June 18.

We had calculated to lay by and let the cattle rest and feed up but after breakfast we thought best to "keep the ark a moving." After five miles travel we came to Willow Springs. These form a small branch which we had followed up for two miles before coming to the springs. The Springs are situated at the foot of Prospect Hill which is a considerable eminence. The land generally is rolling and the road hard and gravely. After crossing two creeks of clear water and following down the second some distance, we camped where the water was brackish. Little or no grass and sage brush for wood. Distance traveled, 15 miles.[22]

Monday, June 19.

On account of the scarcity of grass, we hitched up and put out before breakfast thinking some might be found a little farther on. Were unable to do so until near noon when we arrived at the Sweetwater. A little north of the road is a very strong alkaline lake some two or three miles in circumference. On the margin of this was excellent grass. Emigrants generally are afraid to turn in here, but our experience has been that unless very dry the cattle drink such water very sparingly if at all. During the forenoon drive passed a considerable

---

[22]George McCowen's description of this section of the road is similar to that of Thomas Christy, "Willow spring   About three rods west of the road, water cold and plenty of grass   Prospect Hill (summit) Pleasant view of the surrounding country to the Sweetwater Mountains." Becker, *Christy's Road*, map 37.

number of alkali ponds or lakes around which the ground was white. I picked up some lumps that were near two inches in diameter and pure and white. Much of it is stained more or less by the earth. The Red Buttes are in sight to the N.E.

Our nooning place was near Independence Rock which is situated on the left bank of the Sweetwater. This is quite a noted place. The rock is granite and is 300 yards long and from 75 to 100 feet high and in shape an irregular oval. It has a very weather beaten appearance with small water washed furrows. Saw several names high up on the sides and placed mine there writing it with tar. Five miles from here came to the Devil's Gate. This is a narrow gap or fissure, only a few feet wide from top to bottom of a high hill, through it runs the Sweetwater. Running parallel with this is a narrow valley shut in by high rocks upon which are many names of travelers. High up on a fragment I saw the name of John Briggs (supposedly of Roseville, Indiana, as we know that he crossed the plains). Camped about one and one half miles from the head of the little valley by the river. At the head of the valley is a trading post fixed up the best of any seen yet. It is built of hewn pines, three sides of a square are enclosed by buildings. Met some Oregon packers going home. Distance traveled, 17 miles. Saleratus ponds 173. Road sandy.

[H.M.C. On arriving in the little valley where we first came to the Sweetwater, we at once turned from the road and went down by the river to camp. When the cattle were partly unyoked it was learned that a dead cow was in the river just above where water would have to be dipped up. The oxen were reyoked and moved 100 yards up stream. A little later a small train came in and took the camp we vacated. We were a little sorry for them but not enough so to tell them. This was such a romantic place that we were glad to stop for a day, but that was not the reason of our stopping by any means. If feed and water had not been good there would have been no halt.

The little uneven valley is surrounded by high, stony, precipitous mountains, there being no visible place of egress after once into the fort-like place. These are called the Rattle Snake Mountains on account of the peculiar spotted surface which is caused by a very dark mossy vegetation and weather beaten discoloration which surrounds each individual rock whose face of light grey stands out roundly in the distance making all the range decidedly spotted.[23] Emily, Teresa and some of the young men crossed the river and by taking a circuitous route were able to climb the almost perpendicular mountain directly across the river from camp. They appeared on its crest waving cedar branches and hallooing to attract our attention. They were seen so distinctly that they appeared but a short distance away and yet they were so small and the voices so indistinct that despite our impressions to the contrary we knew they must be a long way off. Uncle Sam was quite put out to think they would show such a lack of discretion in going so far from camp in the Indian Country and said a good deal, but it did not reach them, at least not *then*.

When the cattle were being driven in preparatory to leaving camp, the remains of another cow were found in the edge of the stream among some rocks just above the camp. We decided that a dead cow more or less did not matter. Soon after leaving camp came to Independence Rock and looked in vain for George's name which we knew was there but among the several hundred of others inscribed there it could not be found. Near Independence Rock we saw what appeared to us to be a miniature mule — until it hopped off like a rabbit. We were told that it was a *jack rabbit*. As it was many times the size of any we had ever seen it was a great curiosity.]

Tuesday, June 20, 1854.

It was very cool this morning. One felt comfortable in an overcoat and standing by the fire. The mountains are just huge piles of rock with very little earth about them. One and one half miles from camp crossed a clear branch of clear cool water. Passed cattle that died from the effects of alkali and also a train lying by for their cattle to die or get well of their dose. Passed three men on the road trying to buy flour. They had been hands with a train but had left their boss and were now looking for someone to take them along and feed them. We were not able to do either.

Nooned near the river after passing some bluffs upon one of which I

---

[23]The Rattlesnake Mountains are part of the larger Wind River range of the Rockies. There are several versions of how they got their name. Federal Writers' Program, *Wyoming*, 12–13.

left my name in bold letters. A short distance back the road forked. The right hand keeps near the river, the left is said to be more sandy and I think is a little farther. The roads come together near what is the gravel bluffs. After crossing another small branch we camped. We were within camping distance of the river all day. For the last three weeks we have been passing trading posts nearly every day. We had a visit from some Shoshone or Snake Indians. They are not as hungry as the Sioux nor half as impudent. Distance traveled, 20 miles. Distance from Fort Laramie, 193 miles.

[H.M.C. We went over this bit of road in the night to avoid the heat and dust. It was light enough to see names on the rocks just spoken of in the preceding but too dark to distinguish names that were written well over it with tar. Father and mother tried very hard to see George's name, and I wanted to go back from the stopping place where we took breakfast to see if I could not find it. But as it was five miles there was so much opposition that I was obliged to give it up. How one does remember a disappointment.]

Wednesday, June 21.

The road left the river and did not return for six miles. The road forks here, the left being called the old road, and is deep sand most of the way. The right crosses the river and is more direct and a better road. This is disputed by those who went that way. We took the left and were sorry for our bargain.[24] Stopped for noon where the road comes to the river. The three fellows that wanted flour yesterday got into a train as hands to the disadvantage of another who passed us near Fort Laramie. We heard of him being in several trains, but they let him go as soon as they could get another help. Some let him go and run the risk of finding another. We took a bath in the ice cold water of the Sweetwater. It comes now in almost a direct line from the Rocky Mountains, and they are in sight for the first time, the distance being about 70 miles. They glitter in the bright sunshine and look like immense piles of snow. We passed a place where they say ice can be had

---

[24]Most travelers seem agreed that this was a bad stretch of road no matter which fork was selected. Child's guide describes it as "a sandy and barren tract." Child, *Overland Route*, 27. See also Platt, *Traveler's Guide*, 14, and Becker, *Christy's Road*, map 42.

by digging for it. The ground was miry and the water alkaline. There was plenty of good grass but so miry that the cattle could not get to it, and that is the reason it was there.[25]

During the day we met about 50 persons with 100 horses and mules on the back track from California. Also four wagons of repentant Mormans going to their old home in Iowa. Camped on a barren spot eight miles west and seven miles east of the river which makes a big bend northward while we cut across 15 or 16 miles without any good water. Traveled 24 miles.

July 10, 1857.

[H.M.C. We camped in the barren place spoke of in the preceding. There was a white frost and it was very cold. When gathering up the cattle in the morning a ball of *cooperative crickets* was found a little way from camp. These were the largest crickets we ever saw and were of a yellowish brown color. They were clinging together to keep warm and the solid ball was more than a foot in diameter. We could but wonder which had the best of it, the center ones or the ones on the outside.]

Thursday, June 22.

Feed being very scarce we did not wait to get breakfast. After going three miles came to a small branch and stopped to eat a bite. The water is poor and not to be relied on. After going over two or three big hills, we again came to the river about four miles from the breakfasting place. Here we had to ford and the water came near running into the wagon bed. We had the misfortune to lose our camp kettle which was filled with savory meat for our dinners. After crossing another branch of the river we again took to the hills which are getting to be *most awful long.* A mile and a half farther we came again to the river which we soon forded. I waded the stream some three or four times taking the cattle to and from grass. As the water was up to my waist I found it rather cool work. There are two roads here. One avoids fording the

---

[25]The "ice springs" were considered something of a curiosity and are mentioned in several diaries. See, for example, Morgan, *Pritchard Diary*, 92 and 154 *n* 44; Tyler, *Montana Gold Rush*, B-30.

river by going over the bluffs. The other keeps in the river bottom. We took the latter. We camped where the roads separate. Got good grass by crossing the river. This is eight miles from where we left the river before noon. Distance traveled, 16 miles.

The grass has been so poor of late that our oxen begin to look rather badly so this morning we concluded to lighten the load all we could by throwing away whatever was not actually needed. A few pieces of clothing and our oil cloth suits proved to be all that could be included in this list. After we had gone half a mile from camp it began to rain so I went back, got the suits and we are going to hang on to them now.

[H.M.C.   We heard a number of times of a tramp on the road but he did not strike our camp until we reached here. While the suppers were in course of preparation, the scent of the bacon frying was wafted to his nostrils. He kept getting closer and closer until he was barely outside the kitchen. He claimed to be a Doctor and was the filthiest, most repulsive looking person one could imagine. And worst of all, he was so beset with vermin that they did not permit him to forget the fact for a minute. At this stage of the proceedings, Hugh came dashing into camp on horseback without saddle or bridle (just a rope) and called out to know if anyone knew where a Doctor could be found. "A woman in one of the trains ahead (there were two trains in sight farther up the river) was dangerously ill and they *must have a Doctor.*" The "Doctor" was pointed out and Hugh very kindly offered him the horse as "They were in such a hurry," and he could walk back. The fellow declined the horse and looked *very* incredulous, but he *did* go though with the greatest reluctance. We neither saw nor heard of him again.]

Friday, June 23, 1854.

Shortly after leaving camp the road turned to the hills which are rough being covered with stones that stick edgewise in the ground. About seven miles from the river crossed a small spring branch and on coming to another a mile farther on we stopped to noon. During the afternoon crossed three streams, two of them large with clear swift running water which was very good and cold as the stream was shaded by willows. After passing all this nice water we camped in a hollow at the left of the road two or three miles from the last stream and had *no water* and very poor grass and sage brush for wood. The river bottom is full of campers. Distance traveled, 22 miles.

Saturday, June 24th.

Clear and very cold. We are expecting to cross the pass today and look for warmer weather on the other side. About two miles from camp crossed the Sweetwater for the last time. Near the crossing and not three feet above the water was a quantity of snow. The boys said it "was four feet deep and as cold as ice." Since leaving Fort Laramie we have not been out of sight of snow a whole day at a time.

The road to the pass is a very gradual ascent, occasionally descending a little, so we were actually past the summit before we were aware of it. Before passing it we found two men lying by the roadside holding their mules. They were 60 miles behind their train and sick with mountain fever. We took them in and hauled them about six miles and left them at a smith shop near the Pacific Springs where we stopped for noon. Three miles west of the summit found very good water and a few acres of extremely miry ground covered with excellent grass. Most of the folks are afraid the cattle may mire if turned on it, but we were glad to run the risk.

The road through the pass is *very disappointing* and not at all romantic. There is nothing in sight to merit the name Rocky Mountains — no rocks, no overhanging precipices, in fact nothing our geography led us to believe was there. The Rattle Snake Mountains and Scott's Bluffs are much more to be admired and remembered. Camped five miles from Pacific Springs.[26] Sage brush, poor grass, and no water. By going two and one half miles we got some out of a mud hole that did not lack much of being sage tea. Today's dinner finished our scanty supply of sugar. Rained a little during the night. Rumor says the cholera is among the emigrants on the Platte. Drove 20 miles.

---

[26]Most observers agreed that the pass was disappointing as a "tourist" attraction. Platt noted, "The pass is a slightly undulating plain between mountains several miles apart. The ascent over the pass is so gradual as to be almost imperceptible." Platt, *Traveler's Guide,* 14. See also Morgan, *Pritchard Diary,* 93.

Pacific Springs and Creek, just beyond South Pass, was the first spot at which emigrants observed waters flowing westward to the Pacific. Platt, *Traveler's Guide,* 15; Becker, *Christy's Road,* map 43.

[H.M.C. Soon after we were in camp near here a man and his wife came in and made camp near us. They started out on the trip with a pair of oxen and wagon. One ox died so the wagon bed was cut in two and half of it put on the hind wheels making rather a clumsy looking cart. To this the one ox was hitched and thus they were making their way. They both had to walk all the time. There seemed to be almost nothing in the cart. The woman was in delicate health besides. Aunt Sis said she knew she was hungry so she fixed up something appetizing for her and the woman seemed very grateful. In another place on the road we saw a man with just one ox. His bedding, a pair of boots, and a little wad of provisions were hung across the back of the ox. It is needless to say that he walked.

When driving through the sage brush as we left camp we came upon the carcass of a rather small bear that some one had shot. He had a beautiful coat of long black hair.]

Sunday, June 25.

Four miles from camp we came to Dry Sandy. This has no water in it as the name would seem to imply, yet there is a good bed for quite a body of water which at times must flow through it. There is little growing here except sagebrush. The sandy ground is thickly inhabited by little animals similar to prairie dogs but not quite half as large. Their cry is like that of a small bird. We are beginning to pass dead cattle quite frequently and occasionally some that have been left to die. Sore feet and alkali the prevailing trouble. About 10 miles from Dry Sandy we crossed Little Sandy. This is a fine mountain stream very full now on account of the warm days melting the snow in the mountains. This is the first good water since leaving the Pacific Springs at the pass, about 20 miles.

Two miles from Dry Sandy the road forks. The right is Kinney's Cut-off and the left is the Old Mormon Trail now called Sublett's Cut-off or the Salt Lake road.[27] We took the latter and camped on Big

---

[27]McCowen is somewhat confused about the proper nomenclature for the roads. The old Mormon Trail went to Fort Bridger. The Sublette Cut-Off went due west across a long desert to Ham's Fork. Platt, *Traveler's Guide*, 14; Stewart, *California Trail*, 245.

Sandy almost three miles from Little Sandy. Almost no grass. We kept the cattle on an island and as there were some suspicious looking characters about we thought it best to guard them. So I took a quilt and waded in the snow water three feet deep and made my bed among them and passed a very comfortable night. Here we saw a Missouri Trader that had been living among the Indians for 24 years. Have learned that the traders call the little animals squirrels. Distance traveled, 20 miles.

[H.M.C. This brings us to where I can again take up my own diary.]

July 22nd, 1857.

Time has rendered most of this days doings illegible. There was a journey of 10 miles and a small stream crossed. The road was not good but there was plenty of feed. We took a left hand road supposing it led to a good camping place, but in that we were mistaken.

July 23rd.

The road continued rough and the grass gradually became scarcer until by noon there was no vegetation but sage brush and the water alkaline and alkali everywhere. Stopped but a short time at noon not even turning the oxen out. Five miles farther and the road forks. By consulting guidebooks, we learned that the left was called Sublett's Cut-off or the Salt Lake road and father and ourselves took the right hand one as we did not want to go by Salt Lake for several reasons.[28] When we divided company at the forks of the road there was considerable difficulty in separating the cattle. After we had gone a ways some of ours were found to be missing and two of the party went back after them.

Coming again to where the road forked, we took the left hand one and when night overtook us we had found neither feed nor water, only sage brush and sand. Traveled until 10 o'clock and then stopped

---

[28]According to Emily Horton, the party had originally planned to go by Salt Lake in order to replenish their food supply. But Emily added she was sure "it was Providence that decided us to go back to the other road" for otherwise they might have lingered in the city and been involved in the Mountain Meadows Massacre. Horton, *Our Family*, 21, 30–35.

to wait for the boys to come with the cattle before deciding what to do. Soon after starting a fire voices were heard and then hallooing off to the right. Our boys fired a gun and in a short time the stragglers found their way to our camp. In the darkness they were unable to tell which road we had taken. They had found both grass and water so we were the stragglers. This way seemed too unpromising to continue any longer and none wanted to go back five miles to where the road forked so we recklessly set out across the country through sand and over sage brush. The star light was not bright enough to do more than aid us in keeping the right direction. It is needless to say that the shaking we got was very thorough. Fortunately another road was soon found, and two miles more brought us to a stream known as Little Sandy. It was 12 o'clock before we got settled. From day light to midnight made a long day. How acceptable a good warm supper would have been, but the cold lunch taken hours ago had to serve. Soon hunger and weariness gave way to refreshing sleep.

July 24.

Our camping place was quite as good as if it had been selected by daylight. Plenty of wood and fairly good grass. This stream is about the size of the Sweetwater but not such nice clear water. As the drive yesterday was unusually hard a rest today was readily assented to. The boys amused themselves killing prairie squirrels as they were pleased to call them. I do not know upon what they based their knowledge of the family name of this little zoological whisk about. I am firm in the belief that they are *rats*. They are but little larger than the ordinary rat and resemble them more than anything else. Tenacious of life and extremely quick of motion, they were hard to capture even after being mortally wounded, and if a shot gun was used, they invariably made their escape into the little homes in the sand along the banks of the creek. With a revolver Reel secured quite a number. I protested against cooking rats, but fresh meat has been so scarce and the boys were so sure they were squirrels that they had to be cooked. The pronounced opinion was that they looked too much like rats and tasted too much like fish to ever become very popular as an article of diet.[29]

---

[29]The animals are more commonly known as ground squirrels. Geiger and Bryarly had a similar experience with these small creatures. Potter, *Trail to California*, 139.

There are Missouri trains up and down the creek tonight having come in during the day. Since the party divided there are hardly enough of us to be called a train (only the two wagons), so these Missourians seem to think us of little importance and are crowding us.

July 25th.

Four miles from camp came to Big Sandy which is wider than Little Sandy yet runs but little more water. The high banks are of sand and stone and from appearances are washed at times by great floods of water. Followed down the stream two or three miles and crossed. Three miles farther came to a small patch of grass which was very good. The road was gravely and sandy. In fact it has been the same ever since we crossed the North Platte. Ten or twelve days ago, a young woman in a train back of us died. Last night her mother died leaving seven small children.

Took a long nooning and then after five miles travel camped beside the creek opposite a high bank of stone 40 or 50 ft. high. Very little grass. The cattle are obliged to feed on green willows. Consequently many have died at this point and their bodies lie in the stream and there is no other drinking water. It has come to be the rule that such conditions prevail. We are reminded of the old adage, "One can get used to anything," and again of the calf that died "just as it got used to doing without eating." Are we to share its fate? It is very cold.

July 26th.

Road some what hilly. Nooned two miles from where the road comes to the river. Down the river are some French traders with a great many cattle. Reel gave a little cow and 10 dollars for a three year old steer in very good order. Father traded "Old Blue" (his horse) for a large yoke of oxen (in poor order), a yoke of three years old, and one of four years and bought one immensely large ox for $50. This fits us out pretty well making 4½ yoke for father and 6½ for us.

This afternoon drove one and a half miles down the creek. A man by the name of Dobbins was camped here. He has 30 head of cattle and two wagons. His wife and little boy ride in one and the other is for baggage only. There were three young men with him until this morning when one "Got mad and left." Dobbins made a bargain with them before leaving home. They paid him 25 dollars in advance, had to furnish their own blankets, do the cooking, washing and dish washing, attend to all camp work, getting wood, etc., drive teams which meant walking all day and stand guard at night. His part of the contract was to feed them. Is it to be wondered that "one got mad"? He crossed the plains several years ago and talks as though he thought he knew all the ins and outs of the trip. He proposes that we travel together as our combined forces would insure greater safety from the Indians and still be a small enough train to find feed enough if feed could be found at all. Mother and I do not like his manner and would rather keep to ourselves, but his superior knowledge of our now one great aim in life won the confidence of the men so the matter is settled and we will travel together. Father and Reel are to take turns with the boys in standing guard at night. It may be better to do so but as yet we have not had a guard. Stopped for the rest of the day and will make our first day's travel with Dobbins tomorrow.

The young man who left was perhaps too much out of humor to think of his baggage. Dobbins took the black oil cloth bag and its contents and threw the whole in the river. Mother and I were indignant. This young man now hundreds of miles from home must depend on the generosity of some one, he knows not whom, who is fortunate enough to have a spare shirt. We hear of sandy stretches and desert roads in advance. To lighten the load Reel has thrown away the moulding board, rolling pin, and the one smoothing iron in the camp.

Reel went down the hill and took supper with the French men and their squaws. He traded a pair of shoes that he did not want for a pair of nice moccasins for me. They were made by the Utes and are much nicer then the Sioux Indians make as they put on soles of buffalo hide with stitches half an inch long. The buckskin was smoked in tanning and is a beautiful tan color. A piece of scarlet broadcloth edged with several rows of white beads decorates the top of the moccasin and from either side of this extends around the top of the quarters (if I may use the term) a little drop curtain effect fringed by making fine cuts an inch deep around the edges. To fasten securely on the feet they are tied with a string that is run through little slashes cut in the top. I feel quite proud of them. We did not see an Indian while coming through the Crow and Snake Indian country. They are much more to be feared when they keep out of sight. If friendly they come to make exchanges for sugar, looking-glasses, etc. The Crows robbed a train this year on the other side of the mountains.

The weather is cold enough for October. Overcoats, shawls and a good fire are necessary to keep us comfortable. The mountain peaks are white with snow — beautiful to look at but bodily comfort is more to be considered just now than fine views.

July 27th.

Down by the river the road again forked affording another opportunity to go by Salt Lake. This main road continues to be called Kinney's Cut-off.[30] But few are going by Salt Lake on account of rumors that the Indians are liable to be more troublesome of that route and also because there is a 50 mile desert to cross and on this only 20 miles without feed or water. When five or six miles from where we camped we left the main road and followed one that brought us to water sooner and there is also grass. This has only been traveled this year. A real, truly guide board (a very modest one) informs us that it is 12 miles to Green River. So in coming this way we have saved two miles travel as the distance was said to be 20 miles.

The 12 miles to Green River was over very barren country, there being no vegetation whatever except stunted sage brush. It is spoken of as a desert. The road is deceptive in appearance. It looks smooth and quite level but dear, dear was there ever such a road. It could not have been rougher as there were stones of all sizes yet they were so deeply covered with dust that none were visible. But we had jolts to know they were there. As the cattle dragged their feet along through the dust it rose in clouds and came thickly into the wagons and settled down on everything even getting into the food which was thought to

---

[30]By the late 1850s there was a sometimes bewildering choice of trails in the Salt Lake area. In addition to the Mormon route through Fort Bridger and the Oregon Trail via Fort Hall, there were a number of other routes including the Sublette Cut-Off, the Baker and Davis and Hockaday and Dempsey roads, and the Kinney Cut-Off, all "short cuts" to the main routes. The Kinney Cut-Off, taken by the Carpenters, forked from the Fort Bridger road near the second crossing of the Big Sandy. The Kinney Cut-Off offered better water and was somewhat shorter than the older, and better known, Sublette route. For a description of the various roads see Paden, *Wake of the Prairie Schooner*, 238, 262–63, and Stewart, *California Trail*, 304, 317.

be put away very securely. We did not get to Green River until after dark. The river is very deep and swift and there is a ferry boat for taking the wagons over. A number of trains had crossed and others were camped on the river bank ready to be taken over in the morning. The boys went up the river looking for feed but finding none we camped right in among the other trains and the poor tired hungry cattle were herded at the foot of a very high steep rock.

July 28th.

Search was made early this morning for grass and some being found a mile and a half on the other side of the mountain the cattle were driven to it. The ferryman was not here when the wagons were taken over and was still absent this morning. The boat was kept busy. Some time after breakfast when the last wagon was being taken over the ferryman came. It was apparent that he had been on a spree. His usual charge is $5.00 per wagon and 10cts a head for stock. As we did our own ferrying he thought $3.00 would be the right amount for each wagon but was finally convinced that $1.00 would do. The loose stock was taken up the river where it was less deep and made to swim across. Nothing was collected from the 12 wagons that crossed ahead of us. They left camp about daylight, the ferryman not even seeing them.

The river here is about the size of the Kansas. The water is beautifully clear and green and the smooth light colored gravel could be distinctly seen at its greatest depth. As the ferryman has six boats he is well prepared for serving the trains. The journey yesterday was so hard that we did not leave camp until noon and traveled only six or seven miles. Camped on Fontenelle's Fork of Green River which is a small river about the size of Sweetwater. Willows are thick along the river bank. This insures wood (such as it is) for cooking. There is plenty of grass but as there is alkali on the ground the grass is not very good.

July 29th.

Came five or six miles up the creek this morning and stopped for the day as the cattle seem very tired and we can enjoy a little rest ourselves. The water is very clear and cold and the grass good. Several trains camped here. In one they buried a baby today. The nights and mornings are *very* cold.

July 30th.

One of those "Sublett's Cut-off" roads (by the 50 mile desert) came into our road near camp. The dust is ankle deep and blows about tremendously. Began ascending the Green River Mountains and nooned at Cedar Springs. There was plenty of green brush but no grass. The cattle are not fastideous but take with a relish anything they can get. There was not water enough for the stock. After traveling six or eight miles over rough steep mountains we came down to a small spring branch. Here the old Kinney road came into ours. We have been on the Cut-off. Two or three miles farther and we left the main road turning to the right on a camp road which in two and a half miles more brought us to the foot of a mountain on which is considerable snow. Fairly good grass, spring water and plenty of wood. The mountains here are beautiful yet they are barren except in the little hollows and ravines where there are springs, green bushes and cedar trees.

July 31

A mile from camp crossed a fine spring branch. One and a half miles farther crossed Crow Creek. Both these creeks afford plenty of water for stock yet we saw no good grass by either of them. We came back to the main road and passed a small trading post. Dobbins sold flour at $10.00 per hundred, coffee at 40 cts. per lb. During the forenoon crossed two spring branches both of them having most *dreadful crossings.* Nooned in a little hollow where there was grass but no water. It was up and down hill all the afternoon. Gained five or six miles and camped on Ham's Fork of Green River. No grass at camp but up the creek some distance, at the foot of the mountain, a little was found. Down stream half a mile a Frenchman had a trading post. I let him have some Indian beads. Got enough to pay for bringing them so far yet they are not in demand like coffee, sugar and tobacco.

August 1st.

Stopped again for the day. Some are throwing away to lighten their load. We felt when leaving home that nothing was being taken but the merest necessities yet we find that in our anxiety about the cattle giving out we take a different view of what we may give up without anything more than inconvenience to ourselves. Two miles from camp, up in the mountains, grass knee high was found and the cattle taken to it. We learn here that Uncle Sam's train is two days ahead of us. (They came in on the Sublett Cut-off.)

August 2nd.

This morning Reel bought another ox, paid $25.00 for it. Half a mile from camp began ascending the mountain. The road was steep, stony and sidling. After reaching the top we followed a high ridge occasionally ascending and descending a little. Six miles farther the road crossed a small spring branch beside which is a small quaking aspen tree. Four miles farther we passed through a fine large grove of spruce pine and four miles more travel (having climbed to a great height) the descent began — steep, stony and sidling.[31] At the foot of the mountain a little creek three or four feet wide supplied us with very cold water. Camped three fourths of a mile down the valley, the cattle having to be taken two miles farther to grass which was only tolerably good.

August 3rd.

Immediately on leaving camp we commenced ascending another long steep slope. On gaining the top the descent began which was steep and sometimes rocky and sidling. This brought us into Bear River Valley. After following down a small spring branch for two or three miles we came to the main river bottom. Nooned on the small branch. Good water and tolerably good grass. The river bottom is two or three miles wide and is covered with fairly good grass.

Afternoon traveled six miles. Crossed Smith's Fork of Bear River and camped soon after crossing an old trail. Drove the cattle across the creek to good grass. Where we first came to the stream there was a bridge for which they charge 25 cts. toll. As it was rather rickety and the creek fordable, we chose to ford. Bought some beef at 12½ cts. per pound. The bridge was kept by a Frenchman. Dobbins got him drunk on whiskey at $1.00 per pint.

---

[31]From Mrs. Carpenter's description, this was probably Fir Grove and Hill. Child, *Overland Route*, 33–34.

August 4th.

Our road lay up the river bottom. Passed Houks and Cox and then nooned near them. We were followed until noon by the Frenchmen wanting more whiskey. The "Jinny" train overtook us at noon. Soon after starting come to Thomas Fork, crossed on a bridge but no one there to collect toll. One and one half miles down the river, finding good grass, stopped and camped.

August 5th.

In leaving camp we took what we called "Dobbins Cut-off" and reached the road two miles from the river at the top of a steep sidling hill. Got safely down and came into a beautiful valley in sight of the river and between Farmer's and Houk's. Good road for three miles, then climbed an awfully steep hill and went down a gorge. Farther on turned up another gorge where a rock encroached so on the road that there was barely room for the wagon bows and hubs to pass through. Ascended another slope and steep pitch and followed the ridge for half a mile before going down the rockiest hill in all our travels. On reaching the bottom turned off of the road and camped on Bear River again.

August 6th.

I have been sick ever since we were at Big Sandy and Reel has kept my diary. I now resume. If instead of walking (as Reel did) he had lain in the wagon (as I did) I think he would have emphasized the roughness of the road more than he did. Seven miles from camp crossed a good sized stream and five miles farther came to another and stopped and camped. Did not travel any after eating dinner. Near camp a spring was dug out. The water was so cold that it made the teeth ache. There was excellent grass but the least wood we have had at any camp.

August 7th.

Last night about midnight the Frenchmen from the trading post 30 miles back came for more whiskey. Callers at night are so out of the usual course of events that everyone was awakened by their loud talking. Dobbins let them have some but not enough to satisfy so they followed on after Houk's.

Crossed seven small creeks this forenoon. None more than three miles apart. Took dinner by one of them near some white hills. The tops of these hills appear to be covered with snow, even at a short distance, but instead it is bare white stone. Wild currants were growing here on bushes six or eight feet high. They were larger than the ordinary currant and of a bright yellow color. Some thought them very very fine but although hungry for fruit the color did not appeal to my appetite. While nooning a pack train passed. The entire outfit on mules. They were returning from California. After noon drove five or six miles over hilly road and camped where the grass was good but it was difficult for the cattle to get to the water in the little branch the banks were so steep. We are beginning to have warmer weather.

How we do wish for some vegetables. I can really scent them cooking sometimes. I had an opportunity at noon to eat some of Mrs. Dobbins' cold beans. The boys cooked so much bacon with them that each bean had a rim of grease around it. Oh well, I can plainly see that I am too particular. But then one does like a change and about the only change we have from bread and bacon is to bacon and bread. I sometimes wish I could drink tea and coffee like the rest, especially when the water is not good which so often happens. There has been such poor feed that Sookey's milk is failing. "Woe is me" when it gives out.

August 8th.

Up hill road this morning. Nooned by a little stream of very cold water near a trading post. A little farther on were a couple of white mounds near the road that rose 12 or 15 ft. above the level surrounding them. They were a calcareous deposit from innumerable soda springs. Some of them were arched over with this rocky substance. Some had a curbing around them two or three feet higher than the water and others boiled up like lard and ran over forming little streams that find their way down the rocky surface. Where there is any dampness on the rocks they are the color of iron rust. The water is very cold and tastes like ink.

Sugar Creek is a quarter of a mile farther on. The bottom land to the right is thickly covered with cedars. Another trading post here. It is kept by Americans that say they have been living among the Indians for 10 years. A white woman and some squaws were busy around a camp fire (in front of the little house) preparing a meal. A beef had recently been killed and we saw nothing else being cooked. The woman kept her sunbonnet over her face so we only caught a glimpse of her features. It was thought that the man in charge feared he might be recognized and in imagination we saw a dark stain resting on his character in the far away somewhere but did not think he need have much anxiety about the law or justice overtaking him. It was evident that the woman felt the situation more keenly than he did. We were convinced that they were not there from choice.

After crossing the Soda Water came to the main Soda Springs. They are near the river bank (Bear River). The rocky formation is the same as that surrounding the smaller springs. I learned this from hearsay as I did not go to them. It was so very hot and the dust was blowing directly that way so I preferred staying in the wagon. The course of the river for a mile farther was about west then it makes an elbow around a high mountain and turns due south. Here the diary and guide book informed us were the Steamboat Springs so we were on the lookout. Last year the immigrants filled up the spring and we hear that it broke out in the river and spouts up a foot or two above its surface. A time or two we thought its location was cited [sic] but were not sure. It at least was not very active that day.[32]

Then followed four miles of rocks. Surely wagons never tried to go over a rougher way. It cannot be called a road. Large purple stones were every where with no earth whatever between them. When there is a freshlet the river no doubt leaves its banks at the big bend and long ago swept away everything but the purple rocks. We were sorry they did not go too. After this shaking up, we went a mile and a half to one side on a camp road and stopped for the night. Grass only moderately good. Plenty of wood but it had to be carried up a very steep hill.

---

[32]Soda Springs, near Bear River, were considered one of the most interesting spots along this part of the route. "Visit them," Child recommended, "This water when sweetened and mixed with acid, makes a fine effervescing drink."

The Steamboat Springs, so named because they were said to resemble "the puffing of a steamboat" were a short distance off the trail. According to observers, the water gushed from two to three feet up from solid rock, "foaming, whizzing, sizzling, blowing, splashing & spraying." Potter, *Trail to California*, 145. See also: Ware, *Emigrant's Guide*, 29; Child, *Overland Route*, 36; T. J. Ables, "Letter, Ables's Ranch near Petuluma, Sonoma Co. Cal., October 12, 1857," typescript, Newberry Library, 9.

August 9th, Sunday

A mile from camp we passed the Fort Hall Road. At the time we thought it a camp road and had gone some distance before learning differently. We had thought that perhaps we would go that way, partly I think because George went that route. We did not like to retrace our steps even for a mile and from the appearance of the road we knew that no trains had gone that way this year so we rather reluctantly kept to the Old California Road.[33] Ten miles farther we began to ascend a mountain that was six miles of up and down to reach the other side where there was a stream with a very rocky crossing. The water was good and grass was found on the hills.

Sparks and man came up with some cattle they have been back hunting for the past two days. They are several days behind their company. He says there is talk of a fight between the Banacas and some other tribe. Met four mounted Indians with a band of ponies going at full speed. These are the first we have seen for a long time and it alarms us. The dust now days is something fearful.

August 10th.

Two Indians, mounted on ponies, came into camp this morning. They appeared much excited and made us understand that their tribe, the Banacas, had been fighting with another and six of their men had been killed. We did not know whether to credit the story or not. There was a good deal of anxiety lest the visit boded us no good. They were given breakfast which they ate very hurriedly and then left on the road we were to follow.[34] The ascent of another mountain began. The

---

[33]The Oregon Trail continued north to Fort Hall, a fur trading post on the Columbia. This route was out of the way for California travelers, however, and most, like the Carpenter party, took the Hudspeth or Meyers Cut-Off from Soda Springs to City of Rocks. The route is well described in Dale Morgan, "Letters by 49ers Written From Great Salt Lake City in 1849," *Western Humanities Review* 3 (April 1949): 105.

[34]Carpenter means the Bannocks, a branch of the Northern Piute who roamed the area in and around Fort Hall. Their name, and those of other tribesmen, was frequently mispelled by the overland diarists. The Bannock were occasionally hostile, but whether it was this group or another that harrassed the party is not clear. Later, Helen blames the Shoshone, but Emily claimed they were Arapaho. Ables, who also traveled this route in 1857 noted that "The first depredation committed by Indians was on Head Paths [sic] Cut-Off." See Brigham D. Madsen, *The Bannock of Idaho* (Caldwell, Idaho: Caxton, 1958), and Ables, "Letter," 11.

road was bad all the way, six miles. Then came down to a little creek where there is a Morman trading post. Quite a party of Banacas were here but they kept out of sight as much as they could and at the same time get a peep at us. Very little information could be gained from the Mormons. Two flags hoisted on poles we were told were war flags. They were made of red and green broadcloth trimmed with long white and short yellow feathers and large brass buttons. One had an otter skin stretched across it and all together they were rather tasty.

Drove only two or three miles down the creek and stopped for the day finding good grass and plenty of willows for wood. We begin to think there is too much stopping and resting. The cattle are able to go and we would rather be moving along. Dobbins assures us that we are going fully as fast as we should. He argues that while the grass is good we should let the cattle feed up and a little later we will pass all these trains that have passed us. "Our teams will be in good condition and theirs will be given out." We are not satisfied but Father and Reel think perhaps he is right.

Soon after Dobbins' boy left he engaged a middle aged man to take his place. He gave his name as Scott. We have learned that he is a deserter from Fort Kearny. There have been a good many rumors of Indian depredations, and we have found little messages by the roadside, written in pencil, on the bleached bones of animals such as "look out for the Indians; Indians ran off all the stock of train ahead;" etc. etc. As Indians have not been in sight we have not been really alarmed until those came to camp. Scott appears more anxious than any one else. He says there is more reason to be afraid when they keep away from us. The traders call this stream Porteneu Creek. The mosquitoes are very bad.

August 11th.

Followed down the creek a short distance and then took to the mountains again for six miles. Then came down to Marsh Creek which is a small miry stream. The water moves very little. There is quite an expanse of bottom land that appears to have been covered with grass but much stock has been over it so we are too late to be benefited. The crossing was so very muddy and bad that we wallowed through, no other word would express it. From this marshy flat we again began climbing the mountains. The dust was so deep that it made the pulling hard, yet it did not fly as badly as usual owing to last nights rain. Very cloudy all day and is the pleasantest one for six weeks or more. Seven or eight miles up through the mountains and down again camping on a small stream. I think there is grass.

August 12th.

Up and down all the forenoon. Took dinner by a small stream and followed it the rest of the day. Camped by the creek and near some traders. They say it is 25 miles to the next water.

August 13th.

This morning started through a canon that is seven miles long ascending all the way. To say the road was very dusty conveys but little idea of its condition. We really suffered from it. As soon as the top was reached, we began going down a very long, steep, stony hill. (The guide books says it is five miles down.) Nooned in a little valley where there was little but sage brush growing. More mountain road in the afternoon. Steep and sidling in places. By the time we got to the top of the ridge it was dark and not knowing what was before us (except that it was down hill), stopped and camped there in all the dirt without feed or water. Nothing but sage brush. If it had been light enough to see the road we would have traveled right along.

Dobbins' wagons are always in the lead, then ours, and father's last. With three or more yokes of cattle to each wagon, there is a lot of dust at any time, but today it was worse than ever and seemed to permeate everything. The food was supposed to be put away securely but had its full share. Snuggled up in uninviting beds, with hands and faces unwashed. Weariness and discomfort were soon forgotten in sound sleep that was refreshing even though dust coated.

August 14th.

Left camp at daylight. The road down hill was not at all a bad one. By eight o'clock came to a small stream where we breakfasted. No grass but some back on the hills. Did not start again until afternoon, then drove six miles up hill and down all the way. In a canon a spring that had been dug out furnished water enough for the oxen but had to be dipped for them. Two miles farther and we camped where there was tolerably good grass but no water.

August 15th.

Three miles from camp the road ran by a mountain that was covered with cedar and quaking aspen trees. At the base of the mountain is a very fine spring. Had very good grass at noon but no water. Some distance farther on, came to a little branch which is fed by innumerable springs. A mile farther and it has grown to be quite a large creek. The crossing was very bad. Followed the stream a mile farther and camped near it. In selecting the camp, care was taken to keep at a distance from the willows. Finding that a little trench (not more than a foot deep) came up into camp, the wagons were ordered away from it lest the Indians crawl up into camp. Plenty of wood and good grass. The stock was to be kept as close to the wagons as possible and give them an opportunity to eat. About dusk there was a commotion among them. A speedy reconnoisance revealed nothing save that several head had broken away from the herd and were so frightened that it was with considerable difficulty that they were driven back. *No* cause for this little flurry was visible.

August 16th.

Very cold this morning. The traders report the Indians troublesome through here running off horses and cattle. They say that all the horses belonging to the "Jinny" train were stampeded and that a few miles back a man being out alone was shot three times and killed. His horse and gun were taken. Their modus operandi is to ride boldly up in the daytime, screech and halloo and frighten the stock so that a stampede follows.

After following the stream four miles and crossing, the creek makes a detour. The road, though uneven, kept a direct westerly course. During the afternoon where the road was comparatively smooth, Billy Collin (Dobbins' boy driving the wagon just ahead of ours) whipped up his oxen until their heads were at the tail-gate of the lead wagon, then climbed into the wagon and brought out his old "fiddle." By the time that he was on the ground again the oxen were beginning to lag. As he tuned the instrument he gave the near leader a kick and then, as the others passed, they got a poke in the ribs so they were kept moving. The road has been so rough of late that Billy has had but little opportunity to indulge in this musical pastime and while he drives is the only time he may play there are so many camp duties. Today he sawed "Buffalo Girls Are You Coming Out Tonight" and "Arkansas Traveler." As I do not believe Billy ever read the lines, "Music hath charms to sooth the savage," I consider him innocent of any deep laid scheme in that direction. And then Billy's music was of the "Rend a rock and split a cabbage" variety. It helped to relieve the monotony anyway. The oxen, despite prods and kicks, would not keep up, so the "fiddle" soon had to be put aside for the whip to play its part.

The drive from where the creek was crossed this morning was to be 12 miles. About four p.m. some green patches were sited [sic] in the distance. These we knew were willows by the stream where our day's journey would end. Suddenly, coming from we scarcely knew where, were five well armed, well mounted Indians in the road coming directly toward us single file. Our men hurriedly put on knives and pistols and with guns in hand all went steadily forward. "How" was the salutation of the Indian in the lead, and then they filed silently by peering into the wagons in a very curious manner. They were trying to learn our strength it was said. When they had gone by some 50 yards they dismounted and in a line across the road executed a dance. This was regarded as a bad omen. One of the party was so unlike the others in his every movement that he was unhesitatingly pronounced a white man and if so a Mormon. After the dance they passed out of sight, and we with the greatest anxiety proceeded. We were in a valley of considerable extent with high mountains on every side except in the direction from which we had just come. We felt a good deal like rats in a trap. Leaving the main road we turned to the left and going half a mile up the stream made camp on the east branch of Raft River. The stream is only three to four feet in width, is very sluggish and with a muddy bottom. There are a great many willows along the stream and farther back are large clusters of them. A little opening was selected and with the same care as last night we kept away from the willows. The wagons were arranged in a circle to make an enclosure for the stock. Water kegs, ox yokes, and chains were used in making the connections between wagons. The grass was good.

Usually the cattle are left to graze until they are satisfied, but tonight it was deemed unsafe to leave them out after dusk, so they were brought in early and before their supper was finished. This made them unruly, but after a few ineffectual attempts to get beyond the guard they settled down to rest and there was not a sound upon the night air except the heavy breathing of those tired, half fed cattle that to us were now so indispensable. About 10 o'clock all were suddenly awakened by a terrible commotion among the cattle. They surged this way and that, banged against the wagons in a way to suggest an upset, and all was hurly burly. Some one cried out "Oh them darned Injuns." For a few minutes we thought the Indians were upon us, that our stock would be driven off, and if we were not killed we would be left in a most helpless condition. Our fears were soon allayed. It was found that a colt tied to an ox yoke was the sole cause of the disturbance. The colt, finding the yoke was not stationary, became frightened and went pell mell among the cattle. They in turn were frightened and I am free to confess that we were "equally so." Father's man, an Englishman by the name of John Fosset, was the careless party. This was on a par with his usual poor judgment in whatever he did.

August 17th.

Father was the early guard and took the stock out to graze as soon as it began to grow light. They were some 300 or 400 yards from the wagons. When the sun was just peeping over the top of the mountain there was suddenly heard a hoot and a blood curdling yell, and immediately the Indians we saw yesterday were seen riding at full speed directly toward the horses. As they drew uncomfortably near, Father put his gun to his shoulder as though to shoot, and they instantly moved farther away. (At the time he did not know that but one barrel of the gun was loaded.) He took advantage of the little scare given them by getting between the Indians and the horses which he began driving toward camp. The Indians kept their horses in a run, circling this way and that and hallooing at the top of their voices. As Father did not shoot, they gradually became more venturesome, and each time they passed they drew a little nearer. Again the gun went to his shoulder and again they drew off. This was repeated several times before any from camp could be on the ground. Reel was sound asleep when the alarm was given. He sprang up, barely taking time to put on his pantaloons. While running he tied together a leather belt and a silk handkerchief and on reaching the horses made a loop of the handkerchief around the lower jaw of one of them and sprang on its back using the belt as a guide strap. Father, with his gun to his shoulder, kept the Indians back while Reel rode around the cattle and headed them towards camp. The other boys were soon on hand to help.

The stock having had but a partial feed last night were so intent on getting breakfast that they did not see any Indians at all. Otherwise they would have been very easily frightened off as even the scent of the red skins alarms them. When the Indians found their attempt to get the stock was a failure, they began calling out "How, How, How." But getting no response, they fired six shots and kept circling around keeping their horses in the run until they seemed well tired out. Later they took up a position behind a clump of willows within shot of camp. When the stock was well into camp it was noticed that Dobbins was not with the others. Where was Dobbins? All had been so intent on saving the stock that no individual had been thought of. Where was Dobbins? He was found just as far back in one of his wagons as he could get and there he sat with two guns. When asked why he did not go to help with the stock, he replied that it was not safe to go and leave the women and children alone. The idea was all right. No one else had thought of it, not even the women and children themselves, yet they were quite as safe without him as with him.

Some of the party wanted to leave camp at once but they said we must have breakfast first, so the meal was gotten ready and all the while bullets were whining uncomfortably near. We might just as well have gone at once. No one could eat. Nobody had any appetite and any way the teeth chattered too badly for any one to attempt it. Sometimes the Indians were in sight and sometimes not. A number of times one stood on his horse's back so as to bring his head above the tops of the willows and waved an impromptu flag made of a badly soiled shirt on a pole. Whether this was intended as a war flag or a flag of truce we were unable to decide; but whatever their intention it was all the same to us. The shirt could not have been white enough to restore our confidence.

During the time we were getting breakfast and yoking up, bullets came whizzing through camp. None can know the horror of it who have not been similarly situated. A number of times Father and Reel rested their Sharp's rifles on a wagon wheel and took deliberate aim. Scott begged them not to shoot, telling them that as they valued their lives and the lives of the women and children to desist. "The country," he said, "is full of Indians, and if you kill one of them they will never stop until they have murdered every one of us." The women added their entreaties to his and very reluctantly the guns were put down. Things were hastily put into the wagons and as soon as the cattle could be yoked we left camp. We were not more than a 100 yards away when the Indians rushed in and peered about in every direction to see if anything had been left that they could carry off. Not finding any thing, they began riding after us. As when after the stock, they did not come directly towards us but all the time in a circular way from one side of the road to the other, each time they passed getting a little nearer and occasionally firing a shot. None of the party seemed anxious to shoot except Father and Reel. They could stand it no longer. They must let those Indians see how far their Sharp's rifles would carry. Without aiming to hit them, they made the earth fly dangerously near and so the enemy seem to think for they were much more careful in approaching us. As soon as attention could rest on any thing but *Indians*, it was noticed that the boldest rider was on a large brown American horse belonging to a train ahead. The others had Indian ponies. I think it was this brown horse in the hands of this rascally fellow that made Reel decide to shoot. The Indian crossed the road, in the run, broadside to us, and Reel, getting down on one knee so as to have a rest, took deliberate aim at the horse and fired. Immediately the horse slowed down, and the Indian slid off of his back and ran behind the willows. The horse followed more slowly and limping.

They must have held a consultation as they did not appear again for several minutes, and then followed only a short distance farther when they turned squarely to the left making directly toward a gap in the mountains. We were traveling in a westerly course, but according to the guide book a few miles farther on the road turns due south. So they were going in a line that would intercept our road. This was not reassuring. The brown horse was not able to keep up with the others but they all soon passed out of sight. The expectation of meeting them again made us more alarmed than when they were in sight and shooting after us.

Five or six miles travel brought us to Raft River proper which is but a good sized creek.[35] The road kept near the river and the willows on either side were the largest, tallest, and thickest we have seen any where and came in so closely to the road that there was not room for the drivers to walk beside the wagons and yet every one was keeping a sharp lookout, expecting any moment to be attacked. This was endured for three hours. At noon we came to a place where the willows were not quite so thick so stopped to give the stock a chance to eat as they had little supper and almost no breakfast. They had to be taken across the creek on the slope of the mountain which began to ascend from the creek bank. The mountain was comparatively smooth, without trees, and the only vegetation, a few hundred yards above the creek, was sage brush. Scott was on guard with the stock and went some distance up the mountain until he could see the road where it emerged from the willows at the river crossing which was a mile farther down stream. He said he saw eight Indians go into the willows at that point and could see plainly the glint of sunshine on the gun barrels after the Indians themselves were concealed in the brush. By chopping and clearing away willows and spading the steep banks, it was made possible to get the wagons across. The next two or three miles were traveled on the side of the mountain keeping as near as possible the general direction in which we wished to go. It was very hard for the oxen to pull the wagons over the brush and quite as hard for us to stand the jolting. After three miles of this there seemed no further necessity of keeping on the mountain as we were entirely away from the willows and were just as safe in the road which lay in a slightly undulating open between mountain ranges. An old ox or cow was the only living creature in sight.

We kept to the road for the next four miles and finding neither grass, wood, nor water, we turned to the right and went a mile up the face of the mountain opposite the one we had traveled during the

---

[35]Carpenter's description of the road to the Raft River is similar to that given by Child. The party was now but a short distance from the intersection with the Fort Hall road. Child, *Overland Route*, 37–41. See also Becker, *Christy's Road*, 10.

afternoon. From the road could be seen a patch of green which denoted willows and water. It was nearly dusk before the place was reached. There is a fine spring, plenty of grass, and a nice cluster of willows that partially concealed us from the road. No fires were kindled and we had no lights as we thought that perhaps the Indians had gone for a larger force and knowing that we could not get away were not keeping a watch. So we wished to avoid what ever might attract attention when they returned. The tent was put up as usual but not occupied. The wagons were run closely together, water kegs were taken from underneath the wagons (where they were always carried), and with ox yokes and every available thing were used to make a barracade. As a means of protection it did not look very promising.

We felt the situation most keenly. Such a mere handful of humanity: four men, four women, three young boys, and three children, one my mother's little six month old baby. In *no* way could we turn for assistance. The "Jinny train" was the last one to pass and that was eight days ago. Since then we have seen none and have been traveling slowly. We are confident that we are the last immigrants on the road. Dobbins has kept us back until all have passed. When a train passes over some very dusty road the small particles of dirt rise in clouds and hang over the road for miles. These have been seen sometimes twenty miles, the trains themselves not being visible yet the dust in the air plainly marking their course. The road traveled this past week has been unusually dusty, and we must suppose from our manner of reckoning that all are several days in advance so we realize that we must depend on ourselves.

The night was dark and we sat in little groups and talked in whispers. About nine o'clock Dobbins ventured a little distance from the wagons but came hurrying back and said, "I want the old man (meaning Father) to go down there with his long gun and see what that dark object is." Father went. It was one of the oxen that had strayed a little from the others. A little later a shot was fired down on the road. Our hearts stood still knowing it could be from none but our enemies. The stock was driven in closer and Father went up to the spring where John Fosset was put on guard. He was there but sound asleep. The cattle he was set to guard were driven in, but John was left to look out for himself. He had proven so untrustworthy that we were not much interested in his welfare.

This is my little brother's, Hale's, ninth birthday. Notwithstanding the worry and excitement of the day, some one remembered it. The manner in which it was passed will be a life memory. Father could not trust the boys nor Dobbins to guard the camp so he was on all night.

August 18th (Wednesday)

All safe this morning. We were agreeably disappointed in not having a call last night. Some report having seen Indians and hearing them singing. As we are sure they were not far enough from camp to hear anything more than the rest of us the story is discredited. A few miles from camp we came to a stream which had but a scant amount of water, but by noon reached another that supplied plenty. Here a couple of Mormons have a blacksmith shop. In the next three miles passed considerable alkali. The ground is low and has a marshy appearance and pools of dark coffee colored water are in among the scant grass and weeds. It is a great deal of work to keep the stock away from this water. In spite of all that can be done, they get occasional sips. Another Mormon blacksmith shop.

Here we went into the mountains again but had a very good road. Two miles farther come to a narrow way which they call a pass. At the entrance of this was a newly made grave filled with stones. Near it a bit of board was picked up on which was written this brief account of the unfortunate one. "This man was killed by Indians, Aug. 7th. He was from Iowa and was traveling alone with a wagon and one horse." Emerging from the pass we came into what is known as Pyramid Circle. There was perhaps an acre of partially level land with a good sized stream flowing through it. On this level, and the hills which encircled it, were the most beautiful and wonderful white rocks that we ever saw. This is known as the City rocks and certainly bears a striking resemblance to a city. To be sure it was a good deal out of the usual, for the large and small houses were curiously intermingled and set at all angles, but it only made the place the more charming. There was everything one could imagine from a dog house to a church and courthouse.[36] While the stock was being cared for the women and

---

[36] The City of Rocks, or Steeple Rocks as they were sometimes called, was another often noted landmark. "These are a curiosity worth the traveler's notice," wrote Thomas Christy and he described their "decayed castels [sic] and lofty steeples." Geiger and Bryarly fancied they could see "anything from the Capitol at Washington

children wandered off to enjoy the sights of the city. When they returned to camp a stern and well merited reprimand awaited them. "How could you do such a thing? Did not you know there might be an Indian behind every rock?" etc. etc. We were so spellbound with the beauty and strangeness of it all that no thought of Indians entered our heads. Some of us, at least, are too young and thoughtless for our surroundings. The older ones did not forget to make all the possible arrangements they could for the safety of the camp.

August 19th.

A few miles from the City Rocks the Salt Lake Road comes in. A mile farther came to a creek that has the appearance of being quite a stream at times but there was little water running. Eleven miles from camp came to some fine springs that gush out from underneath a rock. Nooned here and then started over the mountains. Very long, steep hills to go down. One place in particular was so bad that the only wonder is that the wagons kept right side up. Portions of the road were barely wide enough for the wagons. Steep mountains on one side and an abrupt bank on the other and at times very sidling.[37] Camped on a small branch near the foot of the mountain. Good grass and plenty of cedar wood. This has been a tiresome day.

August 20th.

Two miles from camp came to Goose Creek. This is quite a stream with a thick growth of willows along its banks. Three Indians suddenly came from among the bushes and out to the road where the wagons had halted for a few minutes. They did not appear unfriendly. Mother thought best to conciliate the rascals so handed out food. Some of us argued that it would only make them all the more anxious to get what was in the wagons. In leaving they did not follow the road but hastily got into the bushes and out of sight. The road fol-

---

to a lowly thatched cottage." Becker, *Christy's Road,* map 60; Potter, *Trail to California,* 161.

[37]The road described by Mrs. Carpenter lay through Granite Pass, "a magnificent but little known gateway to the Far West." Becker points out that few travelers were aware of this "mile-post," and it received little comment. Becker, *Christy's Road,* 10.

lowed the stream for 20 miles. Good grass all the way along the creek bottom. Had one very bad slough to cross.

August 21st.

Three miles from camp the road leaves Goose Creek and goes into a canon that is four miles long. A little stream follows the canon for two or three miles. This is the last water for 13 miles. The first part of the drive was most dreadfully stony but the latter part was excellent. Billy got his "fiddle" out and sawed for a while. Rock Springs was the next watering place. No grass. The springs are situated at the head of 1000 Springs Valley which has little vegetation except sage brush.[38] Two miles down the valley camped without grass or water. Raining.

August 22nd.

This morning Dobbins was not willing to leave camp until he had his breakfast. When we learned this, and that he had sent one of the boys back two miles for water to make his coffee, we told him we were not going to wait and would not travel at his gait any longer but would rush ahead as fast as the teams could stand it. It is now 18 days since we have seen a train, and we are going to make a desperate effort to overtake the trains ahead. The past six days have been a great strain that we would like to see ended. It seems pretty bad for a little party like this to divide its forces in a hostile Indian country but it has to be done. Dobbins' conduct in wishing to hang back is unaccountable since we know him to be such a coward. Nevertheless we go.

Two miles from camp came to a small hole of water with a mud bottom. Stopped and got breakfast. By the time we got through with that mud hole there was nothing left that Dobbins or his stock would care for. A mile farther crossed a small spring branch and three miles farther came to good grass but no water. In the afternoon came to another small stream of such poor water that the cattle did not like to drink it. Some was obtained near the head of the stream that we could

---

[38]The trip through Goose Creek Valley, described above, is similar to that outlined by Paden, *Wake of the Prairie Schooner*, 375–89. Carpenter's comments on Rock Springs and Thousand Springs Valley near present day Elko City, Nevada, are also similar to those of other travelers. See: Platt, *Traveler's Guide*, 21–22; Becker, *Christy's Road*, map 63; Morgan, *Pritchard Diary*, 160 *n* 70.

drink yet it was not good. More "alkali" water and a great many dead cattle. With the exception of a few days our teams have not been in the lead since on the trip, and being accustomed to follow we very naturally expected it would require a good deal of persuasion to make them keep up the gait at which we wanted to go. To the surprise of all there was no lagging. In their freshest moments they never traveled with such alacrity. I shall always think they understood the emergency. Why otherwise would they, with little urging, keep up a gait at which they had not been accustomed to travel now when they were so worn with travel and half fed.

Traveled eight or ten miles in the afternoon in 1000 Springs Valley which is a great expanse of level country barren of trees. If it were only covered in grass it would be called a prairie, but since it has only a very poor quality of sage brush, I call it abominable. We were not expecting to find the 1000 springs (or however many there may be) right out on this level stretch of land. No inlet, no outlet, just a lot of wells or holes full to the surface with water and covering several acres. "And the green grass grew all around," but unfortunately for us had been well eaten off. For some distance around there was a slight undulating motion which gave rather an uncomfortable feeling of uncertainty as to how long one might stay on top. The stock like ourselves were cautious at first, but thirst got the better of their fears and they drank directly from the wells. Some of the wells were so close together that only the most courageous or "fool hardy" would venture to walk between them, and again they were from 10 to 20 feet apart. The smallest one was two feet in diameter. The majority were 10 to 15 feet and the largest one was 20 feet. One they sounded was 30 feet deep. In the largest they could not strike bottom. There were fish in them six inches long which showed that the water was not alkali, although the surrounding country had a great deal of alkali on the surface. We think there is a lake which has been gradually covered and crusted over first with a growth of water plants and then with loose earth carried by the winds which have a great sweep over this barren waste. Passed many dead cattle near the alkali. Camped right in among the wells. Notwithstanding Dobbins was traveling as fast as he wanted to go, he kept closely after us all day and this evening passed and soon turned off the road and went out of sight.

August 23rd.

This is the dampest morning I ever saw. At least I never saw dew pile up as it was here. The blades of grass were weighed down with it and clothing left outside the wagons was ready to be wrung out. No rain ever left things in such a wet state. Very unpleasant getting breakfast. The boys tell us that Dobbins camped two miles away from us without water. This morning he was well back to the road when he stopped at the wells to water his stock. When he saw us coming, he made all possible haste as he did not want us to be ahead of him. We had made up our minds that we would be. For fully a quarter of a mile the stock belonging to both was kept trotting or loping all the way. One of Dobbins' wagons came in ahead, then came ours, then his other wagon followed by Father's. Just as this occurred, the wagon in the lead curved around a big mud-hole and ours cut straight across. The mud was less than knee deep (not nearly as bad as it looked), but we made the water fly and came out ahead. No sooner had this happened than one of Dobbins' oxen came unyoked and capered off with the loose stock. This stopped his wagons and gave Father an opportunity to come up with ours by going through the mud-hole. We drove on a little way and then stopped and helped his boys get the ox and separate the cattle. In the latter they had considerable trouble because they were used to running together but finally it was accomplished and we moved on.

Eight miles from camp came to some hot springs. The water boils up and is hotter than the hand can be held in. Quite a little stream was running from them. A quarter of a mile up stream from the springs, found nice springs of cold water.[39] Plenty for the stock and pretty good grass yet considerable alkali on the ground. Ten miles farther on the road began a gradual climb in a canon which it followed for several miles. At a turn in the road some white spots far in advance were seen on the mountain side. Our schooled eyes were at no loss to determine what they were. We knew it to be a train although it was too far away

---

[39]These hot springs are also described in many of the guides and diaries. Platt estimated the temperature in the springs at 180°. Platt, *Traveler's Guide*, 22. See also: Child, *Overland Route*, 45; Potter, *Trail to California*, 192; Becker, *Christy's Road*, map 63.

for the cattle to be discernable. No more welcome sight could meet our gaze. None except that little bank of travelers can ever know the inexpressible joy and relief experienced on seeing those old dust begrimed wagons. The weight that was lifted left us buoyant and happy. The train was lying by on account of the illness of one of the party. Had it not been for this we would have had to camp another night alone before coming to any train. Got here at 2 p.m. having traveled 22 miles which was a very good drive with tired oxen.

This train, Sparks, Farmers, and Houks (all large trains) have been keeping close together on account of the Indians. They were uneasy about us knowing how small our train was and that we were the last. We stopped and camped near this train. Somewhat later Dobbins passed and camped on another hill. Some of the boys found a body on the mountain side. It was partially covered with dirt and brush and too badly decomposed for them to be able to tell whether it was a white person or an Indian. It was thought to be a white woman. Four Indians were seen on the mountain. These people claimed one of the oxen Dobbins had picked up. A baby was born in camp tonight.

August 24.

Continued on up hill for two miles before the descent began. After two miles down hill the road forked, the left going through a canon (very bad road), and the right, which we took, is farther but was very good. Traveled seven miles before stopping to noon on a small branch in which there was but little water. Here we came up with Farmer's train which was lying by on account of the illness of Mrs. Wilson, Mr. Farmer's married daughter who had a baby that had come prematurely and some one else that was sick. Mother at once took the baby and is nursing and caring for it.

Aside from wanting company, on account of the Indians, we were very glad to meet old acquaintances. We attached ourselves to their train which moved eight miles in the afternoon and camped in a valley where there was sage brush and grass waist high. The train we came up with claimed one of the cattle that Dobbins had picked up and brought along.

August 25th.

Traveled nine miles in the forenoon and nooned on Canon Creek which is the headwaters of the Humboldt.[40] Good grass all along the valley. Farmer went on ahead for some of his cattle that got with another train. He brought back news of Indian depredations. Four or five days ago some two or three wagons were taken and six or seven men and two women were killed. Only one man escaped. As Uncle Sam's had three wagons and a number of men we are feeling anxious about them. Two men of another train were killed and in another a man was wounded. This latter was guarding stock and an Indian crawled in the grass until near enough to shoot which he did hitting him in the lower part of the leg. There was 300 head of cattle but the Indians only succeeded in running off 60 head and one horse. There is talk of an Indian hunt.[41]

We followed down the valley and camped on the creek. My mind was so distracted by the dust that I have no idea how far we came. The distance seemed interminable. Now that we have joined this train, we must go at the tail of the procession. Nine wagons ahead of us, each with from four to six yoke of oxen dragging their feet along in the dust which was so light that it only needed a breath of air to set it floating in clouds. The air was so thoroughly full of it that our own oxen and driver were at times quite obscured. I put a curtain across the front of the wagon and opened the cover in the back in an effort to get air thin enough to breathe. People back in the states have no conception of a dusty road.

---

[40]Canon or Bishop Creek is a branch of the Mary's River, one of the tributaries of the Humboldt. The trail along the creek was one of several routes to the Humboldt Valley. Becker, *Christy's Road*, map 64; Morgan, *Pritchard Diary*, 163 n 72.

[41]The Indians on this part of the route were considered among the most troublesome on the entire trail. Usually lumped together by the emigrants under the epithet of "Digger Indians" they included Shoshones, Piutes, Utes, and other Great Basin peoples. "They will steal or shoot your stock," warned Child, "and although they appear friendly, they will not scruple to take your stock." Ware furnished a similar admonition, "Their practice is to disable cattle, so as to make it necessary for the emigrant to leave them on the road." Child, *Overland Route*, 46; Ware, *Emigrant's Guide*, 33. On the distinctions between the various "tribes," see Potter, *Trail to California*, 175 n 21.

There is strong talk of starting on an Indian hunt tomorrow. It is said there are 15 trains within four or five miles of us and 200 men. The train that lost the stock has taken an Indian prisoner. Through a Mormon interpreter he has agreed to take the whites to where their cattle are if they will agree not to kill him. It seems to me a very risky business to follow an Indian off into the mountains to meet they know not what. I do not believe that he can be trusted, but the men seem to think there is no danger. There are three lone wagons standing near the willows stripped of their cloth covers, just a little way from our camp. None here know who they belonged to. They silently bespeak a grim tragedy. This morning we moved down the creek nearer the other trains so as to be all together. We are next to Harps. That is where the wounded man is. 30 men well armed and well mounted set off following the Indian who stepped very spritely keeping a close watch all the while as though he expected a shot in the back or something of the sort. If they halted he immediately did the same. If he acts in good faith he is promised a gun and his liberty. Reel is of the party. I was opposed to his going but unable to prevent it. To say the very least it is an unwise thing for those men to follow an Indian out into the mountains in the expectation of getting the cattle back. The Mormon who acted as interpreter has gone. We think he should have been held until the party got back as we cannot regard them as friends.

August 27th.

The train did expect to move today but on account of the illness of the women did not do so. To wait for the Indian hunters was another reason for not moving but that alone would not have prevented it as the horsemen could easily overtake us and every one is so anxious to be getting along. The river here is a good sized stream. There is quite a valley following its course. Not many willows.

August 28th.

The women are no better. All the trains are waiting. It took Father and another man until noon to put an axel in our wagon. This forenoon Wilson's little baby died. Moved five miles in the afternoon to get fresh feed. This afternoon the hunters returned highly elated with their success, having been gone three days and two nights. Went 60 miles into the mountains. They brought back 37 head of the 60 taken. The trip was a very hard one and they suffered from hunger and cold having taken no blankets and no food but a few biscuits in their pockets. The first night they camped on a mountain side near a little brook and some willows. Every precaution was taken so no fires were to be made. The horses were staked out and guards stationed, and the party huddled together in a vain effort to keep warm. A guard came in and in response to the inquiry as to why he did so exclaimed, "My God Cap, don't you know an Indian could crawl up and shoot me and I wouldn't know it." The men finally decided that they might just as well be killed by the Indians as to freeze to death, so they built a fire and made themselves as comfortable as they could.

At the time of a previous writing I did not know that a party went out the next day after the stock was taken. They had no difficulty in following the trail of the stock but did not dare to go as far as the party was small. The trail remained and could still be plainly seen. The prisoner took the party directly to the Indian camp. Before they were aware of its close proximity Indians were seen running to the brush. They seemed to be all women and children. Only one old man was sighted. He ran in some willows that overhung the creek bank and crawled in. They tried to make him come out, but he would not so they shot into the brush and he immediately set up a very queer wail which was thought to be a death chant. It did not long continue. Three women, the mother and sisters of the prisoner, were captured. Reel was riding after one of them when she suddenly dropped to the ground. He was looking ahead when his horse stumbled over her. After dropping to the ground she had crawled back towards him.

The party was mostly Missourians, and some of them were disposed to treat the squaws as the Border Ruffians did the women of Kansas. Fortunately there were enough real men to protect the squaws. Some were for having the squaws killed, but they were not injured in any way only held as prisoners until the party was ready to leave. Eighteen head of the stock had been killed and the carcasses were lying near. The skins were already doing duty as "wickyups." They were sewed together and stretched around poles set in conical form with an opening at the top for the smoke to escape. The hind quarters seemed to be all they were going to make use of. All the rest of the animal was left.

Who can understand such improvidence? They had cut the meat into strips and had it drying in the sun. Reel began eating some of the meat and put some in his pocket. One of the Missourians said, "Just look at the damned Yank." They were all glad enough to eat of the meat and put it in their pockets too. What they did not carry off they burned along with the wickyups. They could not learn what became of the other seven head.

The squaws were told that unless they brought 10 ponies inside of two days that the Indian would be killed. Whether they fully understood it or not they were not certain, but the ponies were not brought. The prisoner was made to drive the cattle back, and some of the party made it as hard for him as they could. He was quite foot sore from running over the rocks. After the cattle were returned to Harp, and the boys had gone to their separate camps, Harp's company whipped the Indian with ramrods raising great welts on his back. Parties interfered and took him to McVay's camp to be set at liberty the next morning.[42]

August 29th.

It was rumored last night that the Indian was to be killed this morning. Before we left camp a little party with the Indian went back on the road out of sight, supposedly to kill him. If not, why was he not liberated at camp?

Wilson's little baby was buried beside the road this morning before we started. The road followed the river all day. There has been a great sameness in river, valley, and country generally so much so I have no idea how far we have come. It was about noon before the men who went back with the Indian came up with the wagons.

August 30th.

Still traveling down the river. Met some surveyors from California. They tell us that Uncle Sam's are all safe but report the Indians very bad. They buried five white men in one grave and three in another

---

[42]The Ables party was traveling along the Humboldt at the same time, and Ables participated in the first search party which captured the Indian "guide." "Afterwards heard that the 2nd company was successful in overtaking the Indians, after following the trail seventy miles," he reported. Ables, "Letter,"15.

near Gravel Ford. There are 30 men in the party. They were attacked but no one was injured.

August 31st.

This morning we came to where the road forks. We took what is called the canon road which crosses the river four times. The first crossing was very deep and 30 feet wide. The canon is several miles long. After going a short distance in the afternoon we came to where the road leaves the river for 17 miles and stopped right there and camped.

September 1st.

Ours was the first train to pull out this morning and we are particularly glad as it will make a difference in the amount of dust that we get. Just before going into the mountains passed the grave where the three men are buried. Their names were unknown. The hills were steep and very stony.

There were four spring branches with very bad crossings that I feared we would not be able to get through. Crossed Gravel Ford and encamped.[43] All creation seems to be here tonight. We are in pretty close quarters but it is all the safer in this hostile Indian country. A man from McVay's train says that the Indian prisoner was given the gun he was promised, some provisions and a blanket & told to go. We are in hopes that it may be so but do not believe it. (50 years after the incident just related, I was told by Mr. Tom Rawles that his father was one of the party that went back on the road with the Indian. Mr. Rawles went to see that the fellow had fair play. He was well armed and they knew him to be a man of good principals and determination and when he told them that whoever molested the Indian should have the contents of his gun they did not dare to interfere. Mr. Rawles was the last one to come to camp. Even after so many years I was very glad to know that the rascal got safely away.)

September 2nd.

This morning passed a grave where three men were buried. A paper

---

[43]The route to Gravel Ford, near Beowawe, Nevada, is described in more detail in Morgan, *Pritchard Diary,* 164 *nn* 73 and 76.

was picked up which stated that their nude bodies were found in the willows 200 yards from where they were buried and that they were underneath a wagon bed. From papers found near by it was thought they were Mormon traders named Jones and Morgan and were killed by the Indians July 21st, and buried by the California packers August 16th. The boys found a white man's skull with a bullet hole above the ear.

Nooned by the river and on leaving it started over the mountains which were steep and dusty. This going down was stony. Camped on grass knee high near where the river turns due north and the road goes straight ahead. The surveyors told us that there was better feed on the north side but that it was farther. We kept straight ahead.

September 3rd.

Traveled fast and at three o'clock stopped by a slough and ate dinner. During the afternoon came to where the road was white with goose feathers for two hundred yards. Portions of a comparatively new wagon, hacked and broken, were barely out of the road and the earth was torn up showing there had been a terrible conflict. There was nothing more, but we understood only too well what it meant. It was night when we got to the river. The willows are very thick and the water deep.

September 4th.

Left the river this morning and did not come to it again until five o'clock. The road has been very rough and full of jump offs and chuck holes and so covered with dust that they were not seen but felt. There has been but little vegetation in sight today except sage brush. Came about 20 miles notwithstanding the roughness of the road. The nights and mornings are very cold. There is frequently quite an ice on the water buckets. The middle of the day is warm and pleasant.

Since we caught up with the trains, seven head of the cattle that Dobbins picked up on the way has [sic] been claimed and taken. At last we know why he wanted to lag behind. His greed is still greater than his cowardice which we thought could not be excelled. For the sake of those few cattle all our lives were risked.

We have learned that parties in advance of us found the body of a nude woman on the bank of the slough that we passed yesterday. A piece of hair rope was around her neck and on one foot was an India rubber overshoe. From appearances it was thought she had been tortured by being drawn back and forth through the slough by this rope around her neck. The body was given the best burial that was possible under the circumstances.

September 5th.

Came seven miles over better road than we had yesterday and stopped at noon at an excellent watering place. We were detained two hours or more waiting for some boys who went back after lost cattle. In the afternoon traveled seven miles more. There was no grass on the way and the road came to the river but once. There was excellent grass across the river so the stock was taken across to it as there was none where we camped. Dry willows very scarce.

Living as we do, I suppose it is permissible to note what the neighbors do and how they do it. The old gentleman Farmer is very good to help "Mother" in the culinary arrangements. He makes the fires, gets out the pots and kettles and the eatables and helps generally while "Mother" makes the bread and coffee. "Sister" is too small to do more than be in the way. When the four sons and men are ready for a meal each for the time being becomes his own cook so there is no occasion for anyone to grumble. Willows are sharpened and slices of bacon speared and held in the fire ad lib. It looks quite amusing.

September 6th.

Two miles from camp went into the mountains again. Most of the way was through a canon. In one place the road while going up hill crossed two perpendicular ledges of rock between two and three feet in height. Seven miles of this and it was all stony. Again came to the river but did not find grass until we had gone three miles. After that the grass was excellent. A good drive had not been made, but there is a stretch without water or grass and no one seems to know how far it is so stopped and camped.

Mr. Taylor's wagon is just ahead of ours and the children amuse themselves peeping out at the back of the wagon. There is one girl at the gawky age. She takes great pride in her little sister less than a year old. We have all taken turns in asking the baby's name just to hear her say, "She is named Myranda, after mother, and Isabell after a queen." (The b-e-l-l to be dragged and with especial emphasis.)

September 7th.

This forenoon we passed what they were pleased to call a trading post. It was made of brush with a wagon cover stretched over it. (Perhaps the cover is from the deserted wagons we saw.) The proprietor had flour, sugar, and coffee for sale. Flour 20 cts. a pound. An ox that had given out Reel sold for 15 dollars. He thinks he did well. Some of the trains are going to cross the river. We will keep to this side. This afternoon passed a trading post which is ten miles from the other. Flour is raising in price very fast. Here it is 30 cts. per pound.

These traders tell us that nine persons were killed where we saw the feathers in the road, and the next train that came by picked up a woman that had been scalped and left for dead but was still alive. They say the Indians traded the woman's scalp to them, and they sold it to her preservers. She was the only one of the party that escaped. (Six years after the foregoing I learned that the lady's name was Hollingwell, if I remember correctly, and that she was brought to her friends at Healdsburg, California. Her disposition they claimed was entirely changed, and after a year or two she died of a settled melancholy.)[44]

September 8th.

A greater part of the way today has been through deep sand. Even the hills we climbed were sandy. All day the road has been back several miles from the river except just where we nooned and camped. Nothing growing near the road [except] sage brush, grease wood, and a shrub we call iron wood because it is so like iron in looks and hardness. It has yellow blossoms and is very plentiful. Fairly good grass tonight.

---

[44]The woman's name was Holloway. According to William Maxwell, who knew her, there were ten people in the party and four, including Mrs. Holloway, survived. He believed the culprits were "generally Shoshones often accompanied by white renegades." Ables also describes the attack and notes that the Indians had been particularly troublesome that year. ". . . it is estimated that fifty persons have lost their lives on this river, the last summer, from the Indians." Maxwell, *Crossing the Plains*, 63–72, 124–26; Ables, "Letter," 15–16.

September 9th.

Passed another trading shanty. They charge $1.00 a pint for vinegar and the same for molasses. Coffee and dried apples are 50 cts a pound. They had a small stock on hand. Either had sold out or knew they could sell but little for not many immigrants can afford such delicacies at such prices. Here we crossed the river (water hub deep) and did not come to it again for 12 miles. Very deep dust all the way. I wonder what is expected to happen to a fellow who swallows twice his allotted amount of dirt (one peck). We are under no apprehension as this outdoor life seems to render us impervious to what would kill ordinary mortals. Only the other day, I saw some rice being warmed over that had been cooked and left standing in the kettle which was brass. There was a rim of verdegris all around the edge. The cooks stirred it in and nobody was even sick from it. "All is well that ends well." Camped by the river at the upper end of Lawson Meadows.[45] Raining and *very* cold.

September 10th.

Followed down the river 13 miles and halted for the day. The road here leaves the river again and there is no grass nor water for 12 miles which would be too long a drive after what we came over this morning. Passed three trading posts today. They are growing more frequent. Bought a scant pound of butter. Paid $1.00 for it. They say they did have vegetables but are all sold out. Very cold all day and is raining again. When it began raining here, snow could be seen falling on the mountain tops. Tonight they are quite white. It makes us fear that we may be caught in the mountains like the Donner party.

September 11th.

This morning the sun came out and made things look more cheerful than they did last night. Aside from chuck holes the road has been good. Stopped and watered the stock as soon as we came to the river, but as there was a scarcity of grass, we drove six miles farther going

---

[45]Evidently Mrs. Carpenter means Lassen's Meadows near present-day Rye Patch Dam. The meadows extended for several miles and were often used to recruit teams for the desert crossing. Federal Writers' Program, *Nevada*, 135; Morgan, *Pritchard Diary*, 165 *n* 80.

through a crooked canon where the road was very sidling. Camped on the poorest grass we have had since on the Humboldt. It is difficult to find enough willows to do the cooking with. For several days there have been 22 wagons in our train. Where there are so many it is much harder to find a camping place with enough of all the necessities.

September 12th.

Went up through another canon and then followed six miles of barren country. When we came to the river again we followed it only a few rods and then went into the hills again. Ten miles of up and down and we came to a slough which we followed three miles before stopping to camp. As soon as the road came down to the level country plenty of alkali was to be seen on both sides of the road. Quite unexpectedly a spring of good drinking water was found. In order to get good grass we had to camp quite a distance from the road.

A lot of company tonight. The camp is full of Indians. These are the first we have seen on the Humboldt except the one that was taken prisoner. They call themselves the "Piutahs." We got some small fish from them which are very good. They also brought a few wild ducks. After seeing the entrails of one thrown away, an Indian picked them up, threw them on the fire barely long enough to warm, and then greedily devoured the dainty morsel. The most of them can speak a little English. It was a great novelty to see them dance, which they did very energetically, but our late unpleasant experience with their neighbors, the Shoshones, was still in our minds and we felt more comfortable when they were gone.

September 13th.

Decided to lie by today as there is such good grass. This is called the Big Meadows.[46] Some are cutting grass to carry along to feed when crossing the desert which is 25 miles ahead. The trader butchered a beef this evening. Got some at 10 cts. a pound. We were never more

---

[46]Big Meadows, near modern Lovelock, Nevada, was another favorite place to stop to rest teams and cut hay for use on the desert crossing. Thomas Christy gives a particularly good description of the area. Becker, *Christy's Road*, map 78.

From Carpenter's comments it would appear that cattle, like hogs, are affected by the mast or fodder on which they graze.

disappointed. We were so hungry for fresh meat and this looked so nice, yet it was so sweet that some of us could not eat it at all. It was so sweet as though sugar had been sprinkled over it. This is from the animal feeding on sugar-cane which is about all there is for stock to live on here.

September 14th.

Came 15 miles and camped at what is called the lake. It is where the Humboldt River spreads out in a lake like body and there is no longer any current. There is little grass and that is covered with alkali and the water is so impregnated with it that it cannot be used for drinking, and what makes the camp still more unpleasant there is no wood. We brought wood and water from the slough where we camped last night. Some are cutting sugar cane for the cattle. They eat it only because there is no grass. The leaves and stalks are covered with tiny green bugs that puncture the plant and then get caught in the oozing sweetness and are held as though cemented. The Indians scrape off sugar and bugs and eat without any further preparation. Some of our party tried eating "Indian sugar" before they knew that a goodly portion was bugs.

September 15th.

When the cattle were driven up this morning two laid down and in a few minutes were dead. A great many are sick from alkali. Drove 12 miles over desert country where there was nothing whatever growing. At the foot of a hill which was directly ahead the road forked. The left was called the Carson Route. This led off through a sag that was less steep and looked much more inviting than the other. Some of the party took this route but for some reason, I know not what, the Farmers and ourselves took the right hand road which was called the Truckee Route.[47] There is a trading post near the forks of the road.

---

[47]As noted in the Bailey diary, there were two routes from the Sink of the Humboldt, one via the Carson River and the other to the Truckee. Most travelers, like the Baileys, took the Carson route, but others opted for the Truckee. See Child, *Overland Route*, 51 and Becker, *Christy's Road*, 11 for descriptions of the Truckee road.

We got some small potatoes at 20 cents a pound that were so very bitter even after a deep paring had been taken off that they were quite unfit to eat, but we were so very hungry for vegetables that we did eat some and were sick in consequence. Onions were 36½ cents a pound.

We crossed over the hill and camped on low bottom land at what is known as the Sink of Humboldt. This is a low sandy basin where the water earlier in the season spreads out over several miles. Just now there is not such a great expance. The water is unfit for drinking and there is no grass whatever for the stock. What is still worse, they all seem to be sick and here we are with a 45 miles desert just ahead. We must push on for if we stay here the cattle will die of starvation. They are talking of starting tonight.

September 16th.

As it takes 24 hours to cross the desert, it was thought best to start in the evening so we left camp an hour before sundown. Traveled fast all night. A little before day came to a hot spring which is said to be half way.[48] Stopped to let the cattle rest and to get breakfast. As soon as it was light enough to see we found that our horse and Father's were not with the rest. Reel hurriedly ate some breakfast and on Farmer's little old pony started back. The spring is six feet wide and 10 feet long, just a big hole of hot water without inlet or outlet. This was the place of all places where people left everything but themselves and not satisfied to merely throw their things away they dumped them en masse into the spring. It seemed to be quite full of wagon tires and all kinds of irons belonging to the outfits. Lying about was an endless amount of ox chains, pieces of wagons, etc. etc. The water had no bad taste, so we dipped up and cooled some for the oxen. As the loose stock would not drink from a bucket or pan they had to go without. The grass brought along was doled out to the oxen. Some of the road up to this point had been quite stony. There had also been sand, and the rest of the way was hard clay. We remained at the spring about three hours. At noon came to a sandy hill where we stopped and gave

---

[48]These springs, about twenty-miles from the fork in the trail, were indeed about half way across the desert. From Child's description, they were small geysers. Child, *Overland Route*, 52.

the oxen some water from the water kegs. A little at a time was put into a pan and held to an oxe's nose. If it had been put in a bucket one ox would have gotten the full amount. It would have been impossible to get his head from the water until all was gone. As it was, it was hard to manage them. They pushed and scroughed to all get a taste.

After ascending the hill it was typical desert all the rest of the way. There was deep sand for eight miles, and the road on both sides was strewn with dead cattle. A number in our train succumbed to the heavy travel and heat. Away off to the south could be seen a beautiful river that looked so cool and peaceful with its clusters of green trees along the bank that we no longer wondered how it was that a lone weary traveler could desert the road for the elusive mirage. It was hard to believe that we were rightly informed. It certainly was a river but too far away for us to reach. It must have appeared the same to the stock as they became unruly and kept trying to break away in that direction. The horses especially were determined to go.

Dead animals by the way became more frequent, and the articles abandoned were continuous. The sand gradually became a little less deep and about the first intimation that we had of the nearness of the Truckee River the cattle began to bawl and those that had the strength to run bolted ahead of the wagons and made for the river dashing down the steep banks and into the water. The drivers followed pell mell and had great difficulty in keeping them from drinking too much of the very cold water. No sooner were they driven out than they rushed right back so they had a lively time for a little while.[49]

The road went down a very steep bank into the river. It was 40 feet wide and two feet deep. It was just sundown when we crossed making 25 hours for the trip. Near the crossing there were some California traders. Here we got some news of the relatives at Grass Valley, California and as one of the traders was going back to California, we sent a letter to George yet hardly expected it would reach him. Drove three fourths of a mile up the river and camped. Not much grass but plenty of bushes for the cattle to browse on. When it began to get

---

[49]Many travelers reported the same difficulty with their stock on reaching the river. See: Waters, "Account of a Trip," 74–75; Maxwell, *Crossing the Plains*, 166–67; Potter, *Trail to California*, 193–94 *n* 9.

dark, we felt anxious about Reel as he had not returned. It was not reassuring to have them say, "He should not have gone alone," and "No one knows what those Indians might do to a lone man for the sake of three horses." He did not return until nine o'clock having ridden 90 miles. The horses had not kept to the road all the way but cut across in a more direct line, yet he had no difficulty in tracking them. When found they were within two miles of the camp we left and were wandering rather aimlessly as there was nothing to eat.

"Lige" Farmer took water back to some of the stock that was left in the sand having given out. They left seven head and we one. Some think it would have been better to have stayed at the sink over night and started on the desert in the morning, so as to have had the most wearysome part (the sand) in the cool of the night. As there was nothing for them to eat at the sink, it is a question whether it would have been any easier for them to have starved 12 hours before starting. The traders tell us it is 12 miles to any better grass so we stayed here for the day. Bought onions, potatoes and beans, the latter at 40 cents a pound. The boys went back for the cattle. Brought in two head. The others were dead or nearly so. Our ox could not be found.

September 18th.

Our ox found himself. He had made his way to the river when the boys were back looking for him. He is so recuperated that he seems in fairly good condition for traveling.

During the 12 mile drive today, we crossed the river 10 times. With one exception the crossings were most *terribly* stony. Many of the rocks that the wheels were obliged to go over were as high as the wagon hubs and so covered with a slippery, mossy substance that it was with great difficulty they kept their feet at all. First one and then another would fall and momentarily we thought the wagon would upset and to make it worse the water was deep. Henry was driving. At the best crossings, he jumped on old Dave's back (Dave was the near wheeler). Sometimes the oxen got in such a mixup that he had to dismount in the middle of the stream. Most of the crossings he waded from start to finish. Once he looked around and smilingly said, "This is the way to drive over the rocks." In turning to his cattle his feet went from under him and he sat in water up to his neck.[50] Between crossings the road was very rocky or for a change we had deep sand. Passed over one piece of road that was the very worst since leaving home. So very stony and sidling that the men worked for some time before a team attempted to cross and then it was with considerable trouble that all got safely over. Camped in Little Meadows. The grass is only tolerably good. More traders here. They tell us that Uncle Sam is only three days ahead and that he has lost 20 head of stock while we have lost but one.

September 19th.

Rested again today. The cattle are weak from the hard travel and require rest. More have given out and were left on the road. The boys have all been off on the mountain side getting small pine trees for whip stocks. The trees are from six to eight feet long and they are busy trimming off the limbs and smoothing up the handle part. This is the first opportunity for getting any since we were at Ash Hollow and what they have been using are worn down to a foot or two in length. A braided lash from six to ten feet long with a good buckskin cracker attached to one of these long whip stocks is called a Pike County revolver. The Missourians know just how to manage one to get the best results. The whip stock is held firmly in both hands, and the long lash is made to circle two or three times above the head and then, with a quick forward motion, there follows a report like a pistol shot, and woe to the ox it reaches. Reel and "Lum" Farmer are experts. They can hit the "bulls eye" (the desired spot) every time. It looks very simple and easy and of course the drivers all tried it but with poor success. Father and John Fossett perhaps had the most disastrous experience of any. It was like what is said of a woman throwing a stone. The lash stopped in the opposite direction from what was intended and it is the

---

[50]The Truckee fords were infamous. "These fords are all very bad," Child reported, "the river being a rapid stream, and its bottom covered with large rocks." Lydia Waters observed that "The wagons sounded like thunder going over them. I was driving as usual, and the soles of my boots were almost worn off, what was left had turned back to the heel." Child, *Overland Route*, 52-53; Waters, "Account of a Trip," 75.

stopping that hurts. Father peeled the top of one ear and John took all the skin off of the top of his nose.

September 20th, Sunday.

A number of cattle have died from eating wild parsnip. It grows here plentifully and as there is a scarcity of grass it is impossible to keep the stock from eating it. The plant looks very much like the garden parsnip. Blood in the urine is the first symptom. The second is death. Life may be reckoned in minutes after it is known they are affected. Did not stop at noon but kept right along until we reached the Big Meadows which made a drive of 12 miles over very stony bad road. Crossed one very bad slough and the river seven times and camped near a trading post. This is the first house made of boards that we have seen for a long time. Good grass here. More cattle left along the road.

September 21st.

Rested again today. The traders tell us there are Mormons 18 miles from here in the Washoe Valley who have improved claims to sell at ridiculously low prices. Some of them came to the trading post this afternoon. They want us to stop here a day or two and go see their places. Brigham Young has ordered all Mormons back to Salt Lake and they must go. One offers his place which includes 80 acres of open tillable land, house and barn, the latter full of hay, all for a horse and gun. Reel wants badly to go and see, and perhaps buy, but the rest of us are suspicious of any thing connected with Mormons. Several more cattle died today.

September 22nd.

Did not stop at noon. Traveled 10 miles, all the way just like climbing over a stone pile. In Indiana we disliked very much to ride over a bit of "corduroy" road, but that was not a circumstance to this. Only crossed the river once today but this *once was bad enough* to make up for any number of times. Camped on the bank of the river. The cattle had to be taken to the opposite side and then only tolerable good grass.

September 23rd.

One of our *oxen* died last night. Four miles more of the stony road and then another crossing was made. The crossings are all so bad that we dread to come to them. Soon after this last one we began to ascend the Sierra Nevadas. The road was up hill and down for eight miles. In many places it was extremely steep. So the going down seemed about as hard on the cattle as the climbing up. Came to a small spring branch called Little Truckee. This we followed and camped right in among the beautiful pine trees. The mountains are thickly covered with large white pine and spruce. Found more grass than could have been expected in such a shady place. Wild parsnip in abundance.

There was one long and extremely steep, bad hill to go down this afternoon. One wagon at a time had to go down and get out of the way before another could start. While we were waiting on the wagon ahead, Reel expressed the opinion that our off wheeler was poisoned. Before we started he was certain. I begged for the ox to be unyoked, but he said, "We could never get safely to the bottom without old 'Star.' " He did his part to the bottom of the hill and after being unyoked died in a few minutes. He was sincerely mourned as he had been one of the most useful and faithful of animals.

Now that we are where wood is plentiful, the boys made up a roaring campfire. A standing, dead, hollow tree was near camp. This they piled full of wood and set going. As the air was very chilly, the warmth and glow of the fire was delightful. All gathered around and enjoyed it for a little time. Then it was seen that there was going to be more fire than wanted. The tree fell with a crash and fire flew in every direction, catching in the dead leaves and branches of other trees. This caused no little excitement and it was only by the combined efforts of all that a big forest fire was prevented. Five cattle died today.[51]

September 24th.

The road today has been better. Traveled 12 miles. Passed several lit-

---

[51]The Carpenter party did not use the Donner Pass but rather the less familiar Henness Pass into Sierra County. The road, built by Patrick Henness and his partner in 1852, went ". . . up the Truckee 30 miles to Big Meadows; thence up a sloping mountain and down a beautiful valley 4 miles then up the old Nevada road to the junction of the roads, 4 miles; then to the Little Truckee 8 miles; then up said river to the Lake and Summit." James J. Sinnott, *History of Sierra County*, 3 vols. (Volcano, California: The California Traveler, 1975), 3:52, quoting Henness' description of the road. See also: Stewart, *California Trail*, 305.

tle streams and for a mile or more was in a little valley where there was plenty of grass. Today passed where there was room for the road to fork for the first time since leaving the desert. The right is the Forest City road and the left the Truckee Route. We took the latter although it is said to be a very bad road. Yet it is more direct to Nevada City near our destination. Camped in a valley two or three miles in extent near a pond or small lake. The grass has been good but is now frost-bitten and dry. We are entirely surrounded by the mountains all of which are covered with tall pines. It is quite cold.

September 25th.

Traveled 12 miles. Water every little way and a fair supply of grass. Passed a hay ranch where some men had a lot of cattle and a cheese factory. Bought some butter and cheese. Two miles from this we came into a valley of considerable extent in which is situated Weber Lake, a beautiful body of water half a mile or more across.[52] It seems to be about round. Camped among the pine trees at some little distance from the lake. We are now within three miles of the summit.

September 26th.

The feed is good so we are lying by to let the cattle recruit. Grass is said to be scarce from here on and after we get into California feed will be very dear. After camping learned that Uncle Sam's were camped one-fourth of a mile farther down the valley. Some of the boys shot some little ducks at the lake. They are quite unlike any we ever saw. Instead of one flat web between the toes there is a little narrow web attached to each individual toe. They were nicely cooked but could not be eaten. Tasted of fish and mud etc. etc. We learned later that they are called mud hens.

September 27th.

Still at the same camp. This evening after supper we were enjoying a sociable chat around a fine camp fire when the boys from Uncle Sam's came. It was several minutes before we recognized George among

---

[52]Also known as Truckee Lake, this lovely body of water is located in eastern Sierra County. Sinnott, *Sierra County*, 3:55.

them. We felt that we were quite excusable for when he left home three years ago we regarded him as a boy. Now he sported a moustache and wore a broad brimmed Mexican sombrero which gave him quite a distinguished appearance. The letter sent by the trader was posted at Forest City and reached him one evening. The next morning he set off on foot for Forest City 40 or 50 miles distant.[53] He arrived there in the evening, found the man who posted the letter, and learned our probable whereabouts, and the next morning started on, reaching Uncle Sam's camp at supper time. We had been resting so much along the Truckee that we were not as far along as was expected but after starting he would have kept on until we were found no matter what the distance [might] have been.

September 28th.

This morning decided to stay a while longer as four other wagons are to remain. They want the teams to get in as good order as possible before leaving. The camp was moved a mile and a half over to the west side of the valley as we may stay some time if the weather continues good. Henry killed a very large hawk. George knew some one who said California hawks were fine eating. Reel believes in experimenting (I do not), but the hawk was cooked, that is all.

October 2nd.

Nothing of importance during the past four days only that after a two days visit George went back to the "diggins." Later Father decided he would not remain here so this morning the family left

---

[53]Forest City, in Sierra County, was one of the area's liveliest mining camps during the 1850s and was a town of considerable size. Nevada City, about forty miles south in Nevada County, was also a large mining community and the center of the county's gold district. It had a population of approximately 800 and a large number of stores and other businesses. Carpenter's nomenclature for the two routes does not conform to the names in use at the time. From the description which follows, the party remained on the main Henness Pass road. Descriptions of the towns are in Hoover, *Historic Spots*, 494; Erwin G. Gudde, *California Place Names,* 3rd ed. (Berkeley: University of California Press, 1969), 111; Hugh B. Thompson, *Directory of the City of Nevada and Grass Valley* (Nevada City: Charles F. Robbins, 1861); and H. P. Davis, *Gold Rush Days in Nevada City* (Nevada City: Berliner and McGinnis, 1948).

camp. I go along as they now think they may stay two weeks longer. One and one half miles from camp crossed the summit. There was some difficulty in locating it, and at once we could see that all water ways led westward. The mountains are very heavily timbered and many of the trees come in so closely to the road that it takes a lot of dodging to miss all of them. Came 12 miles over very bad road.

There were cunning little seal brown squirrels hopping up at every turn, sitting on logs and rocks at very close range, seemingly consumed with curiosity as to what we were there for. Camped by the side of the road near a big camp of men working on a ditch. There is a store and cookhouse. They call the place Milton, also Truckee Ditch.[54] The ditch they are working on follows the mountain side and is to carry water 100 miles or more down to the miners. Father went over to the camp to see if there was any fresh meat to be had. When he started he was told, "If there is nothing better bring back liver or even lights." They were just out and would not have more for a day or two. So to our great disappointment he came back empty handed.

October 3rd.

One ox was gone this morning and Father went to look for him. While he was gone some horsemen came by with a band of cattle. They ran directly to the oxen and we, fearing a general stampede, ran out to keep the cattle back. The men cried out to us to keep back, that the cattle would kill us. But we were so accustomed to cattle that we paid little attention to what they were saying and did turn the cattle away. They explained later that these were wild Spanish cattle and were liable to attack persons on foot and wondered we were not killed. From these men we learned to a certainty that the ox went back to the Lake so we went on without him but it had detained us half a day.

------

[54]Truckee Ditch was one of the extensive system of canals and flumes in the Sierra and Nevada county mining region which was considered "the most spectacular hydralic operation" in the gold country. One of the most important companies was the Milton Mining and Water Company for which the town was named. Hoover, *Historic Spots*, 255–56. Nat P. Brown and John K. Dallison, *Brown & Dallison's Nevada, Grass Valley and Rough and Ready Directory* (San Francisco: Town Talk Office, 1856), 10–13 has an excellent description of the various canals and flumes.

After traveling three miles we came to a little stream on the side of the mountain and as it was eight miles to the next water, we stopped for the night. There was a little grass along the creek, but the cattle are so determined to go back that they have to be chained up and fed hay that costs three cents a pound. Today we passed many places where the water in the big ditch is flumed across deep ravines and little flats from one side hill to another in order to make the ditch as direct as possible. These flumes are set up on a frame work that in some places is 75 to 100 feet high.

October 4th.

Continued to go up and down hill all day. Much of the way was stony. The worst hill was two miles long. After eight miles came to the middle waters of the Yuba. Here was quite a little town with a store, blacksmith shop, and some little shanty residences. It did not take long to do the town so we moved on and camped in Jim Crow Canon.[55] It was fortunate for us that a teamster with a load of hay camped there also as there was little picking for the oxen and he let us have hay. And we would not have known where to get water as the spring was down in a deep ravine completely hidden. Today we met a packtrain and it looked oddly enough to see mules with boxes of goods and groceries piled two or three feet above their backs. There were boxes of soap, sacks of flour and sugar, kegs of syrup, wash tubs, wash boards, brooms, window glass and sash, etc. etc.

October 5th.

The road today was the best we have had since in the Sierra Nevadas as this is the regularly traveled stage road, yet it has been quite rocky.[56] We saw a six horse stage today in a headlong drive down the mountain. To say it looked dangerous is putting it very mildly. Although the horses seemed going at full speed, the driver, in a most reckless

---

[55]Jim Crow Canyon, named for a Kanaka, was near Downieville. The town Carpenter describes could have been any one of the many mining camps in the area. Hoover, *Historic Spots*, 491–92; Gudde, *California Place Names*, 157.

[56]Near Milton the party left the main Henness road and turned south on the Nevada Turnpike which proceeded via Graniteville, Cherry Hill, and Columbia Hill to Nevada City. Sinnott, *Sierra County*, 3:55.

manner, cracked his whip over them and away they went like the wind. We were glad to be traveling by ox team instead of by stage. Passed several saw mills and a number of quite snug looking houses. Camped at Coal Springs where there was a store and boarding house, etc.[57] There is a collection of houses in almost every little valley. Perhaps they call them towns or maybe just camps. When we are up on a ridge they are generally too far away for a very definite idea to be formed of their importance. It was in this way that we caught a glimpse of Forest City. All there is for the cattle is browsing on oak bushes and a few spears of grass.

After a long pull up a steep hill we stopped and watered the oxen at a watering trough in front of a story and a half hotel. The proprietor was very friendly and seemed glad to have some one to talk to. We were invited in to rest and later was shown all the comforts and conveniences of the place. The house was several feet from the ground and there were no carpets so as we followed him about our footsteps reminded one of horses on a barn floor. He followed us to the wagon and with the greatest reluctance saw us drive off. From his garden we were supplied with some cabbage which was sweet, crisp, and tender and as we munched it he had our sympathy for his lonely condition. Yet the slight margin by which I had escaped an offer of marriage was quite amusing.

October 6th.

Rained all day and the road was very muddy. Drove 12 miles all the way up and down hill and the hills are long and steep so much so that we walked. It was nearly dark when we came to Emery's Crossing of the Yuba river.[58] Here was a hotel and toll bridge and a number of little board shanties. The proprietor let us go into one for the night and we found it much more comfortable than being outside in the rain

---

[57]Coal Springs was probably located in Coal Canyon. However, it is not listed by Gudde in either *California Place Names* or *California Gold Camps* and is not included on Sinnott's map cited above.

[58]Emory's Crossing, three miles northeast of North San Juan on the middle fork of the Yuba River, was also known as Emory's Bridge and, as Carpenter notes, was a rather prosperous little crossroads community. Gudde, *California Gold Camps*, 109; Brown and Dalison, *Nevada . . . Directory.*

although there were no battens over the cracks in the walls. An old clock ticking on the wall constituted the furnishings. The baby, now seven months old, got badly frightened on hearing it tick. In fact, she was so afraid of indoors that she was repeatedly taken outside that being the only thing that would pacify her. In our travels she has become a child of nature. Here we got our first glimpse of a queer little human being that we knew no name for until we remembered some pictures in the old school geography. Then we decided he must be a Chinaman.

October 7th.

Rained all night and is still raining this morning. The toll for crossing the bridge was $2.50. Then followed a terribly long hill to go up. Eight or ten miles farther there was another bridge and the same toll for crossing. It has been up and down hill all day. Still it is the best road since crossing the desert. Finding that we were to begin the ascent of the mountains as soon as the bridge was crossed, Mother, Emily, Hale and I (not forgetting the baby), set off on foot although it was raining for we knew that it would be a hard pull for the oxen to get to the top. Soon we were overtaken by a teamster who had been up in the mountains with a load and was going back "empty." He had eight mules to an immense wagon with a bed five feet high and was on a spring seat some little distance above the bed. In fact *we* thought he was *considerably elevated.* Trailing along behind was a wagon of smaller size. In all probability he was not accustomed to seeing women and children walking on the highway in the rain so in a very pleasant manner he invited us to ride to the top of the mountain. We were never adverse to riding but one glance at the big wagon bed showed the utter impossibility of boarding it without a step-ladder and the other was too far from the team to suit our ideas of the relationship between team and wagon, so we declined the invitation and taking a steep cut-off soon were out of sight. When Father came up and related the predicament that he saw the teamster in we were particularly thankful that we declined the invitation. In making a turn on the grade, the trailing wagon went off and rolled over several times in its downward course. Where would we have been "Ah Himmel?"

Three miles from the last bridge we came to Sockumville on Brush

Creek. This is the mine that George is interested in and our destination. A little way back from the bank of the creek and in among some big pine trees are a lot of miner's cabins. They are all one room domiciles of boards with battened cracks and stick chimneys. They face the road, the diggins, and the hill side beyond and in each is a miner who not only puts in regular hours in the mines but does his own cooking and washing. One of the miners lived in a little white house up on the hill side and his wife, in a most friendly way, came and invited Fenny and me to "take tea" with her. She would not take no for an answer, so we went although we were not "hankering" for tea. Corn beef and cabbage would have appealed to us. It did not matter for Mother had beefsteak, potatoes, etc. etc. for us when we returned.

October 8th.

Went to John Swart's little ranch in the suberbs of Grass Valley and in a few days were permanently located there.[59]

October 22nd.

The rest of the train came this evening. They stayed at the Lake until a three inch snow fell, then afraid of being snowed in they broke camp. Farmer's and Uncle Sam's leave for Santa Rosa, Sonoma County, in the coast range mountains. Now that our journey is ended I will merely add that the cattle came near "eating their heads off" on hay at $60.00 to $70 per ton before they were sent off to pasture in the Sacramento Valley and we trust they may never again want for grass or water. As for ourselves, we are quite happy in the thought that all of our earthly belongings are no longer to be packed in an old ox wagon each morning and set treking westward.

---

[59]Grass Valley was a propsperous mining area in central Nevada County. Settled in 1849, by 1857 the town had a population of almost nine hundred and a number of stores and shops as well as five churches, several lodges, a weekly newspaper (*The Nevada National*), and a Grass Valley Brass Band. Thompson, *Directory*, 83–126. Carpenter's sister recalled, "Towards evening we reached Selby Flat on Brush Creek, brother George's present home, where he was engaged in Placer Mining. . . . The next day George went with us to Grass Valley to see cousin Mary Swart's and family and while there George bought their house and large garden plot." Horton, *Our Family*, 45.

The Southwestern Trails, 1869 – 1870

An earnest love of Nature . . . made me look forward with delight to the deserts of the Southern route. . . . Tramping month after month across the great empire of Texas; wandering free and glad beneath the skies of Arizona and New Mexico; beholding now and then the flag of the Republic, flaunting in its wide authority over those lonesome and hungry wastes of the Middle Continent—this is a pleasure to be fully enjoyed.

Stephen Powers, *Afoot and Alone*

. . . traveled on 10 miles and camped just on the other side of the Rocky Mountains. I had thought all along they would be the Elephant but they are nothing to compare with some we have crossed.

Mrs. Maria Shrode, "Journal"

OF all the routes to California, the southwestern trails are the least known and certainly the least well documented. Although accurate figures, or even estimates, for the southern trails are difficult to find, probably these routes never had more than a quarter of the numbers who traveled the northern roads.[1] Spanish and Mexican explorers, missionaries, and soldiers had used southwestern trails for over a century, and during the Mexican War the United States army crossed the region and laid out several wagon roads. Still, few Anglos were familiar with the area. Then came the Gold Rush and many argonauts tried the southern approaches to the mining regions lured on by southern newspaper advertisements and editorials which promised, "the journey can be made in about two months with pack mules and in about three months with wagons."[2] But despite at-

---

[1]One frequently cited figure for the travel through the southwest is the report of a Colonel Corrasco of the Mexican army who noted that about 12,000 persons, half of them Americans, crossed the Colorado at Yuma in 1849. This, in comparison with Mattes' 30,000 estimate for the northern route in the same year gives some idea of the difference in the volume of traffic on the two routes. See: Glen Dawson, ed., *Lorenzo D. Aldrich, A Journal of the Overland Route* (Los Angeles: Dawson's Book Shop, 1950), 7, and Mattes, *Platte River Road*, 23.

[2]*Texas Telegraph and Texas Register*, January 25, 1849, quoted in Benjamin Harris, *The Gila Trail: The Texas Argonauts and the California Gold Rush*, Richard Dillon, ed., (Norman: University of Oklahoma Press, 1960), x.

tempts by towns in Missouri, Arkansas, and Texas to boost themselves as "jumping off" places, emigrants did not rush to the southern trails as they did to the older and better known Oregon and California route along the Platte. Until the Boundary Commission completed its work and the Gadsden Purchase added new territory, much of the southwestern route was through land controlled by the Mexican government and this undoubtedly contributed to the reluctance of emigrants, especially families, to take advantage of the route. Moreover, by 1849, the Apaches' earlier good opinion of the Americans as potential allies against their traditional enemies, the Mexicans, had given way to open hostility, and the reputation of these Indians for cunning and cruelty far outweighed that of the northern tribes.[3] During the Civil War years, Indian depredations along the southwestern trails increased as Federal troops abandoned the line of posts, and Confederate and Union forces clashed at many points in the region. By the end of the war, the entire southwest resembled a gigantic armed camp in which no one and nothing moved safely from place to place without a sizeable escort. To add to the problems of the route, reliable water supplies were difficult to find in the semi-arid southwest. Along the Platte and Humboldt routes the water was not always palatable but it was at least available, which could not be said along the desert roads from West Texas to the Colorado River.

Partly because the southwestern routes were not as heavily used, there are fewer accounts by emigrants and other travelers. Richard Dillon notes that only about two dozen "diaries, travel books, emigrant guides, and reminiscences" exist for even the Gold Rush years (1849 – 50) along the southwestern trails as "against the northern trails hundreds."[4] Odie Faulk, in his popular, but certainly not exhaustive, study of the Gila Road lists some forty first-hand accounts between 1846 and 1870 as compared with Merrill Mattes' seven hundred on the northern roads. Some of the best of the southwestern journals are by army officers and government officials but they tell little of emigration, particularly family emigration, along the southern routes.[5] Nor

---

[3]Dillon, particularly, speculates that "the reputation of the Apaches may have had more than a little to do" with reduced travel in the southwest. Ibid.

[4]Ibid.

[5]See, for example: Ralph Bieber, *Exploring Southwestern Trails* (Glendale: Arthur

are the modern sources as rich and varied as those for the California trail. There are no studies similar to Mattes' *Great Platte River Road* or Stewart's *California Trail* to bring together sources and analyze southwestern travel. The best modern, edited works by Bieber, Dillon, and Dawson are helpful but they deal only with the late 1840s and early 1850s, and Faulk's work, although interesting, is cursory. With few exceptions no detailed studies of the sites and towns along the route have appeared in print.[6]

Several factors may have contributed to the lack of documentation about southwestern routes. Many who went along these trails, particularly after the Civil War, were drovers taking large herds of livestock to new ranges and ranches in New Mexico and Arizona; trail herders had little time to keep journals while they guarded and herded large numbers of unruly animals.[7] The freighters and stage drivers who frequented southwestern roads were more concerned with their loads and supplies than in leaving a literary account, although some of their passengers did describe at least a part of the trip.[8] Moreover, from the few extant accounts one gets the impression that migration along the southern trails had a larger proportion of "poor whites" and that emigrants on these routes may have been less educated and less literate than travelers on the northern routes where literary production was more voluminous. Lieutenant Cave J. Couts reported from the Gila in 1849 that travelers were constantly begging "sugar, flour, molasses, pork and a little fresh beef. . . ." Most of these travelers were south-

---

H. Clark, 1938); John R. Bartlett, *Personal Narrative of Explorations* . . . . , 2 vols. (New York: D. Appleton, 1854); Grant Foreman, ed., *Marcy and the Gold-Seekers* (Norman: University of Oklahoma Press, 1937); and L. R. Bailey, ed., *Survey of a Route . . . : The A. B. Gray Report* (Los Angeles: Westernlore Press, 1963).

[6]Odie B. Faulk, *Destiny Road: The Gila Trail and the Opening of the Southwest* (New York: Oxford, 1973). The best single studies are those of the various federal posts, particularly those like Fort Davis, Texas, which are now National Historic Sites.

[7]An exception is James G. Bell, "A Log of the Texas-California Cattle Trail," *Southwestern Historical Quarterly*, 35 (January–April, 1932): 208–37, 290–316; and 36 (July 1932): 47–66.

[8]See, for example, William A. Duffen, ed., "Overland Via 'Jackass Mail' in 1858: The Diary of Phocion R. Way," *Arizona and the West*, 2 (Spring–Summer, 1960): 35–53, 147–64; Waterman L. Ormsby, *The Butterfield Overland Mail*, L. H. Wright and J. M. Bynum, eds. (San Marino: Huntington Library, 1942); and George F. Pierce, "Parson's Progress to California," *Historical Society of Southern California Quarterly*, 21 (1939): 45–78.

erners, Couts recorded and opined, "If any are left in Arks. [sic] it is more numerously populated than I had anticipated."[9]

Nor does the situation appear to improve in later years. Stephen Powers, an early traveler, observed that many government relief stations had been established to assist impoverished, often starving, emigrants. He also describes a class of people "who are commonly said to 'make their living by moving'" along the southwestern routes.[10] "Pikers," whatever their home state or country, were not inclined to record their experiences even if they had the necessary mental and physical skills.

Despite differences in number of travelers, in the character of the emigration, in climate and conditions of the trail, there are similarities in the northern and southern trail diaries. Both trails were long, wearying, and monotonous. "Distance, mere blue naked distance, and nothing else . . ." described much of the scenery.[11] "It is something refreshing to see even the mail coach," a weary Maria Shrode wrote, "Even an old broke down ox or a flock of snipes will break the monotony of the plains."[12] The Parrish family was so tired of bad roads and stagnant water that they gave up their original plan to go to the gold fields and "resolved to make our home by the first running water we found."[13]

Fortunately for southwestern travelers, there were more "breaks" in the journey than along the California road. The line of forts, trading posts, and stage stations which grew rapidly in number during the 1850s provided brief respites from sand, sage, and rocks. Towns, or at least villages such as Santa Fe, Franklin (El Paso), Tucson, and Arizona City offered opportunities to buy necessary supplies. Occasionally fresh fruits and vegetables could be purchased from traders or Mexican farmers. Most travelers took some time in the towns and villages to visit stores and regain the feeling of being back in "civilization" for a few hours.

---

[9]Cave J. Couts, *From San Diego to the Colorado in 1849* (Los Angeles: Arthur M. Ellis, 1932), 21, 23. See also Harris, *The Gila Trail*, 83–84.

[10]Stephen Powers, *Afoot and Alone; A Walk from Sea to Sea by the Southern Route* (Hartford, Conn.: Columbian Books Company, 1872), 219.

[11]Ibid., 225.

[12]Maria Shrode, "Journal."

[13]Root, *Following the Pot of Gold*, 24.

Southwestern journalists, like their northern counterparts, described the scenery, which if not as spectacular as that on the northern route, still drew its share of compliments. The giant saguaro cactus, the imposing Spanish dagger, mysterious caves and underground springs, rugged mountains, colorful sunsets, exotic mirages—all evoked favorable, and often romantic, comment. Southwestern travelers, male and female, frequently remarked on the potential of the country. "This country needs only industrious people and water to make it a garden" was a typical remark, although where the water was to come from no one was too sure.[14] Like most travelers, the two women whose diaries follow comment on the rich soil and the unique opportunity for successful farming and ranching in many areas. However, neither seems inclined to take advantage of the possibilities.

Although southwestern travelers saw fewer of the native Americans than did their companions on the Platte Road, Indians also came in for their share of discussion. The Apaches were elusive and usually unfriendly, and reports by emigrants were rarely based on first-hand encounters but rather reflect fear and distrust based more on rumor than fact. A general adage along the trail was that if you saw an Apache you were already in trouble. Still few trains were attacked. The desert Indians stole livestock, harassed an occasional small party and kept emigrants on their guard. However, the often-told tale of the Oatman Massacre was one of the few verified reports of emigrant death from Apache warriors. In fact, the story was repeated so often that one begins to suspect it was the only example of Indian "perfidy" the terror-mongers could recall. Reid gives a fairly long description of the Apaches, based partly on observation in Texas and Mexico, and partly

---

[14]William Bell and W. F. Colton wrote extensively on the possible development of the Rio Grande, Gila, and Colorado River valleys where they believed there was an "immense bredth of land capable of sustaining a vast population." William Bell, *New Tracks in North America: A Journal of Travel and Adventures*, 2 vols. (London: Chapman and Hall, 1869), 2: 78–83. Powers also felt the land had great potential, as did Phocion Way. John Reid was more reluctant to believe that the desert could be turned into a garden spot, but J. Ross Browne reported on a plan to rid the Colorado desert of sand and provide water from the Colorado River! Powers, *Afoot and Alone*, 165; Duffen, "Way Diary," 151; John C. Reid, *Reid's Tramp or, A Journal of the Incidents of Ten Months Travel* (Selma, Alabama: John Hardy and Company, 1858), 54; J. Ross Browne, *Adventures in the Apache Country, or A Tour Through Arizona, 1864*, Donald M. Powell, ed., (Tucson: University of Arizona Press, 1974), 48.

on word of mouth. Bell also offers fairly extensive comments on the "wild tribes" of the southwest who, he concludes, are all cruel and vicious and all "doomed to eventual extinction." Such sentiments were widely held by emigrants.[15]

At the Pima and Yuma villages of Arizona, and among the Pueblos of Northern New Mexico, southwestern emigrants did encounter friendly tribesmen whose homes they could visit as they traded for corn and vegetables or fresh horses. "Everyone who visited the Pima Village had a good word for the Pimas," Dillon reported.[16] If that is not entirely true, at least the comments of the emigrants were generally favorable. Some, like J. Ross Browne, found them a noble people and admired many of their customs. Some, like Maria Shrode, saw a field for the missionary and teacher, while others, including Harriet Bunyard, thought them "dirty and detestable" and were anxious to leave their area.[17]

The Anglo population of the southwest also came in for a good deal of unfavorable comment. Miners, ranchers, and other frontier dwellers were often considered rude, uncouth, and possibly dangerous by the traveling population. One journalist went so far as to describe the residents as engaged in "riotous living, fierce gambling, buffonery, staggering and beastly drunkeness."[18] Thus it is not surprising that emigrants rarely lingered in the towns along their route.

Nor did the United States Army fare much better in the esteem of travelers. In the post Civil War years, several companies of Negro troops were stationed in the southwest, and they were frequently described in the journals as "lazy and ignorant." Since many of the emigrants were from the South, their comments are not surprising,

---

[15]See Bell, *New Tracks*, 1:178–89; Reid, *Reid's Tramp*, 171–79; Powers, *Afoot and Alone*, 209–10; and Duffen, "Way Diary," 156, for fairly typical views of the Apaches.

[16]Harris, *The Gila Trail*, 80–82, and *n* 73.

[17]Browne, *Adventures*, 105–13; Shrode, "Journal"; Harriet Bunyard, "Diary of a Young Girl." Powers described the "relief and satisfaction" with which he reached the safety of the Pima villages where he felt "almost at home." Of course he concluded in an ethnocentric vein that "the men are entirely worthless, but they are kind and peaceable." Powers, *Afoot and Alone*, 216. For good descriptions of the Pima see, in addition, Bell, *New Tracks*, 1: 158–77, and Reid, *Reid's Tramp*, 228–30.

[18]Powers, *Afoot and Alone*, 200. See also Browne, *Adventures*, 133–34; Bell, *New Tracks*, 2: 93–94; Duffen, "Way Diary," 159.

but Northern writers, too, satirized the appearance and speech of the "Buffalo Soldiers."[19] But all frontier soldiers, black or white, came in for a good deal of uncomplimentary comment. They might be guarding Uncle Sam's domains, but the class of men who enlisted in the post-War army did not inspire a great deal of confidence. Powers commented on "this unmitigated farce of military protection," and another diarist opined that the emigrants would be better off without the soldiers.[20]

Of all the ethnic groups encountered by travelers along the southwestern routes, the Mexican Americans seemed to have evoked the most comment. Every journalist had something to say, however briefly, about the Mexican's strange language, customs, and dress. Many of the accounts have long digressions, usually critical, on Mexican mores and manners. Typical Anglo stereotypes of the Mexican-American as indolent, dirty, and ignorant appear with depressing regularity. Bell compared the population unfavorably to the "Roman Catholic, Irish peasantry." Barsina Rogers French believed that the Pueblo Indians "seem to be more industrious than the Mexicans" and "have a better idea of building a town."[21] Many farm families were amazed by the different agricultural practices and noted the Mexican's "primitive" methods of plowing and the lack of fences. Only a few travelers offered any positive comment.[22] Throughout the period of Anglo emigration and settlement in the Southwest, Anglo-Mexican relations remained distant, and the two peoples viewed each other with mutual suspicion. Susan Parrish's family even encountered a taste of reverse discrimination at Tucson where the Mexicans, "bitter against the Yankees" refused to sell them needed supplies and food.[23]

The Southwestern route had its share of problems. Disease and accidents brought sudden, and often painful, death. Graves along the way were dutifully noted by journalists as were the frequent quarrels, sometimes ending in physical violence, that marked every overland

[19]Bell, *New Tracks*, 1: 188; Reid, *Reid's Tramp*, 123; Couts, *From San Diego*, 22.
[20]Powers, *Afoot and Alone*, 200; Bunyard, "Diary."
[21]Bell, *New Tracks*, 2:67; Barsina Rogers French, "Journal of a Wagon Trip from Evansville, Indiana to Prescott Arizona, April 8–September 3, 1867," ms., Huntington Library, 34–40.
[22]Powers, *Afoot and Alone*, 163–67; Reid, *Reid's Tramp*, 225–26, 143–50.
[23]Root, *Following the Pot of Gold*, 8.

journey. Difficult passes, rocky canyons, bad water, and dangerous fords marked the slow progress along the overland trail whether north or south.

There were several approaches to the main southern route, the Gila Trail from Tucson via the Pima villages to Yuma. Some travelers chose one of the many routes across Texas. Others took a Mexican tour via Parral, Monterrey, or Monclova while others traveled south through Santa Fe or west along the Arkansas River. Still others, like the diarists whose accounts follow, took the Butterfield Overland Mail route or one of the many cattle trails to the main route. Once on the main trail, however, there were fewer alternate roads than on the northern route. From El Paso or Tucson to the confluence of the Gila and Colorado rivers, trains stayed on the main road or risked the possibility of running short of grass and water for the stock.[24]

The two diaries which follow reflect the closing years of overland wagon travel. By the late 1870s, improved steamship transportation and the opening of transcontinental railroads made other modes of travel cheaper and easier as well as faster than ox and mule wagons. These two diaries also reflect conditions on the southern route in the post Civil War years, conditions quite different from those encountered by the forty-niners whose diaries constitute much of the published documentation on the southern trail.

The diarists are both from East Texas; both were Confederate sympathizers. Harriet (called Hattie by her family) Bunyard was nineteen and unmarried. With her parents, three brothers and two sisters, and a number of unrelated families, she traveled in a train captained by her uncle, Isaac Stewart.[25] Maria Shrode was forty-four, the mother of eight children. Many members of the train, captained by her husband, were relatives and close friends from Hopkins County.[26]

The Stewart train proceeded west along the Butterfield Overland stage road and the line of reopened army posts. The young diarist had little use for "the feds" and was amazed to see white and black soldiers

---

[24]On the various approaches to the trail, see Harris, *The Gila Trail*, ix, and Faulk, *Destiny Road*, 61–66.

[25]"Diary of Miss Harriet Bunyard," Percival J. Cooney, ed., *Historical Society of Southern California Quarterly*, 13 (1924), 92.

[26]Maria Shrode, "Overland by Ox Train in 1870," *Historical Society of Southern California Quarterly*, 26 (March 1944), 5–6; *Handbook of Texas*, 2:685.

serving together. She found the Tonkawa Indians an interesting people, but the Pima and Maricopa she dismissed as "detestable." An opinionated young woman, she is generally complimentary of the neat and clean dress and homes of the Mexican-American population.

The Shrode party, with a large cattle herd, chose a less direct route. From Hopkins County they moved northwestward to Denton County where they joined John Chisum's "Jinglebob" cattle trail to Coleman County. At Fort Concho they briefly joined the Butterfield road to the Pecos where they turned north to Fort Stanton, New Mexico, following another famous cattle trail, the Goodnight-Loving. They then swung south to the main road. Unlike Hattie Bunyard, Maria Shrode had little to say about Negros or Indians, but she did comment frequently on the Mexican Americans and particularly remarked on their farming practices and crops.

Despite the difference in their ages and marital status, both women have similar comments on the overland experience. Their camp duties seem to have been fairly minimal, and both write at some length on the problems and pleasures of the journey. It is monotonous and long but not without its pleasant aspects. In California, both families were met by relatives who helped them get established. David Shrode, a master wagon builder, established a successful wagon and blacksmith shop in Duarte where the Shrodes became well-known and respected citizens. Their children, Jake, Major, Charlie, and Sara, David's children by a previous marriage, and Maria and David's four, Helen, Viola, Jennie, and Lee, were all active in community life. Jake became an outstanding horticulturist, Helen and Viola graduated from Los Angeles State Normal school and taught for many years in Los Angeles County. Lee and Jennie both studied medicine at the old Los Angeles Medical College. Harriet Bunyard and her family, which included her father, Larkin, her mother, Frankie Stewart Bunyard, three brothers and two sisters, settled near El Monte where Harriet died in 1900. Unfortunately, little more is known of their life in California. Harriet's diary was preserved by her younger sister, Fannie Bunyard Lewis, and portions of it were published in 1924.[27]

---

[27]Shrode, "Overland," 6; Bunyard, "Diary," 92.

April 25th & 30th
have almost completed
our preparations for the
much talked of journey friends
and neighbors have been
So kind in assisting us
long will they be remem-
-ered,
May 1st Bid a kind adieu to my
much loved Texas home
although the road was very
muddy we had a pleasant
drive long will it be
remembered arrived at our
Stewarts in the evening
12 miles distant will
remain there until monday
this being Saturday
M 3d all in fine spirits
Started early traveled 15

Harriet Bunyard

Diary of a Young Girl

Collin [County, Texas][1]
April 25th & 30th.

Have almost completed our preparations for the much talked of journey. Friends and neighbors have been so kind in assisting us. Long will they be remembered.

May 1st.

Bid a kind adieu to my much loved Texas home. Although the road was very muddy, we had a pleasant drive. Long will it be remembered. Arrived at Uncle Stewarts in the evening — 12 miles distant.[2] Will remain there until Monday, this being Saturday.

May 3rd.

All in fine spirits. Started early, travailed 15 miles. Crossed the East Fork of the Trinity and Little Elm. Had no trouble. Camped on a high, beautiful prairie. Passed over a broken, hilly country. Two men were hung near the camp the evening previous and were said to be still hanging. [They were] hung for stealing.[3]

---

[1]Collin County, Texas, is located in the blackland prairies of northeast Texas between Grayson and Dallas counties. In the late 1860s the population, mostly small farmers and ranchers, numbered about 14,000. During the Civil War the county was badly disrupted and many of the buildings in McKinney, the county seat, burned. Following the war, a number of Confederate sympathizers, including the diarist's family, migrated west to escape what they considered the brutalities of the Reconstruction government. H. Bailey Carroll and Walter P. Webb, eds., *The Handbook of Texas*, 3 vols. (Austin: Texas State Historical Association, 1952-1976), 1:375. For a view of the county in the 1860s, see *The Texas Almanac and Emigrants Guide* (Galveston: W. Richardson & Co., 1867), 91-92.

[2]Possibly the diarist's uncle was Isaac T. Stewart, one of the founders of Stewart's Creek Settlement on the east side of Big Elm Creek in southeastern Denton County. Ed F. Bates, *History and Reminiscences of Denton County* (Denton, Texas: McNitzky Printing Co., 1918), 37.

[3]Although the nineteenth century accounts do not record this particular incident, local historians do note that the post Civil War years were turbulent in Denton County and there was much lawlessness, particularly horse and cattle stealing. Vigilante justice was also common. Bates, *History and Reminiscences*, 123-25.

May 4th, Denton [County].[4]

Started early. Travailed over a beautiful, sandy prairie. Arrived at Pilot Point[5] about twelve, stopped, ate dinner, and purchased some necessary articles. Had some photographs taken. Lud (?) Turner insisted that some of the girls should stay with him. He said he had no companion, but no one would take pity on him and stay. Left town about 3:00. It was rather dusty being sandy soil. Splendid water here. Crossed a small creek. The road was very rough, but all made it safe through. Passed through the Cross Timbers.[6] They have a rather picturesque appearance—post oak timber with small prairies. Crossed Big Elm. Crossing was good. Camped up on the prairie. It was dark when we camped, everybody tired. Travailed 18 miles.

May 5th.

All ready waiting for some emigrants now camped on the other side of the creek. They are from Arkansas, 4 wagons, two hacks, 10 men. Makes in all 10 wagons, 4 hacks, 20 men. This is a lonely looking place. Several small houses in sight. Red sandy soil. Travailed 7 miles, crossed Duck Creek and stopped to eat dinner. It is a very pretty stream [with a] rocky bottom. Just ready to start when Mr. Stewart's wagon tongue got broken. Made another. Went two miles, camped by a little branch near Bolivar.[7] Stayed one day. Went fishing with one

---

[4]Denton County, immediately to the west of Collin County in the Eastern Cross Timbers (see note 6), was settled in the 1840s. By 1869, the county had a number of schools, businesses, and churches and a newspaper, the Denton *Monitor*. *Handbook of Texas*, 1: 492; *Texas Almanac, 1867*, 99.

[5]Pilot Point, a small community in northeastern Denton County, was founded in 1854. The rich prairie land and good water at nearby Dripping Springs attracted settlers, and by 1869 the town had a growing population and a number of stores and other businesses. *Handbook of Texas*, 2: 379; Bates, *History and Reminiscences*, 58–59.

[6]During the nineteenth century, the term "Cross Timbers" was given to two broad belts of timber, mostly post oaks and black oaks, which extended from Oklahoma to the central portion of Texas. The Eastern, or Lower, Cross Timbers, which the diarist is describing here, ran through Denton County along a line slightly west of Sherman to Dallas. The Western, or Upper, Cross Timbers, approximately 15 miles to the west, is described later in the diary. *Handbook of Texas*, 2: 885. See also Edward E. Dale, *The Cross Timbers, Memories of a North Texas Boyhood* (Austin: Univeristy of Texas Press, 1966), 4–5.

[7]Bolivar, fourteen miles northwest of Denton, was established in 1859. In 1867, the United States government built a telegraph line from Sherman, in Grayson

of the ladies living in Bolivar. Caught some small fish. I would not like to live here. Sold some things that we started with in order to lighten our loads.

Denton County, May 7th.

Two more young men joined the train making 22. Crossed Clear Creek. Passed two vacant houses. Suppose the Indians was the cause of them being left. Came to Denton Creek. There had a little bad luck. Wagon turned over, no serious damage done. Went 2 miles farther and camped by a little branch. Here the water falls 15 feet from beautiful shell rock. Trees growing down there with their tops just even with the level of the land. Such a good place for Indians to hide. Passed three vacant houses. They look very desolate. The country has a wild appearance.

Wiss [Wise] Co.[8]
May 8.

Quite a pleasant wind blowing from the east this morning. Started early, traveled 21 miles over such a rough road through very thick post oak timber. Came in sight of Government Mills.[9] There, at a branch, we found a broken wagon loaded with very large cottonwood log. Prised the log off, taken the wagon away, and passed over in safety. Here are quite a number of small houses all made with the plank standing on one end. Also covered with plank. They are all close together

---

County, to Fort Belknap via Pilot Point (see note 5) and Bolivar. The road along which the Stewart train traveled was sometimes called the "wire road" because of the telegraph lines paralleling the route. *Handbook of Texas*, 2: 379; Bates, *History and Reminiscences*, 84–89.

[8]Wise County, immediately to the west of Denton County, was organized in 1856. During the Civil War the area was subjected to frequent Indian raids, and many settlers fled eastward. By 1867 the population had declined to 400, thus accounting for the many deserted homes and farms noted in the diary. *Handbook of Texas*, 2: 926; *Texas Almanac, 1867*, 174.

[9]Government Mills, or Government Saw Mill, was located on Sandy Creek northwest of Decatur and, as the name implies, was one of the many government sawmills established throughout the area to provide lumber for the construction of Fort Richardson and other government activities in the area. It was also known as Slab Town. Rosalie Gregg, ed., *Wise County History, A Link With the Past* (Quanah, Texas: Nortex Press, 1975), 144. See also J. C. McConnell, *The West Texas Frontier*, 2 vols. (Palo Pinto, Texas: n.p., 1933–39), 1:103–105.

and form quite a romantic appearance. Camped near by in the timber. Stood guard tonight. How I wish there was no wild Indians.

May 9th, Sabbath morning.

What are my friends in Collin doing this morning? Going to church I will suppose. Started and drove 2 miles to water for the stock. Camped in a very nice place. Will remain until Monday. Every appearance of rain. All hurrying to get tents stretched and fixed before the rain. One lonely looking little house in sight. The people that live there are part Indian. 8 more wagons with 10 men joined us this morning. They were camped at Decater [sic][10] waiting for company. Appointed Uncle Stewart captain of the train.

May 10th & 11th.

Rain prevented us leaving until Tuesday when we drove 14 miles. Passed where there had been a little village but was but one family there. All left on account of the Indians. The country is very broken, high hills covered with large rocks that look like houses in the distance. I am now sitting on the hillside on a large rock while the clear notes of the Whipporwill is ringing in the still twilight. Evening, when a memory of the past comes o'er us.

May 12th.

Came 7 miles and camped in a small prairie surrounded with timber and high hills. We went to the top of one of the hills. Found many large curious rocks there. The top was almost covered with level rock while on the sides was great stacks that looked like they had been placed there by the skill of man. Crossed West Fork of the Trinity. Had no trouble in crossing.

---

[10]Decatur, or Taylorsville, was the county seat of Wise County. Once a prosperous community on the Southern Overland Mail Route, Decatur suffered from Indian raids and depopulation during the Civil War period. After the war there were frequent strong disagreements between Union and Confederate sympathizers, and soldiers from Fort Richardson were stationed there during most of the late 1860s. *Handbook of Texas*, 1: 479; Cliff D. Cates, *Pioneer History of Wise County* (Decatur, Texas: n.p., 1907), 154–56.

May 14 & 15.

We are now camped by a nice clear branch and good spring up on a hill with splendid cold water. Jacksborro [sic] is in plain view.[11] One hundred miles from McKinney to Jacksborro. Federal's quarters are the nicest part of town. Elm and musquet [sic] timber, sandy soil with rocky hills is the general appearance of the country. Mostly timber except some small prairies. The people here are kind and accomodating. It is reported that there has been some Indians seen not far off, but we have seen none. Some of the girls went up in town today. Others went fishing but did not catch many. Two of the federal officers visited our camp. Nice looking men. They say if we stay here until the evening of the 16th that they will visit us with their brass band.[12]

May 16th, Sabbath evening.

We have travailed about 15 miles today. Passed through Jacksborro and over the rockiest road that I ever saw. It is quite a romantic looking country. High hills as far as I can see covered with small timber

---

[11]Jacksboro, the county seat of Jack County, also suffered from severe Indian depredations during the Civil War period and many residents fled eastward. In 1867, the Federal government established Fort Richardson at Jacksboro to guard the overland trails and mail routes and protect the growing cattle trade. By 1869, the post was nearly completed and included six sets of barracks and ten sets of officer's quarters as well as a hospital, powder magazine, bakery, and other outbuildings. *Handbook of Texas*, 1: 631, 900; Herbert M. Hart, *Old Forts of the Southwest* (New York: Bonanza, 1964), 168–69. Two interesting accounts of life at Fort Richardson and Jacksboro during the 1860s are: H. H. McConnell, *Five Years a Cavalryman or Regular Army Life on the Texas Frontier* (Jacksboro: J. N. Rogers & Co., 1889) and R. G. Carter, *On the Border with McKenzie or Winning West Texas from the Comanches* (Washington: Eynon Printing Co., 1935).

[12]At Fort Richardson, the party picked up the old Butterfield Overland Mail Route. Established in 1858, the company operated a semi-weekly stage, mail, and passenger service to California before the Civil War disrupted operations on the southern route. See LeRoy R. Hafen, *The Overland Mail, 1849–1869* (New York: AMS Press, 1969) and Roscoe and Margaret Conkling, *The Butterfield Overland Mail, 1857–1869*, 2 vols. (Glendale, California: Arthur H. Clark, 1947). The *Texas Almanac* for 1869 lists the following stops and distances on the upper part of the old stage road which are remarkably close to the figures given by the diarist: "Fort Richardson, a 6 company post, 35 miles to Fort Belknap, 30 miles to Fort Griffin, a 6 company post, Griffin to Phantom Hill 65 miles, Phantom Hill to Chadbourne 60 miles, Chadbourne to Concho 45 miles." *The Texas Almanac and Guide to Texas for 1869* (Galveston: W. Richardson and Company, 1869), 156.

and large rocks. Oh, how hard it did rain and blow last night. There is a very cold northwest wind blowing this evening with indications of rain. Several families from Bosque (?) and Denton County have overtaken us. There is now 45 men in this train.

May 17th.

Two men passed by camps last night going after the doctor for some wounded men that had been in a fight with the Indians. There was 12 men out herding stock. They had no arms but pistoles [sic] and 50 Indians, well armed, dashed upon them and killed and wounded 5. One of the wounded died this evening. Killed every one of their horses. This fight occurred on Salt Creek 5 miles above where we are now camped. The men that were wounded are at a ranch one miles from camp. Several of the boys went to see them this evening. They suffered so much before they had any attention. Suppose that the rest of the wounded will get well.[13]

The stage passes from Belknap to Jacksborro, the distance of 38 miles, and is guarded by 5 Indians of a friendly tribe. They look so Indian like with two large rings in each ear and beads strung all about them. Travailed 15 miles today over nice road and beautiful prairie.

May 18th, Young Co.[14]

One yoke of oxen was missing this morning. Therefore we have moved only one mile to better range. An old vacant house here and very good water. Found the oxen but too late to go any farther so will remain here until morning.

May 19th.

Started late, travailed 10 miles. Passed Fort Belknap.[15] The houses

---

[13]This skirmish should not be confused with the more famous "Salt Creek Massacre" or "Wagon Train Fight" which took place several years later in Young County. The diarist's description of the events of 1869 corresponds closely with the report by McConnell in *West Texas Frontier*, 2: 238–40.

[14]Young County, immediately to the west of Jack County, was organized in 1865 and included Young Territory which extended all the way to the New Mexico line. Like other frontier counties, Young suffered from frequent Indian raids during the Civil War years and by 1869 the white civilian population had been reduced to 135. *Handbook of Texas*, 2: 948.

[15]Fort Belknap was established in 1851 on the north bank of the Salt Fork of the Brazos near present day Graham, Texas. It was closed in 1859 when the Indians on

are very much dilapidated here. Many chimnies [sic] standing alone. Not more than 6 families living there. It is a very pretty place for a town if it was only improved. Crossed the Brases [sic] River. It is a beautiful stream with no timber immediately on its bank. Live oak, musquet & elm with sandy soils as the general appearance of the country with the greatest quantity and very good variety of wild flowers, some of them most beautiful. Camped about 3 miles from town. It is 35 miles from Belknap to Fort Griffin.

May 20th.

Detained again on account of stock. Some of the boys caught some very nice fish in the Brases. Started after dinner, went 6 miles, camped in a nice place in a small prairie surrounded with post oak timber.

May 21st.

Very warm and cloudy morning. Started early, made a drive of 17 miles. Had a splendid road. Had nothing but branch water and it was warm and not clear. The Collin Co. boys killed an antelope this evening. The meat resembles that of a kid.

May 22nd.

Camped in one mile of Fort Griffin on the east side of the Clear Fork of the Brasses. It is a very pretty stream with large pecan timber on the banks. I think we will get some nice fish here.

May 26th.

Will leave here this morning. Have passed away the time very well since we have been here Sabbath morning. We hitched up our ambulances and drove up to the fort. Feds have very nice quarters there. The

---

the nearby reservations it was designed to guard were moved to Oklahoma. In 1867, efforts were made to re-establish the post, but the lack of a suitable water supply forced the government to abandon its efforts. For a few years, the site was maintained as a picket post for Fort Griffin. The community of Fort Belknap which grew up near the post was the first county seat of Young County, but most of the population fled during the Civil War years. One source lists 67 inhabitants in 1870. *Handbook of Texas,* 1: 140; Hart, *Old Forts,* 20–21. For an earlier description by an overland emigrant girl, see Maggie Hall, "The Story of Maggie," ms., Bancroft Library, 4.

citizens houses are very inferior—small log huts. Have splendid spring water.[16]

Here Indians have caused more disturbance for the last 5 months then they have for several years. Little girl living here that the Indians taken and kept 8 months. Her friends bought her. Whilst they had her they picked a round ring of powder in her forehead as large as a ten cent piece. It makes a black ring and cannot be taken away. Suppose they done it that they might know her again. They had her little sister but would not sell her. The friends think that they will sell her this year. The little girl said that they were very kind to them. The Indians killed their mother when they captured them.[17]

In our drive Sabbath morning we went half mile from the fort to where were camped a considerable number of Tonk Indians. Was but a few that could speak English. Their little huts covered with hay and dirt and a door just large enough for one to pass through. They were all busy at work. They had Commanchie [sic] scalp. They hate the Commanchies and fight them all the time.[18]

We then called at Mrs. Campbell's. Spent an hour. Went back to camp. Here we got plenty of pickels [sic] and beans to do us through. We also had some nice fish from the river Wednesday morning.

---

[16]Fort Griffin was established in 1867 on the Clear Fork of the Brazos in present day Shackelford County. An extensive post, Fort Griffin eventually had quarters and support facilities for six companies of troops. In 1869 the post was garrisoned by four companies of cavalry. *Handbook of Texas*, 1: 626; Hart, *Old Forts*, 146–47. For a good picture of the post in 1869, see Carl Coke Rister, *Fort Griffin and the Texas Frontier* (Norman: University of Oklahoma Press, 1936), 59–76.

[17]Although this particular incident is not mentioned in Rister's detailed study of Fort Griffin, such reports of recovered Indian captives were common during the post Civil War years.

[18]The Tonkawa Indians of Central Texas had a tragic history. Placed on the Brazos Indian Reservation near Fort Belknap in 1855, they were attacked by white settlers. In 1857 they were moved to Indian Territory but in 1862 their villages were attacked by a combined force of Delawares, Shawnees, and Caddos and they were almost exterminated. After several years of wandering, the remaining 97 Tonkawa settled near Fort Griffin where they served as scouts and guides for the army. Long-time allies of the Anglos, the Tonkawas were traditional enemies of the Comanches and, in fact, were occasionally accused of eating them. The diarist's description of the Tonkawa village is similar to those of other contemporary observers. See: *Handbook of Texas*, 2: 789; W. W. Newcomb, *The Indians of Texas from Prehistoric to Modern Times* (Austin: University of Texas Press, 1961), 113–53.

May 27th.

Will start this morning. Got late start but everything was rested and we travailed 18 miles over a rough rocky road. We have a splendid camping place this evening with fine range. Our teams are in better order now than when we started. There is quite a number of emigrants in near us and with us now.

May 28th.

Left camp early. Travailed over beautiful road. Found some cranberries, the first I ever saw. They are splendid. Travailed 16 miles and camped by a nice running stream and fine spring with cold water which is quite a treat to movers. There is a grave near this spring. It has no inscription on it, therefore we know nothing of the inhabitant thereof. Someone perhaps that, like us, was in search of a new home. How I should regret to leave one of my friends on the roadside in a strange land. We have not passed a house since we left Fort Griffin which is 35 miles.

All ready and started early when to our surprise about 30 Feds from Griffin rode up just as the last wagon was leaving the camps. They halted the wagons and searched them for some carbean [sic] guns that some of the train had purchased. They did not find them, and therefore we had to stay at the same camp. Came back and stayed there all day. The Feds camped on the other side of the branch and watched around all day. That night about 8 o'clock they came to our camp and arrested several and kept them all night. The guns were brought up that night. They were bought from a citizen at the fort. The Sargeant had stolen them and given them to the citizens to sell. The Sargeant was arrested and one of our men were taken back to the fort that night to testify against the citizens that sold them, and the others that had purchased were taken next morning to the fort. Imagine our anxiety. Although neither father or brother had purchased a gun, yet friends in the train had. But as fortune favored us they did nothing but take their testimony and permitted them to return to camps the next evening only detaining us two days. They did not give back the money that they paid for the guns.[19] I was very glad as we were detained that we were at such splendid water.

---

[19]The official reports make no mention of the guilty sergeant or the return of the men from the train to Fort Griffin. According to the post returns, "On the 27th, 1st

May 30th, Sabbath morning.

Although we do not wish to travail on Sunday, we will have to leave here today as our stock are beginning to ramble. Camped again. Travailed about 12 miles. Passed Phantom Hill. Is but two houses there but many chimneys standing where houses have been. They look so lonely. Stage stand here.[20]

Country broken, musquet and chaprell [sic] bushes with a few scattered elms are the only timber. How strange it seems to travail all day and not see any houses. We hear of Indians being seen at every fort, but we do not apprehend any danger from them.

It rained a hard shower this evening, also some hail, which renders camping rather unpleasant. We miss our nice spring tonight as the water is not very good. Are camped tonight on a high prairie and in sight, on another hill, is another large train camped.

May 31st.

Started early, traveled 20 miles. Came in sight yesterday of high peaks of the range of mountains. Was in sight all day. Camped just opposite it tonight. It is a noted place and is called Indian Pass. Here the Indians pass through the mountains. Some of the boys went to the top. They looked to be about half as high as they really were. A large rock seems to cover the top of the peak. It is on the left side of the road. Found some beautiful cedar trees here.[21]

Lt. P. W. Pocheu, 1st Cavalry, 1 Sergt., 1 corp, and 24 pvts, 4th Cavalry, left Post and proceeded on the Fort Concho Road to overtake and search an emigrant train then on that road and supposed to have Govt arms in their possession which had been stolen from the Post. Returned on the 29th after having searched the train & found in their possession part of the aforementioned Govt. arms.'' *Returns from U.S. Military Posts, 1800–1916*, National Archives Microcopy 617, "Fort Griffin Texas, July 1867–May 1881," Roll 429 (Washington, D.C.: National Archives and Records Service).

[20]Fort Phantom Hill was established in 1851 near the junction of the Elm and Clear Forks of the Brazos. Sometimes called the Post on the Clear Fork, it was abandoned in 1854 but continued to serve as a stage station and picket post for Fort Griffin. The main buildings were burned at the time the post was abandoned, thus the many chimneys noted by the diarist. Today the site looks much as it did in 1869. *Handbook of Texas*, 1: 630; Hart, *Old Forts*, 43–44.

[21]The train was traveling through the Callahan Divide, a range of mountains extending from east to west through present day Nolan, Taylor, and Callahan

June 1st.

Passed stage stand this morning. Travailed 8 miles, most of the way with mountains on each side of the road. Had to camp here in order to have plenty of water. Have a clear, running branch, very good water. Found some gooseburries [sic] and green grapes. Made some pies of them.

June 2nd.

Camped in sight of the mountains yet. Been passing them all day. Something resembling a grave was found on the top of one of the mounds with a pile of rock by it with white cloth wrapped around the rock. We do not know what it was for. Found a great many buffalou [sic] hides near the camp. Suppose that they had been stretched there last winter. Have not seen any buffalou yet. Seen some little prairie dogs today. They resemble a squirrel. Have not come to a large town of them yet. Had some fish from the creek that was near the camp this evening. Have travailed about 13 miles today.

June 3rd.

Started early. Passed old Fort Chadbourne.[22] I was very much dissapointed. I expected to find people living here but the only inhabitants was a few colored soldiers and one Mexican keeping the stage stand. All of the houses that I saw was made of rock and there was some nice looking dwellings here. And it would be a beautiful place if it was only inhabited by nice people and some improvements made. It is 105 miles from Fort Griffin to old Fort Chadbourne.

We are still camped in sight of mountains. When I was at home I

---

counties and dividing the waters of the Brazos from those of the Colorado. The mountain referred to might be any one of several prominent peaks including Church Mountain (3,000 feet), Bald Mountain (2,250 feet), or Buzzard Mountain (2,410 feet).

"Indian Gap" was later the site of Buffalo Gap, the first county seat of Taylor County. *Handbook of Texas*, 1: 272, and 2: 717.

[22]Fort Chadbourne was established in 1852 to protect the route from Fort Smith to Santa Fe. Abandoned during the Civil War, it was reoccupied in May, 1867, but evacuated as a regular post later that year because of an inadequate water supply. Thereafter it was used as a stage station and picket post for Fort Concho. The small community of Fort Chadbourne grew up around the old post and had a population of 25 in 1880. *Handbook of Texas*, 1: 622; Hart, *Old Forts*, 45–46.

thought that I liked the mountains but they look so lonesome way out here where a bird is scarcely ever seen. We have had very cool, pleasant weather to travel. So far today has been warm and the road very dusty. Came about 15 miles today.

June 4th.

Some stock missing this morning. Moved 4 miles, crossing the Colorado River. Camped on the west side. It is a very pretty stream. No timber on the banks as far as I can see. We crossed so near the head that it is very small. The boys caught some nice fish from the river. It is 30 miles from the Colorado to Fort Conchio [sic]. Some feds from [erased] camped on the river near our train. They were going to [erased]. Also another train of emigrants that was behind us came up with us and camped on the right side of the road while we were on the left. There is no emigrants ahead of us.

June 5th.

Found all the stock and all ready to start early. Had light shower of rain yesterday evening and still cloudy with quite a pleasant wind blowing this morning. Made a good day's drive. Had to leave the road one mile to get water sufficient to camp with and then it was not good.

June 6th.

Oh, we have had such splendid road. The levelest prairie that I ever saw. Crossed North Fork of the Conchio. Passed through the fort. It is a beautiful place for a town and there is some very nice buildings there principally made of rock. Here we seen the colored troops standing around among the yankees regardless of color or grade.[23]

North Conchio is a small stream with very nice timber on its banks.

---

[23]Fort Concho was established in 1867 at the junction of the North and South Concho rivers at present day San Angelo. One of the most important posts on the frontier, it was the center of the line of posts between El Paso and the northeast border of Texas, and it was also part of the southern defense line which ran westward to the mouth of the Rio Grande. *Handbook of Texas*, 1: 622; Hart, *Old Forts*, 178–81. A good picture of the post and life there in the 1868–70 period is J. Evetts Haley, *Fort Concho and the Texas Frontier* (San Angelo: San Angelo Standard Times, 1952), 137–43.

The Negro soldiers at Concho and at other posts were part of the two cavalry and four infantry regiments for blacks authorized by Congress in 1866. Most of the black

The main stream is considerable larger. Here we had some large fish and are camped near the bank tonight. We will travel up this stream 45 miles. It is 85 miles from Fort Conchio to Fort Griffin.[24] There is a splendid spring not far from where we are camped. Two or three company of infantry soldiers are now camped at this spring 2 miles from the fort.

For the last two or three days we have had wild carrots in great abundance. The little prairie dogs bark and frisk about as we pass by their dwellings which are all subtaranean [sic].

June 7th.   •

Nothing of interest passed today.

June 8th.

Camped again near the Conchio. Been washing and rearranging things generally. Will leave here this evening and make a short drive in order to reach the desert of the river in two more days. Here we found another large, cold spring surrounded with willow trees.

The cattle got scared last night and stampeded but not very bad. They got scared, we suppose, at a dog. They did not all run off. Quite an excitement was raised in camps. We did not know but what the Indians were about.[25] Part of the boys went in pursuit of them while others tied horses to the wagons. They did not go more than a mile until they succeeded in bringing them back. No one was hurt. Will leave here this evening. We have two men in our train that have travailed the road before. This is a great advantage.

---

troops in Texas in 1869 were members of the Ninth Cavalry and the Twenty-fourth Infantry. See William H. Leckie, *The Buffalo Soldiers: A Narrative of the Negro Cavalry in the West* (Norman: University of Oklahoma Press, 1967) for a discussion of the Negroes' service and the reaction of Texas settlers to their presence.

[24]This is one of the few places in the diary where the distances given by the writer are inaccurate. The distance from Griffin to Concho via the stage road was about 170 miles. Evidently the diarist meant 185, rather than 85, since she had already noted, on June 3rd, that the distance from Griffin to Chadbourne was 105 miles.

[25]Stampedes were frequent, and dangerous. Although sometimes set off by the approach of strangers, Indian or white, they often occurred for no discernable reason. A traveler on the northern road to California attributed many of the stampedes to "that awe of the wilderness . . . and its effects on the nerves" of cattle as well as men. Maxwell, *Crossing the Plains*, 108–109.

June 9th.

Camped in a nice place near the river. Had showers of rain this evening which was quite an advantage. High hill near the camp and on the right of the road. Not near so high as some that we had passed but it was near the road and myself and several others went to the top. There we found something that looked like a grave that had been there a long time. It had rock piled around it.

Have had very little sickness in the trains so far. One man sick now. Has been very sick. I hope he will get well.

June 10th.

Camped again on the river. We are not far from the head and it is getting small. 10 miles from where we are, we cross the river and then we strike the desert. Had another shower of rain this evening. All seem to think that we will have plenty of water [on the desert]. The boys have caught so many nice fish.

June 11th.

Near the river again. Found plenty of gooseberries but did not find a very nice camping place. So many musquet bushes.

June 12th.

Started very early. Went 12 miles, camped in very nice place. Will start across the first desert tomorrow. They say that we will have plenty of water most of the way. The sick man is improving. Think he will be well soon. I think that this is beautiful country.[26]

---

[26]The train was now traveling along the San Antonio-El Paso stage road which joined the Butterfield route at Fort Concho. The region is normally quite dry during the summer months, but contemporary accounts agree that 1869 was an exception. "There is considerable travel over this portion of the road," reported one observer. "Immense droves of cattle have passed over this road this season, the abundant rains affording a good supply of stock water and the grass is all that . . . could [be] desired." *Texas Almanac, 1869*, 155. For a contrasting picture of the area during a dry year see Stephen Powers, *Afoot and Alone*, 142. Powers notes the many dead animals along the route due to drought. For an excellent description of the country see Conkling, *The Butterfield Overland*, 1: 365–66, 370.

June 13th.

Rained very hard last night which makes it very pleasant travailing this morning. Passed this morning where a United States soldier was buried. He started across the plains intending to overtake a train of emigrants that were going to Calafornia [sic] and failed to do so and therefore starved for food. When he was found, he had canteens with water in it by him. He was trying, it seems, to get back. Found plenty of water. Camped early in the evening. Musquet bushes is the only timber in sight.

June 14th.

Came 4 miles, stopped by a pond of water, ate dinner, done some cooking, filled our barrels with water, and started early after dinner. It is 35 miles to the Pecos which is the next water. We travailed up until after midnight. Had a beautiful road and bright moonlight. Most of the time had very good grass and a little brush for wood.

June 15th.

All ready to start. Early this morning gave our horses some water out of our barrels. They were not very thirsty. Arrived at the river early in the afternoon. Nothing had suffered for water.

Passed through the Castle Mount. They are the prettiest mountains I ever saw. Not a bush can be seen, nothing but scattern [sic] grass. Some of them resemble houses, very muted, in the distance. Passed Central Station yesterday. Nothing but Negroes there guarding the stage stand.[27]

---

[27]The party was now in the Castle or King mountain range in present day Upton County. The point at which the stage road ran through the mountains was known as Castle Gap and was considered "one of the mountain gateways to West Texas." Powers, traveling the same route in 1868, also noted the romantic beauty of the area. "This is no mountain, neither yet like a castle . . . and, seen far off looks like the vast pile of the Tuileries. Castle Gap is a pass of peril, of awful and sublime grandeur." Powers, *Afoot and Alone*, 140. See also Federal Writers' Program, *Texas: A Guide to the Lone Star State* (New York: Hastings House, 1940), 545–55.

At Central Station, thirty miles from the head of the Concho, the San Antonio-El Paso stage road swung south to the Pecos while the Butterfield route crossed the Pecos farther north. *Texas Almanac, 1869*, 156; Conkling, *The Butterfield Overland* 1:364.

June 16th.

The Pecos is a narrow, deep, and muddy stream with no timber on its banks. It is now level with the banks. Very bad tasted [sic] water. There is a skiff that the mail is crossed in, and we have permission to cross our things in it. Commenced crossing as early as we could get all the stock to the ford. They would put the things out of the wagons into the skiff and then tied ropes to the wagons and crossed. One wagon came uncoupeled [sic] in the river. Another broke the rope that was on the tongue, but those on the opposite side still had holt [sic] of the other ropes and the men swam in and brought all safe to shore. Got all the wagons and the plunder over about three o'clock and then commenced crossing the cattle and horses. Just about the time all the wagons were over, brother Dan and Ed Stewart with several others jumped into the river to try their speed swimming. The current being very swift, Ed Stewart cramped and was sinking the last time when they caught him. In trying to rescue Ed, Dan came very near drowning, being so near exhausted. The skiff was pushed to them and they got in and came safe to land. How we all were frightened, but luck for us, all came safe.

Mr. Bottoms had a mule drowned in trying to cross, the only thing that was lost. They kept crossing until about 10 o'clock in the night. When anything would start down stream they would plunge in and bring them out. It is only a few places that the stock can get down to the water without going in overhead. We crossed the river at Melville camp.

June 17th.

Had but little trouble in crossing the remainder of the stock. Got them over and commenced reloading about twelve o'clock. The men have labored faithful in getting across the river that has so much been dreaded. All is over safe now, and I am truly thankful. Will go 7 miles this evening and camp again on the river. While we were loading, the train that was behind came to the opposite bank. I can sympathise with them. for I know that they dread crossing this stream.[28] It is kept

---

[28]Just as the Platte crossing was dreaded by emigrants on the northern route, so the Pecos crossing was one of the great perils on the southern route. See Powers,

full by the melting snow from the mountains. It is 85 miles from Conchio to Pecos River.

June 18th.

Made a long drive and camped in a beautiful place by a sulphur spring. The water is very cold but I do not like the taste. This is said to be a noted place for Indians as there is plenty of water here. There are some little Indian huts not far from the camps. We are still among the mountains. The highest growth that is to be seen is a shrub called the Spanish dagger which is from 4 to 6 feet high with long blades some 2 inches broad and 3 feet long terminating at both ends. One end has very sharp stiff point.

June 19th.

Drove over nice road and passed by some beautiful mountains. Are camped near a stage stand where is a Negro guard and one white man there. We get water out of a very good spring. A train of Mexicans and also one of Negro soldiers passed by our camp today. They are going to San Antonio.[29]

June 20th.

Sabbath morning finds me in camps and will remain here until Monday morning. This morning is warm and cloudy. I wish we would have a shower of rain as the road is very dusty. It is 240 miles from where we are now to El Passo [sic]. When we get there we are half way to Calafornia. Spent the day in reading and talking.

June 21st.

Rained some last night. Is raining this morning bad. Very hard rains

---

Afoot and Alone, 142, and Reid, *Reid's Tramp,* 111–12. The Melbourne (not Melville) Crossing, located where "the San Antonio road via Fort Clark intersected the upper road from Fort Concho," was thirty miles below the better-known Horsehead Crossing. Camp Melbourne was garrisoned by a company of infantry. *Texas Almanac, 1869,* 156; Conkling, *The Butterfield Overland* 1: 364.

[29]The party was camped near the Escondida Creek mail station about thirty-one miles from the Pecos. In 1869 a detachment of cavalry from Fort Stockton was stationed there. *Texas Almanac, 1869,* 155.

ahead of us which makes the air cool and the road pleasant. We passed by a grocery and camped near the fort.[30] Several Mexicans live here but very few white people. Passed in sight of three farms, none of them had any fence around them. There is a large farm three miles from the fort. The Negroes working it for the government. No timber at all here. They burn roots all together for firewood. I do not think this is a pretty country. Have fine spring here. The water is a little brackish.

June 22nd.

Came 9 miles today. At Leon Holes plenty of water and splendid grass.[31] Very good wood. Has been an old fort here. Mexican family camped with us tonight. They are going to Fort Davis, 60 miles from here. They travel by themselves and do not seem to be at all afraid. This is a beautiful camping place and pretty surrounding country.

June 23rd.

Cool and pleasant morning. All ready to start early. They told us that there was plenty of water in about 12 miles of where we were so we did not fill our barrels, only filled our small kegs. But to our dissapointment, the water was all dried up, and we had to go 25 miles in the place of 12, so we had no drinking water all evening. We found some water standing in a pond but not enough for our stock. It was then an hour after sunset but the moon was shining brightly so we camped and put all our stock in the carell [sic] without letting them eat any as they all wanted water. So we started next morning before

---

[30]Fort Stockton was established in 1859 to guard the San Antonio-El Paso road. Evacuated during the Civil War, it was re-garrisoned in 1867. The nearby community of Fort Stockton clustered around Comanche Springs, a famous spot where the water gushed "from the bowels of the earth like a sea monster." Reid, *Reid's Tramp*, 118; *Handbook of Texas*, 1: 632; Hart, *Old Forts*, 128–29. Even today water flows from the springs at a rate of "more than 30 million gallons daily." Federal Writers' Program, *Texas*, 641. For other descriptions of these "peculiar desert springs," see Duffen, "Way Diary," 49, and Powers, *Afoot and Alone*, 143.

[31]Leon Springs was another well-known watering place about sixteen miles from Fort Stockton. Powers described the springs as "strange weeping eyes of water, flung down like bits of the sea." Powers, *Afoot and Alone*, 145; Federal Writers' Program, *Texas*, 642. The "fort" mentioned in the diary was probably a picket post for Fort Davis.

breakfast and went 8 miles to Barilla Springs.[32] Here we found cold, pure water at the stage stand, and spring up in the mountains.

June 24th.

Remained here until evening. Filled our barrels with water and went a short distance to better range. Ma is sick, has the flux. Quite a number of the train has the same complaint.

June 25th.

We are now traveling through a long and narrow gap through the Olymphia Mountains.[33] Some places there is just space enough for the road. There is solid places of rock, 40 feet perpendicular and nothing at all on them. They all look like they had once been very hot. On the top of these mounts, some of which I suppose are near a mile from the level, we find low bunches of live oak trees. Rained hard last night. Found a nice place to camp, plenty of wood but no water. We had water with us. Camped about one o'clock, found plenty of wood and water.

Ma is some better. Part of the train went on this evening. 9 families remained here until morning as our teams need rest so much.

June 26th.

Started early. Passed some of the prettiest mountains. They are strait [sic] up about 50 feet with here and there little bushes and the river

---

[32]Barilla Springs, in the Barilla Mountains, thirty miles from Fort Davis, was typical of the stage stops in the region. "The stage stands of adobe were all built on the same plan. They were usually placed on a rise . . . of ground, which permitted the stage-tender to see several hundred yards in every direction. On either side of the broad entrance was a large room. In the rear . . . was the corral or patio. The walls of the corral were twelve or fifteen feet high, two or three feet thick, and constructed of adobe brick. . . ." Carlysle G. Raht, *The Romance of Davis Mountains and the Big Bend Country* (El Paso: Rahtbook Co., 1919), 130.

[33]The diarist refers to the Limpia, or Lympia, Mountains, part of the Davis Range, an irregular mass of forested peaks covering an area about fifty miles long and forty miles wide in present day Jeff Davis County. This area usually drew favorable comment from travelers. Ibid., 88; Powers, *Alone and Afoot*, 148–49. Like the diarist, Phocian Way also thought the mountains to be of volcanic origin. Duffen, "Way Diary," 49–50. The trail at this point ran through Limpia Canyon, a wide valley between the hills through which ran the clear Limpia Creek.

running over them. Full of nice flowers. Branch running along the foot of the mountains and nice springs. Camped with mountains near on each side and a spring on the right of the road. The train that left are about 3 miles before us. Some of them are in haste to get to El Passo and we do not wish to push our teams. It is 28 miles from Barilla springs to Fort Davis. We are now in 6 miles of Fort Davis.

June 27th.

Ma is better this morning. Man passed camps last evening and told us that 4 mounted Indians and 8 on foot had taken all the mules and horses at the stand at Barilla Spring Friday about twelve o'clock. He was on his way to the fort after soldiers. They passed by last night going to try and recover their horses. Some mockison [sic] tracks were seen in the road just ahead of us. This is their main passage, they say. I do not think they will ever attack us. They will get our horses if they can.

If I was at home I think I would go to church today. The time has passed much pleasanter than I expected on the road. We will move a short distance this morning to fresh grass for the stock. Camped in a nice place by the side of a high mount.

June 28th.

Will remain here today to wash as we have such nice clear water. Beef above of 300 head passed camps this morning on their way to Calafornia. They are from Stockton.

There has been a great deal of rain through this country which makes the range fine. This pass through these mountains is called Wild Rose Gap and it is very appropriate name as there are so many wild roses in the little vallies.[34]

---

[34]Wild Rose Pass was a favorite camping spot on this road. Lieutenant W.H.C. Whiting, one of the first white men to explore the area, recalled, "Wild roses, the only ones I had seen in Texas, here grow luxuriantly. I named the defile 'Wild Rose Pass' and the brook the 'Limpia'." Quoted in Robert M. Utley, *Fort Davis National Historic Site, Texas*, Historic Handbook Series #38 (Washington, D.C.: National Park Service, 1965), 3–4. Also see: Reid, *Reid's Tramp*, 119.

June 29th.

Passed through Fort Davis.[35] It is a pretty little place by the side of the mountains. The valley is wide here and the mountains small. Here are found vegetables. Very high, roasting ears one dollar and 50 cents per dozen, butter one dollar per pound, eggs the same per dozen. This is a beautiful valley. We have a delightful camping place tonight. There is such a nice spring here and splendid water in abundance running out of the mountain. 9 miles from Fort Davis. Several full stores here. Some white people and Mexicans and Negroes. There are 400 soldiers here. They played their band as we passed the fort.

June 30th.

Are camped tonight at Barrel Spring, 18 miles from Fort Davis.[36] Not a very nice place to camp. Grass is not very good. We passed some nice groves of live oak trees today. Very little timber in this country. There is a stage stand here. 12 Negroes guard it.

July 1st.

First intended staying at Barrel Springs until tomorrow but there was a train of negroes from the Pinery that were hauling lumber to

---

[35]Fort Davis was originally established in 1854 to protect the El Paso-San Antonio road and control the Comanche and Apache Indians who roamed the area. Evacuated by Union troops in 1861, it was reoccupied in 1867 by the Ninth Cavalry and the Twenty-fourth and Twenty-fifth Infantry. In 1869 ten sets of officers' quarters, two barracks, and a number of outbuildings, most of adobe, had been completed. The nearby village of Chihuahua had a population of 150 Mexicans and twenty-five Americans. Utley, *Fort Davis*, 202–29; *Handbook of Texas*, 1: 624; Hart, *Old Forts*, 55–59. For views of the fort and the surrounding country, see: Powers, *Afoot and Alone*, 150–51; Duffen, "Way Diary," 50; Reid, *Reid's Tramp*, 119–20; and the delicate water colors and sketches by a soldier stationed at the post in Arthur T. Lee, *Fort Davis and the Texas Frontier* (College Station: Texas A&M University Press, 1976).

[36]Barrell Springs, twenty-two miles southwest of Fort Davis, provided a permanent supply of water from seepage springs in the rocky hillside. One theory for the name is that officers from Fort Davis sank barrels in the bed of the ravine near the spring to collect water. Conkling, *The Butterfield Overland*, 2:31. For a description of the country between Fort Davis and Eagle Springs (note 41 below), see Powers, *Afoot and Alone*, 152–53.

Stockton and another train of Mexican camped at the same place.[37] They had whiskey and the negro soldiers got drunk and commenced cutting up so we harnessed up and left when the sun was not more than one hour high. We travailed 3 miles and made a dry camp. There we found plenty of good grass. We knew they had the advantage of us. If we had killed any of them then we would have been detained sometime. If nothing more these military posts are a great pest to emigrants.

July 2nd.

Camped at Dead Mans Holes, 13 miles from Barrel Springs.[38] Is another stand here, 2 miles from the camp. Good spring at the stand. There we get water to use. There is water at the camps for the stock. This is a wide, nice valley. No timber except some small brush.

July 3rd.

Will remain at Dead Mans Holes until morning. Have spent the day in sewing and cooking. The train that was behind came up this evening. They will remain here a few days as many of their cattle are lame and worn down. Our teams are all in good plight for traveling. We have had plenty of rain. Have a shower most every evening which is very agreeable.

July 4th.

Started off this beautiful Sabbath morning and will travail 9 miles. Here we found plenty of very good water in ponds. It has been many days since we was out of sight of mountains or in sight of timber of any consequence. We have beautiful level road all the time. To see the

---

[37]The Pinery probably refers to the Pinery Stage Station much farther to the north in Guadalupe Pass, although it might refer to one of the areas near Fort Davis where timber was cut for fort construction. Conkling, *The Butterfield Overland*, 1: 389–90; Utley, *Fort Davis*, 7, 20.

[38]Dead Man's Holes and stage station was located in a valley on the north side of El Muerto Peak, thirty-five miles from Fort Davis. According to local legend, the name came from an unknown man found dead near the spring in 1854. Conkling, *The Butterfield Overland*, 2:33; Reid, *Reid's Tramp*, 122.

cactus and Mexican daggers you would think that there was no scarcity of timber.[39]

July 5th.

Several carriages, three wagons, one lady, several men passed this morning on their way to El Passo from San Antonio. No wood, have not even small brush.

July 6th.

Camped at another pond of water. Better luck than we expected finding water. There is also plenty of wood here. Passed Van Horns Wells this evening. Could get no water here. Is stage stand here. It is 32 miles from Dead Mans Holes to Van Horns Wells.[40]

July 7th.

Travailed all day and had to make dry camp. We had a sufficiency of using water with us and they found enough for the horses. 4 of the men went ahead this evening to hunt a camping place. They seen 4 bear.

This is a dangerous place for Indians. Has been mockison [sic] tracks seen all about here. There was a fire seen about 9 o'clock on the top of the mountain. Supposed it to be an Indian camp. Tied all our horses to the wagon and never let the cattle leave the carell. We are camped in 6 miles of Eagle Springs.

July 8th.

Started before breakfast and came to Eagle Springs. Here we found

---

[39]It is rare for overland travelers not to comment on the nation's birthday and to have some sort of celebration. However, it is likely that most of the members of the train were former Confederates and not yet ready to return fully to the celebration of the Union they had so recently fought.

[40]Van Horn's Wells, another major watering place on the trail about seventeen miles from present day Van Horn, Texas, was named for Colonel James J. Van Horn who was stationed in the area from 1859 to 1861. The Wells were considered the "most dependable water source on the road from Limpia Creek to the Rio Grande." Conkling, *The Butterfield Overland*, 2: 34; *Handbook of Texas*, 2: 831; Reid, *Reid's Tramp*, 122.

plenty of water for all the stock by dipping it with the buckets which was soon done. This spring is by the side of a high mountain. 19 miles from Van Horns Wells to Eagle Springs.[41] The teams that is ahead did not get any water here there was so many of them together. It is 35 miles from here to the next water that we know of. If the other trains did not find water before they got there their stock must have suffered greatly.

The health of our little train is very good at present. We have 20 men, 11 wagons, 8 families with us. They say that we can see the river from the top of the mountain. The negroes here have been very kind to us. The spring does not run off. It rises and fills up as it is dipped out. There is quite a number of Indian warriors said to live not far from Eagle Springs.

July 10th.

Left Eagle Springs on the 9th about 2 o'clock. Travailed until an hour by sun, made coffee and rested awhile and started. Travailed until 11 o'clock. Had a splendid road and all went on without trouble.

Started early next morning. It was then 14 miles to the river. We passed through a narrow cannon [sic], just sufficient room for a road. High mountains on each side. We arrived at the river about two o'clock. Our cattle was very thirsty but all made the trip very well. I am proud to say that we are at the Rio GranDe [sic]. It is said to be half way to Calafornia. The road is very dry and dusty now but every appearance of rain.

July 11th.

Camped near the river. There is some timber on the banks of the river, the first we have seen since we left Conchio except a few scattered live oak. I do not admire this country. Has not been much rain here, therefore grass is not very good. It is 2 miles from the camps to

---

[41]Eagle Springs, located at the base of Eagle Mountain near present day Sierra Blanca, was often used as an outpost for Fort Quitman. In earlier years Indians were particularly troublesome on this part of the route. Reid's party was attacked at the Springs, and Way also mentions trouble in the area. Reid, *Reid's Tramp,* 122; Duffen, "Way Diary," 52. See also: Conkling, *The Butterfield Overland,* 2:37; *Handbook of Texas,* 1:532; Hart, *Old Forts,* 130.

Fort Quitman.[42] We are in Texas and can see Mexico. Can see nothing but mountains and rocks. We will make short drives now for some time so the stock can have time to recruit.

July 12th.

Passed through Fort Quitman. Got some small june apples there. Did not see any white women there. There was many Mexican women, some very nice looking and dressed very nice. Some nice looking white men. Beautiful groves of cottonwood trees around the fort. All the houses were perfectly flat on the top. Camped by a lake near the river. Had a very hard rain last night which was much needed. Came to this place Sunday evening. Will stay here until Tuesday morning.

July 13th.

Started after supper and made a nice drive by moonlight. The days are getting so warm that we cannot travail only early of morning.

July 14th.

Started this morning before breakfast and went to a good camping place. Had a large cottonwood tree that afforded us nice shade. Started this evening about an hour by sun and travailed 12 miles and camped. The nights are pleasant for travailing. Mexicans brought some nice fish to the camps for sale. There was a little Mexican hut near our camp and plenty of cottonwood and musquet timber on the road. The roads are extremely dusty.

July 15th.

Had a shower of rain last night, it makes travailing more pleasant. Started before breakfast again. Travailed 5 miles and stopped near the river. Will now get breakfast. We have fish for breakfast. Started near sundown. Had not went more than half mile when Mr. Coughrans wagon axel broken. Taken his load in the other wagons and fixed his

---

[42]Fort Quitman was established in 1858 on the Rio Grande River seventy miles from El Paso. The post was evacuated by Union troops in 1861 and reoccupied in 1868 by three companies of cavalry and one of infantry. Built of whitewashed adobe, the post maintained several out stations to protect the San Antonio-El Paso road. *Handbook of Texas*, 1:630–31; Hart, *Old Forts*, 130–31.

so that it would travail and made a drive of about 8 miles. Passed by Mexican's village. There are a good many Mexican huts along the road. Found no grass, therefore had to go to another camping ground.

July 16th.

Started before breakfast and passed by stage stand and did not find very good grass. The men are now very busy fixing the wagon. We will not have much more grass until we get to El Passo. As we passed by the houses last night one of them was very brilliantly lighted. It looked very nice from the road. White man with a Mexican wife was living there. We will start at 2 o'clock.

Went 10 miles, camped just at dark.

July 17th.

Had nice shower of rain last night. We travailed near the river, sometimes in three steps of the water. Banks are very low and sandy. In one place the river rises where the road once was. In some places very boggy and in some places that they had to mind the stock away from. The road was very dusty and warm travailing. For some days past, Mexicans come to the camps most every day. Some of them make a very good appearance whilst others ought not appear at all. Where we were camped yesterday was a stage stand and several Mexican huts. One of the Mexicans had a large herd of goats and cattle. They do not care as to houses, just so they have shade.

Travailed short distance. Bought some onions, pears and apples from a Mexican. Passed several huts, some of them have some corn growing with no fence around it. There was a Mexican family camped where we camped. One of the prettiest little Mexican children. The pears and apples were cheap. He offered wheat for three dollars a bushel. I think that this would be pretty country to live in.

July 18th.

Have very nice place to camp. Started early, made a long drive. Passed through three Mexican villages. The first contained many small houses and several very nice ones. Plenty of green apples and pears and onions are brought to us very cheap. The road wound around so that it was some distance from the place we went in at to where we left

town. Their corn and gardens have no fence around them and therefore our loose stock was much trouble. The next town the road was
strait and not so far through. I have heard the name of these towns but
cannot remember them.[43]

We had to travail until dark to get where we could camp. Had a
hard rain this evening, very muddy camping. Eleven miles from here
to Franklin.[44] We have seen many buggys pass with nice looking
white men in them. There is high sand hills through this country.
Nothing for stock to eat but weeds.

July 19th.

Started before breakfast. Went in 7 miles of Franklin, stopped, and
got breakfast. Passed through Fort Bliss which is 15 miles from
Socoro.[45] Here is U.S. post and on a short distance farther is Franklin.
This is a beautiful place, so many nice shade trees. Several white
families live here. The town is near the bank of the river and just opposite this on the other side of the river is El Passo. We stopped some

[43]The villages mentioned are San Elizario, Socorro, and Ysleta. San Elizario was
founded in 1772 as a mission and presidio. Until 1814 the Spanish and Mexican
governments maintained outposts there. The town served as the county seat of El
Paso County from 1850 to 1876. Socorro was also named for a mission settlement,
Nuestra Señora de la Concepción del Socorro. Founded in 1682 for Piro, Tano and
Jemez Indians who fled New Mexico following the Pueblo Revolt of 1680, the town
continued as a bustling settlement until the late nineteenth century. Ysleta was also
founded as a mission for Indians who fled New Mexico. It is often described as the
oldest permanent settlement in Texas. It has been almost encompassed by modern El
Paso. Federal Writers' Program, *Texas*, 562–64; *Handbook of Texas*, 2: 549–50, 633,
949. For descriptions of the towns in the 1850s and 60s see: Powers, *Afoot and Alone*,
165–66; Reid, *Reid's Tramp*, 136–37; Duffen, ''Way Diary,'' 53.

[44]Franklin was established in 1848 at the site of a store and ranch owned by
Franklin Coons or Coontz. In 1850 a post office was granted and the name changed
from Coon's Ranch to Franklin. Along with Magoffinsville, Hart's Mill, and
Concordia, Franklin formed the present day El Paso, Texas. *Handbook of Texas*, 1:
407; C. L. Sonnichen, *Pass of the North* (El Paso: Texas Western Press, 1968), 124–45.
For a much earlier view of the area and the villages below Franklin see Harris, *The
Gila Trail*, 51–57. See also: Powers, *Afoot and Alone*, 167–68; Reid, *Reid's Tramp*, 138.

[45]Fort Bliss was established in 1848 at Smith's Ranch, which is now downtown El
Paso, Texas. The post site was moved several times before the present site was
determined. In 1868–69 the fort was located in Concordia, several miles from the
place visitors see today. *Handbook of Texas*, 1:620–21; Hart, *Old Forts*, 83–86. Powers
visited the post in 1868 and thought it rather attractive. Powers, *Afoot and Alone*,
167.

time in Franklin. Purchased flour for the remainder of our journey. We bought at 7$ in greenbacks. The merchants treated with wine and the children with candy. After making the necessary purchases we went one mile and half and camped by Mr. Von Pattersons. Here we were treated with great hospitality. He has a mill. In all of his buildings he has 48 rooms. His wife is Indian. She is head of her tribe. They are very wealthy. They came to the camps and we went to the house with them and they treated us with wine. We then bought wine of him next morning. He had on hand 400 gallons of wine. He lives in a beautiful place near the river.[46]

We received a letter from our friends in Calafornia. They write cheering news to us.

July 20th.

We have a bad road. But little grass for our stock for several days. It is now 9 miles to grass and water. Mr. Von Pattens [sic] wished very much for us to stay a few days with them. I would liked to have stayed, but we will have to hasten on. We found a very pretty place to camp on good grass. Passed over rough country this morning. It is 95 miles from where we first struck the river to El Passo or Franklin. Total distance from San Antonio to El Passo 654 miles. It is about 750 miles from McKinney to El Passo.

July 21st.

Still at the same camp. Have been washing and baking light bread.

------

[46]The reference is to Eugene Van Patton, an influential Republican leader in the El Paso area. The site described is undoubtedly Hart's Mill which was confiscated from Confederate sympathizer Simeon Hart at the end of the war. Van Patton later relocated in Las Cruces where he was closely associated with Albert Jennings Fountain. Letter, Leon Metz, Archivist, University of Texas at El Paso to Sandra L. Myres, March 1978. See also: Sonnichen, *Pass of the North*, 170–72; Arrell M. Gibson, *The Life and Death of Colonel Albert Jennings Fountain* (Norman: University of Oklahoma Press, 1965), 122–27; 233–37.

The El Paso district was famous for its wine which was described by one contemporary as "held in high estimation, even by connoisseurs. A large quantity of wine is annually made, the best qualities of which are pronounced equal to the Catawba. . . ." *Texas Almanac, 1869*, 103.

July 22nd.

Still at the same place. Left the old camp this evening. It was not a pretty place to camp, too many bushes. The Mexicans stole one pair of cows from Jim Stewart and run them across the river. The boys went across after them but failed to find them.

July 23rd.

Started late in the evening and camped at a beautiful place with fine grass. It is 16 miles from here to El Passo. Made an early start this morning. This is a beautiful valley with the Rio GranDe rolling majestically between the cragged looking mountains.

Travailed until twelve, stopped rested awhile and let the stock graze, and ate supper. We then started and travailed by moonlight about 8 miles and found very good grass.

July 24th.

Started after breakfast and came to where some Mexicans were living. They are very nice looking people, white as anybody. Us girls called in to see how the house looked. They gave us some apples to eat and was very kind. Their house looked so nice and clean inside. They have black Mexicans for servants.

It is now 15 miles to where we cross the river. Got supper and travailed some distance. Had nice moonlight to travail by. Camped in 3 miles of La Crusa [sic]. Passed by an old fort. Some Mexicans living there. The old fort looked very desolate.

July 25th.

Passed through La Crusa. It is a very pretty situation for a town, but the buildings are not pretty. The church bell was ringing as we passed through, and the Mexicans were crowding to the chapel. They were all dressed very nice with large bright colored shawls over their heads and shoulders. They were carrying their musical instruments with them to the church. Bought some nice cabbage and onions here.[47]

---

[47]Las Cruces, New Mexico, was named for the crosses erected on the graves of a number of massacred oxcart drivers. Settled in 1848, it was a prosperous town with a

We arrived at the crossing of the river about 10 o'clock. The train that left us are camped 5 miles on the other side of the river. There is two families on this side. Their captain's wife is very sick and could not cross the river. They forded the river. We intended crossing this evening, but alas how little do we see of the future. It pains me to pen the incident. A young man that was with Uncle Stewart by the name of John Thomas accidentally shot himself with his six shooter. He was twirling it around and revolving it and it went off. The bullet went in on the right side through his breast and come out in his back on the same side. Oh how it grieves me to think that anyone should happen to have such an accident so far from home. He has no relatives in this train. Has one brother in a train behind. Most of the men think his case hopeless, but I still hope. We have sent to town for a physician. The accident happened about one o'clock. He will have the assistance of our prayers.

The captain's wife is very sick this evening. Sad, sad facts, our friend died this evening between sundown and dark. He suffered greatly while he lived but was perfectly himself all the time. He refused to die easy.

July 26th.

Have dressed him very nice and sent to La Crusa and had his coffin made and grave dug. The corps [sic] left camp at 11 o'clock. His brother that is in the back train come up in time to see him buried. Buried him at La Crusa. He was taken when he little expected to die.

We have crossed the river and come up with the trains that had left us. We had no bad luck crossing. All forded it. Stopped after dark, rested 3 hours and started. Travailed all night, came to water this morning.

---

fine hotel, a theater, and a branch of the Loretto Academy for Girls. The fort mentioned in the diary was Fort Fillmore, built in 1851. The fort was occupied by Confederate troops in 1861 and was briefly re-garrisoned by Union troops in 1862. Later in the same year the troops were moved to Mesilla and Fillmore was not re-occupied. Federal Writers' Project, *New Mexico: A Guide to the Colorful State* (New York: Hastings House, 1953), 259; Hart, *Old Forts*, 82–83. For other views of Las Cruces in the late 1860s see Powers, *Afoot and Alone*, 170–71.

July 27th.

Tanks have been made here for the purpose of furnishing water to emigrants. They sell the water at 10 cents a drink. Has two trains and one beef herd watered here today. He has made near one hundred dollars today. It is 18 miles from here to the river and about 30 miles to water ahead which is Crooks Canon. They say that this is the most dangerous place that we will have to pass.[48] We crossed the river 3 miles below LaMisjalla [sic].[49]

July 28th.

Started late in the evening, travailed until about 3 o'clock, stopped and slept awhile. The road was part of the way through the mountains. Had no trouble in travailing.

July 29.

Started early and drove until about 3 o'clock. Arrived near Fort Cummins.[50] Here we find splendid grass and water. It is called 35 miles from here to where we got the last water, but we made good time and the stock did not suffer. There is 2 large beef droves camped here.

Had a nice shower of rain this evening which was very agreeable for

---

[48]The diarist is referring to Cooke's Canyon which was indeed considered one of the most dangerous places along the southern route. William Bell, who was in the area in the fall of 1867, heard that the Indians were so bad in the area "that even the soldiers dared not stir a mile from the post, and it was 'just a toss up' whether any traveller got through it alive." However, Bell admitted, the rumors seemed to have been more frightening than the Indians. Bell, *New Tracks,* 2:19. See also Powers, *Afoot and Alone,* 178; Conkling, *The Butterfield Overland,* 2:115–18.

[49]La Mesilla was the Mexican capital of Arizona and Sonora. The town and surrounding valley became part of the United States as a result of the Gadsden Purchase. The Mesilla crossing is descibed in Duffen, "Way Diary," 150–51. See also Conkling, *The Butterfield Overland,* 2:107.

[50]Fort Cummings was established in 1863 near Cooke's Springs, fifty-three miles west of the Rio Grande on the Mesilla-Tucson road. The post was to restrain the Apache Indians and guard the "most dangerous point (except for Apache Pass) on the southern route to California." Robert W. Frazer, *Forts of the West: Military Forts and Presidios . . . to 1898* (Norman: University of Oklahoma Press, 1965), 98. A good description of the post is given in Bell, *New Tracks,* 2: 24–25. See also Conkling, *The Butterfield Overland,* 2: 118.

this soil is very dusty. No timber here, nothing but small brush to burn. Still among the mountains.

July 30th.

Leave Fort Cummins this evening. Will drive through Cooks Cannon this evening. Did not travail very late but the road was rough. We have travailed from Fort Davis to Franklin with 6 families and 20 men. From Franklin to La Crusa we had only 3 families. The others stopped to wait for their friends that were behind. We then had 14 men. At the crossing we overtaken the train that left us at Fort Davis. We did not join them at Cummins. Their train had to wait on account of sickness so 5 other wagons joined us and we went on. We now have 25 men. We would have travailed as we was, but the road from here to Tucson is said to be dangerous.

July 31st.

Are through the worst of the cannon and nothing has happened. Came safe through and are camped at Membris Creek.[51] We left the town to our right as this is the best way. Membris is a small clear stream with cold springs along the banks. There is something over 7000 head of stock camped on this stream, part going to Calafornia and some not so far. There is a small train of emigrants camped here from Llano Co. Texas. They travailed up the Pecos 300 miles, and when they crossed they were attacked by 75 Indians. They lost one man killed. This man lived in Calafornia and had come after his friends. They had 600 head of beeves. Ths Indians wanted their beeves. They had had a hard time.

August 1st.

Left Membris this evening. We now have 25 men. Travailed 10

---

[51]Mimbres Creek had its source in Grant County, New Mexico, north of present-day Deming. The stage station, near which the train camped, was eighteen miles northwest of Cooke's Springs and was described as having "great groves of cotton-woods and willows" in a valley known as one of the most "inviting regions" on the southern route. Conkling, *The Butterfield Overland*, 2: 119–20. The "town" mentioned by the diarist was Rios Mimbres. Powers, *Afoot and Alone*, 180. See also: Duffen, "Way's Diary," 152–53; Federal Writers' Project, *New Mexico*, 375.

miles, most of the way after night. There was several men or Indians seen on the side of the road but they left. We did not learn who they were. Every man had gun in hand ready for a fight but fortune favored and we had no fighting to do.

August 2nd.

Will drive to water this morning. Arrived at Ojo Lavaca or Cow Springs.[52] Has been an old fort. The Indians burned the roof off of it the other day. Did not find very plenty of water here but enough to answer our travailing purposes. Rested awhile, ate dinner, and started on. We have 55 miles to go now without water for our stock. Camped tonight near the mountains. By no means a pretty place.

August 3rd.

Passed an old fort, got some water to drink.[53] Plenty for the horses but none for the cattle.

August 4th.

Travailed last night. Had a beautiful road. This is a pretty valley. About 12 o'clock in the night several Indians were seen on horseback. This frightened me some. No moonlight, nothing but starlight. How quiet the train travailed tonight. The Indians did not molest us. Camped about 2 o'clock.

August 5th.

Have reached the place for water, Stevens Creek, but have to dig out the spring. So all went to work and the stock got some water but not enough.

All had plenty of water by 12 o'clock and we will leave this evening. Our cattle suffered some, but none failed. It is 35 miles to the next water. There is a peak or mount here 300 feet high called Stevens Peak. Stevens had a fight with Indians sometime ago at this place and

---

[52]Cow Springs, or Ojo de la Vaca, was sixteen miles from Mimbres crossing at the junction of several east-west and north-south routes. Conkling, *The Butterfield Overland*, 2: 141–42; Duffen, "Way Diary," 154, Powers, *Afoot and Alone*, 181.

[53]In all probability this was not an "old fort," but the abandoned stage station at Soldier's Farewell. See Maria Shrode diary, note 38.

hence its name.[54] Had beans and pie for dinner. We had cool, pleasant time to travail the road that was destitute of water.

Arazonia

August 6th.

Good luck, we found water 12 miles from the peak and did not have to drive so far. We was glad to find good grass and plenty of water without going so far. Passed through Stens Cannon.[55] The rocks were very high on either side and so near the road. Good place for Indians to make an attack.

The train that we left behind came up this evening. One of Dr. Barnes children died last night. It had hooping [sic] cough and cronic diareah [sic]. Has been 2 deaths in that train. Another babe died with the same complaint.

August 7th.

Quite a number of beeves have come up to this place for water. Some of them do not look very well they have gone without water so long. Made dry camp tonight.

August 8th.

Will pass through Apache Gap today. There is a fort and 300 soldiers. Here the cannon is the deepest and longest that we have ever passed through, but the road is very good. Came just opposite the post and camped. Here is plenty of good water and very good grass. There is quite a number of graves here, most of whom were killed by the In-

---

[54]The reference is to Stein's Peak or El Peloncillo, "a monument and a conspicuous landmark for a distance of more than thirty miles east on the road." This was the last stage station in New Mexico. It was not named for a man killed by Indians, as the diarist claims, but for Major Enoch Stein of the U.S. Dragoons. Powers climbed a portion of the peak which Way described as a "sugar loaf looking mountain." Conkling, *The Butterfield Overland*, 2:127–29; Powers, *Afoot and Alone*, 188–89; Duffen, "Way Diary," 156. William Bell, like the diarist, comments on the long, dry *jornada* from Stein's Peak to Fort Bowie. Bell, *New Tracks*, 2: 41.

[55]Stein's Pass or, as it was better known, Doubtful Canyon. See Maria Shrode, "Journal," note 39.

dians. They are digging gold here. They supposed that there is very rich mines here.[56]

August 9th.

Started very early this motning. Oh, what a rough road we have come over this morning. Coming up out of the cannon it seemed as if we never would get to the top of the mountain. We gained it at last, and then we had a nice road and beautiful valley, such nice green grass. There had been a great deal of rain here for the last few days.

We started before breakfast and have now stopped to get dinner. It has just rained very hard. How glad I will be when we get to Tucson. It is 110 miles from Apache Pass to Tucson. Travailed until near sundown, made dry camp.

August 10th.

Started this morning and had a good road. This is beautiful country. If there was wood and water here this would be a desireable place to live. Arrived at Sulphur Springs about 11 o'clock.[57] Will water here and drive on. It is 25 miles from Apache Pass to Sulphur Springs where we camped last night. There was no wood at all here but we found surplus plank enough to cook with. Started about 5 o'clock, drove 10 miles.

Started after breakfast on the 11th, drove within 4 miles of the Pedro River.[58] Could go no farther after dark on account of the short cannon

---

[56]Apache Pass, or Puerto del Dado, was known as a notorious hideout for Apaches and was considered one of the most dangerous spots on the route. Powers described it as the most "awful and stupendous piece of natural savagery on the whole route. . . ." In 1862, the government established Fort Bowie in the Pass to protect the emigrant road and mail route to California. When Bell was there in 1867 he reported that the post was garrisoned by "one small company of 40 men" and three officers. During his brief stay, the mail carrier and one of the post's officers were killed by the Appaches. Powers, *Afoot and Alone*, 190; Conkling, *The Butterfield Overland*, 2:133–38; Bell, *New Tracks*, 2: 44–49.

[57]Sulphur Springs was the "only water" available between Apache Pass and Dragoon Springs. Located near present-day Cochise, Arizona, it is still used for watering livestock. Conkling, *The Butterfield Overland*, 2: 140; Federal Writers' Program, *Arizona: A State Guide* (New York: Hastings House, 1940), 436–37.

[58]The crossing of the San Pedro River, twenty-one miles from Dragoon Springs, was located about one-half mile from the present-day town of Benson, Arizona. The

between there and the river. Arrived at the river in due time. The road was narrow and rough but short. Here we find good grass and water, small musquet for wood. The Pedro is a small, shallow stream with sandy banks with no timber on its banks. There was a beef drove camped here yesterday. Some of the men that was with the drove had a difficulty and a man was killed. I do not know his name nor any of the particulars. We see his clothes and his grave near our camps. We will stay here a few days to recruit our stock. There is 2 beef droves camped here. Was 2 beeves killed yesterday by lightning during a hard rain. It is 35 miles from here to Sulphur Springs.

August 13th.

Moved our camp to a better place. The evening we moved it rained very hard and next morning where our old camp was the ground was covered 2 feet deep with water so we just moved in time. The river was overflowed. 3 families with a beef drove have not crossed the river.

August 14th.

Started this evening at 2 o'clock, made a nice drive and camped on a high, nice place. Rained all night. I think that it has rained on or in sight of us for 2 weeks. Passed through a short cannon.

August 15th.

It still cloudy with every appearance of rain. Will start early this morning and make a good drive as the road is hard and level. Went 3 miles and found water in some ponds making it 14 miles from the river. Here we rested and got dinner. We then drove 10 miles and camped in a nice place. Had plenty of wood and water. Stand with a number of soldiers stationed. The road is surrounded with mountains.

We travailed through a valley of high grass. This is fine range.

---

mail station here was at the junction of several trails. In 1870, a toll bridge was built at the river crossing. Conkling, *The Butterfield Overland*, 2: 149–50. For other descriptions of the San Pedro Valley and crossing see: Powers, *Afoot and Alone*, 192–94; Duffen, "Way Diary," 158.

There is a stand here and some farms along the river. We had one mess of white head cabbage. Vegetables are high.

August 16th.

Camped in one mile of Muscal Springs.[59] Here the Cenega [sic] swamp sets in. The road is muddy and bad. Crossed the River Cenega several times. It was swimming yesterday but is not very deep today. It is 9 miles through this swamp. Had a steep, hard hill to pull this morning. Got through the swamp about 1 o'clock, stopped to rest and get dinner. 31 miles from San Pedro to Cinega [sic] Creek. The Cinega is a small, swift-running stream with some cotton wood timber on its bank. We crossed it 4 times today. The bottom is gravelly and good crossing.[60]

Come over some more bad road this evening. The hills that we came over today has pulled our teams harder than any place that we have ever crossed. Camped before sundown.

August 17th.

Oh, what a hard rain fell last night and what vivid lightning from every point. Only one tent left standing so we had to dry our beds today and therefore will not leave here before 12 o'clock. This is a high, dry place to camp. 15 miles from here to Tucson.

August 18th.

Started after breakfast. Arrived at Tucson about 8 o'clock and camped on the east side of town. Did not find good water nor much grass. This country is thick with musquet bushes. We will stay until morning.

---

[59]The writer is referring to Mescal Springs, a short distance west of the San Pedro Crossing. From Mescal Springs, the road ran through Mescal Wash, crossed the present-day boundary between Cochise and Pima counties and then went on through Pantano Wash to Cienega Springs. Conkling, *The Butterfield Overland*, 2: 152.

[60]Cienega is a Spanish word meaning a marshy place or, as the diarist calls it, a "swamp." The Cienega Springs stage station was located in modern Pima County near the town of Pantano which was once called "La Cienega." Ibid.; Federal Writers' Program, *Arizona*, 382–83. Powers described the country from the San Pedro to Tucson as "Three thousand square miles of detestable chapparal desert. . . ." Powers, *Afoot and Alone*, 195.

August 19th.

Passed through Tucson. Got some nice watermelons here. This is a beautiful place, some nice houses here. Goods are much cheaper than I expected to find them. Groceries are dear. There is quite an excitement in town about a silver mine that has lately been discovered near this place. It is said to be the richest ever found. Received a letter from friends in Calafornia at this place. They are in fine spirits. I am getting impatient for our journey to come to an end, yet it cheers me to think that every day finds us nearer our destination. It is 520 miles from here to the city of Los Angeles.[61]

Drove about 8 miles from town, found good grass and water, a running stream and nice spring. Will stay here until morning. This creek is called Pond Creek. Sheep ranch here and a few Mexican huts. (Well, it is called 18 mile station.)[62]

August 20th.

Drove 9 miles today. Found good water but not much grass. It is 28 miles to the next good camping place, so we will travail tonight. The sun is now an hour high and they are fixing to start. The weather has been extremely warm for the few days past. The round cactus trees that grow here are quite a curiosity to one that never has seen them before.[63] These Mexicans will be very friendly, but if they get a chance

---

[61]Tucson was one of the oldest settlements in Arizona. In March, 1856, the town became part of the United States (as part of the Gadsden Purchase) and was soon a major stop on the San Antonio-San Diego mail route. After the Civil War, many Americans arrived, not always of the better element, and the town had a reputation for vice and crime. In 1869, the population was predominantly Mexican although the character and size of the city was changing. For good descriptions of the town Powers dubbed "the Chaparral City of the Union," see: Powers, *Afoot and Alone,* 199–201; Reid, *Reid's Tramp,* 221; Browne, *Adventures,* 131–38.

A number of gold and silver strikes were made in the vicinity of Tucson during the later 1860s and early 1870s, and the city was filled with miners. See Powers, *Afoot and Alone,* 199–201 and Browne, *Adventures,* 22.

[62]This was probably the Francisco Puelas ranch near present-day Rillito. Pointer Mountain Station, eighteen miles from Tucson, was located near the ranch headquarters. Conkling, *The Butterfield Overland,* 2: 161.

[63]The reference is to the saguaro or sahuaro, the remarkable giant cactus of the Arizona desert. These huge plants, many more than one hundred years old, have attained a height of more than fifty feet. Their ability to store water is second only to that of the barrel cactus. At this point the train was traveling though the eastern

to steal they are sure to use it. Left camp at sundown. Had good road and beautiful moonlight to travail by.

August 21st.

Came about 9 miles last night. Found a pond of water sufficient for our stock and some grass but not the best. Plenty of wood and pretty place to camp. Remained here until late in the evening. Travailed until after midnight.

August 22nd.

Camped at a high peak called Pecatch that can be seen 15 miles the other side of Tucson.[64] It is 45 miles from here back to Tucson. There

---

limits of the area which today is part of the Saguaro National Monument. Federal Writers' Program, *Arizona*, 383; Conkling, *The Butterfield Overland*, 2: 164.

[64]The correct name is Picacho Peak, but the Pecatch spelling was common among the English-speaking visitors. The Butterfield Overland Mail maintained a stage station at the base of the peak which was "a prominent and picturesque landmark." Browne, *Adventures*, 130; Conkling, *The Butterfield Overland*, 2: 162; Powers, *Afoot and Alone*, 206.

Picacho Peak

is a pond of water here but our stock will not drink it. 3 miles farther there is more water said to be better than this. It can't well be worse. This is a warm and cloudy morning.

Found plenty of water and grass. Three Mexican wagons camped here. 2 woman with them. They say that there is great danger of Apache Indians here. Three men were killed near here 3 weeks ago. There is high mountains on each side. 9 miles farther will find us out of danger of Indians so we will travail tonight.

Was hard rain ahead of us this evening so did not travail very late.

August 23rd.

Did not turn our stock out of the carrell as there is no grass here. We wait to go to grass early. Travailed 3 miles and found some grass. Passed Blue Water Wells.[65] The water was cold and good but the grass was scarce and in bunches. Started at sundown and came to plenty of water and some grass better than what we had. There is a stand at Blue Wells. Some groceries here to sell, but they are very dear.

August 24th.

Are camped near another stand 12 miles from Blue Wells. There was a Pemore [sic] Indian here today. He had his face painted and long strings of beeds [sic] in his ears. He was very friendly, but all he wants is a chance to steal our stock.[66] We have found some good grass and plenty of rain water standing in ponds.

---

[65]Blue Water Wells was the next stage station northwest of Picacho Peak. It was located on the north branch of the Santa Cruz wash near present-day Toltec. In the 1850s, the stage company sank a well at the station to furnish a sufficient amount of water even in dry seasons. According to army reports of the 1860s, both grass and water were usually available at the site. Conkling, *The Butterfield Overland*, 2: 164–65; Powers, *Afoot and Alone*, 210–11; Browne, *Adventures*, 128.

[66]Pemore and Pimo were frequent nineteenth-century Anglo spellings for the Pima Indian people who lived in the Gila and Salt River valleys of Arizona. A traveler in 1858 described the Pima men as dressed "generally in the costume of Adam, with a dirty loin cloth in place of the fig leaf. . . . Their faces were painted an ebony black and their lips a rich red." New York *Herald*, November 19, 1858, quoted in Conkling, *The Butterfield Overland*, 2: 166. Bell gives an excellent description of these people and the allied Maricopa. According to his figures there were 4,117 Pima and 518 Maricopas in the area in 1858. Bell, *New Tracks*, 1: 168–77. See also Reid, *Reid's Tramp*, 222–24 and Hall, "Story," p. 13.

August 25th.

Started late and came 6 miles and stopped. The days are so very warm, but the nites are pleasant so we are laying by in the day and travail at night. It is 6 miles from here to the river.

August 26th.

There is no grass here so we will go on to the river. Arrived at the river about 12 o'clock, found some grass but it is short and salt grass so it is not good for our stock. There is some Mexicans and Indians living here. There is a white man here. He says that he will show us where there is good grass in the morning.

This place is called Sacatone village.[67] Here is where you first strike the Gila River. This river is a swift running stream, muddy. Plenty of willow and cottonwood timber along this stream. Peomore Indians are thick here. How detestable they are! All the men riding and the women walking and carrying all the load.

August 27th.

The men have found splendid grass one mile and half from camps on the opposite side of the river so we will remain here until Sunday. We reached here on Wednesday. It is 36 miles from this place to Pecatch Canion [sic]. We have found very little grass since we left Pecatch except we have very good well water to drink. The pond water down this river is more or less alkali, all of it. We did not let the stock drink it. We will travail down this river 27 miles.

The Indians are passing by here all the time. Some of them ride nice ponies. Most of the men ride and the women walk and carry the load. How detestable they are. I will be glad to get out of sight of them.

August 29th.

Left Sacatone late in the evening. Travailed 11 miles, passed many Indian huts. Camped within 1 mile of Peomore village.[68]

---

[67]The Sacatone village and mail station was approximately twenty-three miles from Blue Water Wells. Browne gives an interesting account of the village and its inhabitants. Browne, *Adventures*, 125-28. See also Conkling, *The Butterfield Overland*, 2: 165-66.

[68]Pima Villages was a designation for a series of ten Indian settlements along the Gila. A peaceable people, the Pima did not engage in wars against the whites and

August 30th.

Passed through the village this morning. There is a steam mill here, post office and huts all around. Came to Maricopa Wells before we had breakfast, a distance of 12 miles. There is a store here and two or three companies of soldiers.[69]

Oh, what warm weather. We are camped one mile from town. There is very good grass here, mostly salt grass. Poor water, most of which is mixed with alkali.

August 31st.

There is quite a pleasant wind blowing this evening and indication of rain. They are fixing to start. Will not get off from camps before sundown. We have to go 45 miles more without water so we will travail most all night. Mericopa [sic] Indians brought some melons and a few roasting ears to the camps today. They are an ignorant, silly looking people.[70]

September 1st.

Did not get to travail last night as a pony was missing. So we came one mile on the road west of town and camped here. We found good grass, not very good water. This is everything but a pretty country. Nothing but gain would ever induce any person to stay here. It is suited only for Indians to live in. We will start about 3 o'clock this evening as it is cloudy and not very warm.

---

generally had a good reputation among emigrants and other travelers. Unlike the diarist, Browne admired these people and their customs some of which he believed "might profitably be introduced into our own judiciary system." His description of the villages includes a number of sketches of the people and the villages. Browne, *Adventures*, 105–13. Also see the earlier description in Benjamin Harris, *The Gila Trail*, 80–81 and note 73.

[69]Maricopa Wells was an important stopping point for emigrants since it was the last permanent water supply before entering the "Forty Mile Desert" between the Wells and Gila Bend. In 1869, as noted in the diary, there was a trading store, blacksmith shop, and small hotel there. Conkling, *The Butterfield Overland*, 2: 169–70; Browne, *Adventures*, 102–103.

[70]The Maricopa were a Yuman tribe who lived south of the Pima along the Gila River. The Pima and Maricopa were allies in various wars and, like the Pima, the Maricopa were a generally peaceful, agricultural people. See note 66 above.

September 2nd.

Had a very pleasant time to drive and made good use of it. We drove 20 miles, stopped 3 hours before day, rested and slept, got breakfast and started. Drove about 10 miles, stopped to rest until the cool of the evening. We have found no grass of any note since we left Mericopa Wells. We have nice shade to noon in today. We will drive to water tonight.

September 3rd.

Did not get to water last night. Drove within 8 miles of Gila Bend, the watering place, and as it was very late they concluded to wait until morning to drive to water. Arrived here very early. The stock had not suffered much. There is a ranch here. Three American women living here. 'Tis a brushy, ugly place. There is no grass here but they tell us that there is plenty in 3 miles of this place. It is 45 miles from here back to Mericopa Wells.[71] This we came without grass or water.

September 4th.

Left Gila Bend this evening and drove 5 miles. Here is a good well, cold good water. Several white men living here and one American lady. Was one American lady at Gila Bend. We stopped here on account of some stock that are lost on the desert. The boys have gone to hunt them. There is some grass here. We have not seen any Indians since we left Mericopa Wells. I would not be sorry if I never did see another one.

September 5th.

The road was very dusty last night. There has not been much rain here lately. There is plenty of musquet and cottonwood timber here. They do not have any cold weather here. The gentleman that is living

---

[71]Gila Bend grew up around an old Maricopa rancheria founded by Father Kino in the late seventeenth century. This area of the road was described by Reid as "miserably desolate," and Powers labeled his trip through this part of the county "The River of Despair." Conkling, *The Butterfield Overland*, 2:171–72; Reid, *Reid's Tramp*, 230–31; Powers, *Afoot and Alone*, 224–25. A contrasting view of the Gila Valley is presented by William F. Colton in Bell, *New Tracks*, 2: 68–82.

here is making preparations to make a crop. He intends planting in 3 weeks from now. He is prepared to irrigate. He started to Calafornia last year, got this far and both his daughters married and he stopped here. All the people that live through here seem to have plenty of money but money would be no inducement for me if I had to live here. Man and his wife that was in this train stopped here to stay awhile if not all the time. Their anticipations of Calafornia are not so great as mine or they would never have stopped here.

Several young men that were in trains behind passed by here this evening. They are going horseback. Found all the stock so we will leave here this evening.

September 6th.

Left camps at sundown, drove 9 miles and stopped for the night.

September 7th.

Came to water in 2 miles and found a pretty place to camp and some grass. This place is called R. Kenion's Station. It is 17 miles from Gila Bend. Mexicans live here.[72] We have to use the river water. Our trains and stock in general look very well. Came through short Kenion's road. Is rough, about 8 miles.

September 8th.

Drove 10 miles, made dry camp. Found splendid grass and let the stock graze awhile. We would have like to stayed here day and night with this good grass but there was no water there so we came on to Oatman Flat. We taken the right hand road and came the turnpike road. There is just room between the mountains and river for the road. It has been dug in the side of the mountains so as to be safe. This road is 14 miles nearer than the one that went around the mountains

---

[72]Kinyon's Station, originally called Murderer's Grave, was seventeen miles from Gila Bend. Powers, with his usual flare for the dramatic, described the country between Kinyon's Station and Oatman Flat as a "fearful plain . . . chasmed and rent with ravines, 'depe diches and darke and dredfulle of sight'. . . ." Powers, *Afoot and Alone*, 229; Conkling, *The Butterfield Overland*, 2: 174–75.

and then that road is very rough and hard on oxen's feet. Had to pay light toll.[73] This is the warmest place that I ever saw.

September 9th.

Started from the station at sundown, and I think that we had the worst road that we have ever had but it was not very lengthy. Long, steep hills. We came 6 miles and found plenty of good grass but our stock did not have much benefit of it, there being no water here.

September 10th.

Started early and came to Berk's Station.[74] Here we found plenty of good water and very good grass. White people living here. The 28th of July this station was burned, caught by matches. Three times it has been burned and twice destroyed by water from the mountain and river. The weather is so warm here that matches kept in the shade will catch unless kept in something that will not burn.

September 11th.

Left Berk's Station in the evening. Is another stand in 5 miles of this place but we did not stop there. We came on to Stanwick's Station 12 miles from Berks.[75] Arrived at Stanwick's Station very early this morning. Stanwick's Station is a pretty place. Gentleman keeping batch there.

---

[73]Oatman Flat, a "thousand acres of bottom land almost surrounded by a perpendicular wall of black volcanic lava," was the site of a bloody massacre in 1851 in which the Royce Oatman family was killed by Apaches. The massacre is described with fair accuracy in the Shrode diary. Conkling, *The Butterfield Overland*, 2: 174–81 and note 46.

[74]Burk's Station was located on the south bank of the Gila in present-day Maricopa County. Browne described the station as "a small hacqual [sic] on the bank of the river, occupied at present by two soldiers who have charge of the Government hay." Browne, *Adventures*, 99; Conkling, *The Butterfield Overland*, 2: 181.

[75]Stanwick's Ranch, Flap Jack, or Flat Creek as it was variously called, was settled by a "Dutchman" named Stanwix in 1858. The present-day town of Stanwix in Maricopa County is eight miles southeast of the old stage station. Conkling, *The Butterfield Overland*, 2: 182.

September 12th.

Did not leave here last evening as some of the stock were missing, so we will leave this morning.

September 13th.

Made a drive of II miles. Found good grass and plenty of water. There is no station here. Passed an old station yesterday, but it was uninhabited.

September 14th.

Started late, passed Texas Hill Station, 16 miles from Stanwick's. Very good well water here. Filled up some kegs with water, then drove 5 miles to grass.[76] Pond of salt water here. Will stay here until morning.

Got late start again, came 5 miles to the river, nooned here and there was no grass here at all. Started this evening.

September 15th.

Started in the evening. Passed Mohawk Station in the night.[77] Had a very gòod road. 17 miles from Texas Hill to Mohawk Station. How glad I will be when we cross the Colorado River.

September 16th.

Had heavy sand road to pass over today. We made dry camp last night. Arrived at Antelope Station about II o'clock in the morning. We are camped near the river but there is no grass here. There is some grass 2 miles from here. Will have to drive the stock to it. There is a mountain just opposite the station that is 300 feet high. Nothing growing on it at all.[78]

---

[76]Texas Hill, or Grinnell's Station, was located near a bluff on the Gila River about two miles from a small butte known as Texas Hill. Ibid., 2: 183–84. Also see Browne, *Adventures*, 81.

[77]Mohawk Station, originally called Peterman's Station, was located in the Mohawk Mountains on the south bank of the Gila in present-day Yuma County. Conkling, *The Butterfield Overland*, 2: 184–85.

[78]Antelope Peak Station was located on the west side of Antelope Peak near the modern town of Tacna. Ibid., 2: 186. For an earlier description and a sketch of the station see Browne, *Adventures*, 82.

September 18th.

Intended starting last evening, but the cattle got away and we did not get all of them so we are still at the same camp. The weather has not been so warm for the last few days. Stationers all keep whiskey along here. 4 men that belong to the beef herd was so much intoxicated today that they knew not what they were doing. They charged and pitched around awhile, shot at the station's keeper, and then left without doing any damage to any one. 16 miles from Mohawk to Antelope.

September 19th.

Found all but three of our stock so we will leave Antelope Station this evening. Started before sundown, went to Mission Camp tonight, 16 miles.[79] The night was pleasant for travailing, but the road was extremely dusty. This morning was like winter, and I am so glad to see the change.

September 20th.

Have to drive to grass this morning, that is if we can find any. Drove three miles and found some grass and cane for the cattle to graze on. There are wagons passing the road all the time hauling to the stations. We have had deep, heavy sand most of the time since we first struck the river and will continue for 75 or 100 miles farther.

September 21st.

Drove within 2 miles of Gila City last night.[80] An old stand here. Passed Gila City today and came 6 miles farther. Found no grass,

---

[79]Mission Camp Station, near present-day Wellton, was so named because it was supposedly located on or near the site of several missions founded by Father Eusebio Kino. Browne, impressed with the magnificent view of the Corunnian Peak at the station, sketched the site. Conkling, *The Butterfield Overland*, 2: 189; Browne, *Adventures*, 78–79.

[80]Gila City was the site of an old placer mining camp about a half mile northwest of present-day Dome. The mining boom was relatively short lived, but the name Gila City was retained. Browne describes the place as "very pretty, encircled . . . by volcanic hills . . . and pleasantly overlooking the bend of the river." Conkling, *The Butterfield Overland*, 2: 190–91; Browne, *Adventures*, 76.

246 / HO FOR CALIFORNIA!

bought hay to feed the cattle. We have lost a good many cattle now, and I fear we will lose many more as grass is so scarce. Nothing at Gila City but one station. It is now 14 miles to Fort Uma [sic].

September 22nd.

Drove within one mile of Fort Uma last night. Had a splendid road. Passed through town today. The fort is a beautiful place on a high hill that commands a full view of Arizona City.[81] The fort is on the other side of the river and Arizonia [sic] City on this side. Goods and groceries are cheap here. Very few pretty houses in the city. Dissa-pointed several times when I got here. First, we got no letter and then we were expecting to get vegetables when we got here but there is very few here. They are expecting 3 boats every day that will bring vegetables.

September 26th.

Camped 6 miles from town at the crossing on the Colorado. Found some grass and cane for the stock. Very pretty place to camp. The Colorado is 150 yards wide I suppose. Muddy but it is good tasted [sic]. There is no timber on the banks here. Very thick brush and high weeds all the way from town down here. A boat came up, but brought no vegetables. The Gila passes into this river just at Fort Uma. The musquitoes are very bad here.

We next have a desert of 40 miles without grass so we will stay here several days. Our stock did not look well when we got here. I do regret having to lay by when we get so near. We have travailed down the Gila River 228 miles. It is 320 miles from Arizonia City to Tucson and it is 250 miles from Arizonia City to Los Angeles.

---

[81]Fort Yuma was established in 1850 on the east side of the Colorado River about half a mile below its confluence with the Gila. In 1851 the post was moved to the west bank of the Colorado opposite the little settlement of Arizona City. During the 1850s the town became increasingly important as hundreds of emigrant trains camped there waiting to cross the Colorado. The brief mining boom of the 1850s also brought an increased population and dance halls and gambling houses mushroomed. River steamers belonging to the Colorado Steam Navigation Company began supplying the area in 1852. This service, mentioned by the diarist, continued until the completion of the Southern Pacific Railroad in 1876. Good descriptions of the fort and town are in Browne, *Adventures*, 55–66; Powers, *Afoot and Alone*, 235; Bell, *New Tracks*, 2: 82–83.

September 29th.

We have now been camped at this place 3 days and have had so much trouble with the stock since we came here. The brush and weeds are so thick that we cannot ride through it. We will cross the river today. There has been Indians here every day since we came to this place. They bring little melons here to sell.

October 1st, 1869.

We have been camped in Calafornia at last. There is a stand here and an American man and lady lives here. This side of the river looks no better than the other. Nothing but mountains and sand and brush. Some of our stock that we could not get that we will have to leave on the other side of the river as there is no grass here to graze on. There was a death in the camp on the 30th, an infant, 10 months old, of Mrs. Collins. They are from Arkansas. It was a pretty corpse. They buried it near the station under a tree. Poor little child, it is now at rest.

We bought some nice apples, onions, and potatoes from a gentleman that is just from Los Angeles in Calafornia. He gives a favorable report of that country.

October 2nd.

Left yesterday about 10 o'clock. We will have no more grass of any consequence for 40 miles.[82] Our ferriage and feed for our cattle cost 30 dollars what time we stayed at the station.

We drove 6 miles and came to a Mexican ranch. Here they told us that if we would drive 6 miles that we would find good grass. So taking their word, with an Indian for pilot, we drove about 4 miles and found some grass and water but it was so boggy that we could not have watered and the Indians were numerous. What could we do, nothing but turn around and go back to the Mexican's ranch. So we started back about one hour high and made the trip safe back not long after dark. Here we bought green corn to feed with. Had some watermelons today.

---

[82]On both the northern and southern routes, emigrants had to face a long desert march near the end of their journey. The forty-mile Colorado Desert was described by one traveler as "a vast desert zone west of the Colorado, a forbidding waste of heavy trackless sands and shifting dunes." Conkling, *The Butterfield Overland,* 2: 211–27. For other descriptions of the route in the 1850s and 60s see: Reid, *Reid's Tramp,* 236–38; Browne, *Adventures,* 47–51; Powers, *Afoot and Alone,* 237–39.

There is sand hill after hill to be seen to the west with nothing at all on them. We are most ready to start again. We will travail tonight. The little Indian huts are thick. I will be glad when I get out of sight of them. They burn all their dead, and if they chance to have a horse it hast [sic] to be burned alive with them. When the dead body is burned they eat the horse and reserve a portion for the spirit that is gone for when it returns.

We came to a station, 14 miles, last night. Had a heavy, sand road most of the way. This is the most destitute country of grass that we have ever travailed over. We will not feed at this stand but will start in the morning and go to the next one, a distance of 18 miles.[83]

October 3rd, Sabbath morning.

We travailed most all day. Reached the stand in the evening, finding plenty of barley and hay to feed with. Remained here until the next evening. We went to the next stand that night. Feed with hay and barley.

October 3rd. [Note: There is some confusion of dates here.]

We reached New River.[84] This river is caused by the rise of the Colorado. It is not running now, but there is ponds that is sufficient for the stock. There is a well here, but the water is not good. Here are found plenty of musquet beans and dry grass for the stock, the first

---

[83]The first station mentioned was probably Cooke's Wells, opened by Colonel Phillip St. George Cooke in 1846. The wells were enlarged and deepened by the Overland Mail crews, and the site also served as a mail station. The second station mentioned was probably Gardner's Wells, about fourteen miles from Cooke's. Browne noted there were four stations on the Yuma-Carrizo route, Cooke's Wells, Gardner's, Alamo Mocho, and Indian Wells, where the water was "tolerably good." Browne, *Adventures*, 50. See also: Conkling, *The Butterfield Overland*, 2: 217–18, 221; Reid, *Reid's Tramp*, 237.

[84]As the diarist notes, New River was the new channel of the Colorado River which broke through its banks and inundated the region in 1849–50. Along with the wells mentioned above, it was one of the few watering spots along the desert road. At New River, Powers encountered a family of "Yankees" who ran a station and small store which offered "cans of fruit . . . sardines, pocket handkerchiefs, little cloth packages of cut tobacco, and a vast array of California wines. . . ." Powers, *Afoot and Alone*, 239–40. On the importance of the river to emigrants, see Conkling, *The Butterfield Overland*, 2: 221–22, 224–25, and Couts, *From San Diego*, 18–22.

they have had since we crossed the river. There is few goods and groceries here. It is 45 miles to the crossing of the river. We have found plenty of water on the desert.

October 6th.

We will leave New River this evening. 15 miles to the next stand.[85] Here we find dry grass and beans for the stock and plenty of lagoon water, some better than the last we had. Remained here 2 days. Leave this evening.

October 8th.

So we now have 32 miles to go without water. We will go 15 miles tonight. There we will find some grass.

October 9th.

Had a heavy sand road last night. Got here about midnight. Will start at 3 o'clock this evening and drive to water tonight. The nights are very cool and pleasant. We will soon be across the much dreaded desert and we found the road much better than we expected. If you ever do travail this road you need not believe half the things that people tells you.

October 10th.

Reached the water about 3 o'clock in the morning. But very little grass here. Bought hay to feed with. Beautiful little running branch. Here are groceries to sell. Here it is 18 miles to grass.[86] We will go there tonight.

---

[85]This was probably Indian Wells, about two miles from present-day Silsbee, California. The exact location is not clear from the diary and the writer might also be referring to Laguna Station five miles west of Silsbee. Conkling, *The Butterfield Overland*, 2: 223, 225.

[86]The train had reached Carrizo Creek near the boundary line between Imperial and San Diego counties. Named for a native cane which grew along its banks, the creek was a "shallow clear running stream" and the area offered "abundant water, grass and wood" to weary desert travelers. Ibid., 2: 227; Reid, *Reid's Tramp*, 238.

From Carrizo to the northern boundary of San Diego County there were six stage stations: Carrizo, Palm Springs, Vallecito, San Felipe, Warner's, and Oak Grove. A brief description of the road and each site is in Hoover, *Historic Spots*, 342.

October 11th.

Arrived at the stand just after sunrise. Travailed all night, found very good grass and water. An American family living here. 25 miles across the mountains there is a settlement of Americans, the first settlement that you come to. It is on the San Diego road.[87]

October 13th.

Have rested two days. We will leave for the next stand this morning, 18 miles distant from this place. We will go there tonight. They say that we will have no more bad water to use. I think we have used our full share of it and we are now done with the dust and sand. There has not been any rain here this summer.

October 19th.

I have not opened my Journal for some time and have nothing to give as a reason for neglecting my writing. We had a pleasant camp at St. Phillipps [sic] with plenty of grass and water but we had some rough road to pass over before we got there. Stayed there two days. It is a small valley with mountains all around and heavy timber on the sides and top of the mountains. Mexican family living here and some white men. Grocery and a few goods.[88] 15 miles from there to Warner's wranch [sic]. Here is a very nice American family. This is a very pretty place. We have had plenty of potatoes and cabbage, very large, since we came here. This is the best grass that we have had for 300 miles. We have also had some large apples and delicious grapes.[89] Had a few sprinkles of rain this morning and it is still cloudy.

---

[87]The travelers had reached Vallecito, an important stopping point along the road. The American woman referred to may have been Mrs. John Hart, widow of the station and store owner at Vallecito. Powers titled the valley as an "oasis" after the long desert crossing, and Browne described the road from Vallecito to Laguna as "a continued feast for the soul of an artist." Conkling, *The Butterfield Overland*, 2: 229, 233; Powers, *Afoot and Alone*, 243–44; Browne, *Adventures*, 45.

[88]The reference is to San Felipe, eighteen miles northwest of Vallecito in the San Felipe valley. Both Browne and Powers noted the beauty of the area although Powers reported that "California-like there was a flowing bar in the station, but of things to eat, not so much as a cracker." Powers, *Afoot and Alone*, 245–47; Browne, *Adventures*, 45. See also Conkling, *The Butterfield Overland*, 2: 236.

[89]Warner's Ranch, one of the most popular stopping places along the California road, was originally the home of Jonathan T. Warner and was noted, in earlier years, for the hospitality of its owner. Although Warner lost the property in 1861, his

Left Warner's wranch after dinner, drove 9 miles and found a fine camping place. Passed through a beautiful valley.

October 21st.

Camped by a nice little stream of water. Had very good grass.

October 24th.

We have been camped 2 nights and 2 days near a stand called Oak Grove.[90] Here we have splendid grass but not very good water. Two of the boys have gone on horseback to the Monte to make a selection of places.[91] We will leave this morning. We are expecting to meet our friends.

We are camped tonight in a pretty place. Two families of Negroes live here. Here we got plenty of nice cabbage, the largest head of cabbage very cheap. These Negroes are wealthy.

The boys met our friends and one of them came back. Met our sister and brother today. Oh, how glad we all are to meet again.

October 26th.

All camped by a lake called Little Lagoon.[92] Mexican wranch here. Had a splendid road all day. This lake is 8 miles long and 5 miles wide.

---

successors continued the use of the name. Conkling, *The Butterfield Overland*, 2: 238–41. For more details see Joseph T. Hill, *The History of Warner's Ranch and Its Environs* (Los Angeles: Priv. pub., 1927).

[90]"Oak Grove describes itself," wrote Powers, "being a little wooded bain beside the brooke, among these unfading hills." The site, sixteen miles northwest of Warner's is one of the few old stations that has been preserved. The building still retains much of the atmosphere of earlier times and is now operated as a tavern. Powers, *Afoot and Alone*, 253; Conkling, *The Butterfield Overland*, 2:241–42; Federal Writers' Program, *California: A Guide to the Golden State*, rev. ed., (New York: Hastings House, 1967), 540.

[91]El Monte, where the family evidently intended to settle, grew up around the home and hotel operated by Ira Thompson. The area, thirteen miles east of the modern Los Angeles Civic Center, and its settlement are described in Root, *Following the Pot of Gold* and Powers, *Afoot and Alone*, 268–69. For a brief history of this spot "at the end of the trail," see Hoover, *Historic Spots*, 165.

[92]Although the diarist refers to the lake as Little Lagoon this was undoubtedly Laguna Grande or La Laguna, a stage station located at the northwestern corner of Laguna Grande or Lake Elsinore. A description of the road from Carrizo to La Laguna in 1880 by William Collier is reprinted in Hoover, *Historic Spots*, 291. See also: Conkling, *The Butterfield Overland*, 2: 246; Federal Writers' Program, *California*, 524; Powers, *Afoot and Alone*, 257–58.

October 28th.

Crossed the Santeanna River [sic] yesterday. Had no trouble in crossing. The bottom of the river is quicksand but there had been a good deal of crossing so that the bottom was firm. We here passed over a beautiful valley today.

The party had nearly reached its destination which may explain why the diary stops so abruptly at this point.

David S. and Maria H. Shrode

us Traveled 18 miles & camped near Laguna Station at a well down in a dry branch water salty Wed 21st Traveled over Sandy road found a little grass Thur 22nd Moved on to Mountain Springs where we found white folks & a John Chinaman for cook Friday 23rd Started on up the Mill— mountains found very good road for 2 miles took a right hand road in in order to cut off a 2 or 3 miles and when we had gone the other way had to unload till the hills were so steep got to mothers Station where we camped on a Spring branch plenty grass & water Sat 24 Traveled on camped at an old ranch belonging

to Mr Hayden Sunday 24 went on toward B... met him on the road He knew us Some Dist Hollowell Chrismas Gift got to the mountains like to send for a yoke of cattle to pull our wagon up the hill got to Baltimore allright found them all well and looking for us had a good dinner prepared for us which was very acceptable Staid there a week moved down the valley 12 miles here our mules were stolen by the Mexicans and they refused to give them up

Mrs. Maria Shrode

Journal

May 16 [1870].

Mr. Shrode bought John Cant's horse for $75 in gold. Today have traveled over some very fine farming country, land black and rich, some beautiful farms. Grass good, water plentiful. Camped at Hopkin's Store.[1]

May 17th.

Smallpox in the neighborhood created some excitement among mamas and papas too.

May 18th.

Started on. Traveled a little over the roughest road I ever traveled in my life. We passed through what is called the Devil's Race Tracks. Two mile heat [sic] and then to a little town called White Rock.[2] There I traded a little. Goods high. That night camped near Hog Eye. One man said the hog was there yet but the eye was pruned out.[3]

May 19th.

Camped on the head of the Sabine River and everybody and his wife and all their children went hunting strawberries. We had to herd the cattle on the prairie without any fence or pen, so we made a fence on one side with our wagons to herd the cattle. That night they stampeded twice.

---

[1] The first page of the diary is illegible. The party left Sulphur Bluff on or about May 10, 1870, and for the next few days were traveling in Hopkins County. For Sulphur Bluffs and the surrounding area, see D. H. Hare, *The Tell of Time: People, Places and Things of Sulphur Bluffs and Hopkins County, Texas* (Hereford, Texas: Pioneer Book Publishers, 1972), 5–23, 34–37.

[2] White Rock was a small community in Hunt County northwest of present-day Greenville. It was settled about 1880, but evidently there was a small population concentrated in the area prior to that date. *Handbook of Texas*, 2: 897.

[3] Although there were several locations in Texas called Hog Eye, the reference here is probably to a location on Hog Creek in southern Grayson County. See Fred Tarpley, *Place Names of Northeast Texas* (Commerce, Texas: East Texas State University, 1969), 80.

Next morning started on. Traveled about 16 miles over rough roads and through thickets. The cattle stampeded three times in the day.

May 20th.

Camped within 5 miles of Kentucky Town where water was plenty but wood was scarce.[4]

May 21st.

Layed over for the cattle to graze.

May 22nd Sabbath.

Stayed at the same camp. Miss Sue Settle was sick. Sunday evening Brother Settle preached a very good sermon under an Elm tree to a very respectable congregation. I thought of the Isrealites while marching to the land of Canaan. The people behaved very well and paid very good attention to the word preached, and I hope the seed soon may bring forth a hundred fold.

May 23rd, Monday.

Moved on leaving Brother Settle and family at a Mr. Aldreages until Sue got better.

May 24th Tuesday.

Traveled about 15 miles over a fine farming country. Toward evening got on a hill or long ridge. We could see all around as far as the eye could reach. Saw Sherman eight miles distant to the right.[5] Camped on the headwater of Little Elm. One of our men killed a white black snake. It looked just like a black racer only it was white.

That day traveled over fine grazing country. Good grass and plenty of water strongly impregnated with iron.

---

[4]Kentuckytown was a small community in eastern Grayson County. Settled in the 1830s, it was located on the stage road between Jefferson and Sherman and was a thriving and prosperous village until the coming of the railroad in the 1880s. Ibid., 8; *Handbook of Texas*, 1: 950. Also see Mattie Davis Lucas and Mita H. Hall, *A History of Grayson County, Texas* (Sherman, Texas: Scruggs Printing Co., 1936), 68–69.

[5]Sherman, established in the 1830s, was the first county seat of Grayson County. Its location on the Overland Mail route and the Texas Trail from Fort Washita made Sherman an important trade and distribution center. *Handbook of Texas*, 2: 604; Lucas, *History of Grayson County*, 80–81. An excellent description of Sherman and the surrounding countryside in the 1870s, is D. H. Pope, *Sherman and Grayson County* (Sherman, Texas: Democrat Printing Office, 1873).

May 25th.

Camped within five miles of Pilot Point in Denton County on a boggy creek.[6] One yoke of cattle got in the bog twice and had to be pulled out. Staid there two nights and branded all the cattle in one brand and washed, visited each other, and had a very pleasant time.

May 27th.

Camped one and a half miles of Big Elm. Laid over til Monday morning.

May 28th.

Received fifty odd head of cattle into the herd. While we was laying over some washed, some watched the camps, some fished, some visited, and some of the boys herded cattle. Some went hunting and some went in bathing and looked like somebody else when they came in they was washed off so clean and looked so fresh.

May 29th was Sabbath.

May 30th Monday.

Had a very hard rain and storm. Had to hold our tent pole to prevent it capsizing. One of our men killed a mule-earred rabbit and dressed it and we had a nice fry. Rained till two o'clock, cleared off late in the evening. Went to bid Brother Joe Gregg farewell. He started home in company with his nephew, Josiah Gregg, Jr.

May 31st.

Traveled 10 or 12 miles. Camped on Dry Hickory. Had a delightful camp ground in a grove of elms with good water.

June 1st.

Started on, but through the contraryness [sic] of Bob we had to stay about two hours on a high hill. While we waited, Sarah and I walked a mile to a high knob where some one had piled up some rocks and made a pillar about four feet high. We piled another pile still higher and wrote our names and the day and month and year and walked back

---

[6]See Bunyard, ''Diary,'' note 5.

to our wagons and was ready for starting when the balance came up. We then traveled on and crossed Denton Creek and went about 2 miles to another little stream called Oliver and camped where there was plenty of wood and water and excellent grass.

June 2nd.

Laid to on account of Mr. Scott being sick. Here Bob came back after his cattle. If we would not leave Scott he was going to take out his cattle and go on and leave us.

There it rained and stormed at night. We had to hold our tent to keep it from breaking the ridge pole. Next morning the cattle was scattered everywhere. We had lost about 70 head.

June 3rd.

Moved on 7 or 8 miles and camped by a fence in the prairie. Had to burn pieces of fence rails for firewood.

June 4th.

Laid over waiting for Brother Settle. Got a letter from him. Sue was no better. He did not think she could live but a few days longer. This morning our cattle broke out of the pen and scattered everywhere, but they found the most of them. Last night it rained again and it is raining now.

June 5th Sunday.

Still in the same place. Went to Prairie Point to preaching.[7] Heard an excellent sermon from Rev. 24:17 preached by a L. Brother by the name of Bradford B. Hunnicut. He is on this circuit but has been prevented from attending to his work on account of sickness in his family.

June 6th Monday.

Still in camps. It is still raining. Friday Mr. Shrode started back to meet Brother Settle and has not come back yet.

---

[7]Prairie Point was a small community in southwestern Cooke County just a few miles north of the Denton County line. *Handbook of Texas*, 2: 406.

June 7th Tuesday.

Still waiting for news from Brother Settle. Jake was sick yesterday and was taking medicine. He is some better today.

June 8th Wednesday.

Still in the same camps. Last night it rained and stormed tremendiously [sic]. I never slept until after 2 o'clock in the morning. I was uneasy about Mr. Shrode. Jake is better.

June 9th.

Mr. Shrode has got in. Miss Sue Settle was no better, no hopes of her recovery.

June 10th.

Still at the camps, water bound. Can't cross the West Fork of the Trinity River.

June 11th.

Moved down to the river Sunday morning. The river had fallen about 7 inches. Saturday we stopped an hour or two at Prairie Point. There I was invited to dine with Mrs. Hane, quite an accomplished lady. She has a good school and is a good teacher from what I learned by her patrons and from observation. After dinner she gave us two or three tunes on the piano. This is a beautiful country and a wide field for emigrants and for the Herald of the Cross.

June 12th Sunday.

Laid by on the Trinity still till they made a raft to cross on.

June 13th Monday.

Fixing to start for the river. Crossed the river on the raft. Moved on two or three miles and camped.

June 14th, Tuesday.

Got to Veal's Station.[8]

---

[8]Veal's Station, in Parker County, was on the mail and stage route between Weatherford and Decatur. Cates, *Pioneer History*, 155; H. Smythe, *Historical Sketch of Parker County and Weatherford, Texas* (St. Louis: Louis C. Lavat, 1877), 32.

June 15th Wednesday.

Camped on the waters of Clear Creek. That night it rained and stormed and lightened and thundered tremendiously. Seven of the boys were out til after midnight with the cattle. I did not sleep any till the rain was over. O, how weak and small I feel in a storm away out here on these high bold prairies in a tent. But God in his mercies has taken care of us so far, and I do not doubt his kindness in the future if we will only trust him.

June 16th Thursday.

Still in camps, waterbound by the Clear Creek. We have the best of water and wood, the wood being dead liveoak. There is a good mast here, the little bushes are not over a foot high, laden with acorns.

June 17th Friday.

Moved on across the creek. Took the wrong road and traveled about four miles out of our way. Found we were wrong, turned round and took the back track and came to the right road, but one of the teamsters turned a wagon over in turning around. But it did not do much damage except bursting a couple of flour barrels open, so we picked up the things and reloaded and traveled on. Camped in a live oak grove. Rained a little that night.

June 18th Saturday.

Moved on to Dennis Pen and camped on Rucker's Creek in Hood County 10 miles from Camanche [sic] Peak and two miles from the Brazos River.[9]

June 19th Sunday.

Still in camps waiting for the river to run down. It still rains on us everyday a little. This part can come up with Arkansas for hills and

---

[9]Dennis Pen was the forerunner of the small town of Dennis, eighteen miles southwest of Weatherford on the Brazos River near Rucker's Creek. Comanche Peak, a high (1200 feet), flat mesa in what is now Hood County was an important early landmark. *Handbook of Texas,* 1: 385, 491; T. T. Ewell, *History of Hood County Texas from Its Earliest Settlement to the Present* (Granbury, Texas: Granbury News, 1895), 6.

vales and rocks. Poor soil, but plenty of good wash water and some good springs.

June 20th.

Today is my birthday. I am 44 years old. We are still in camps.

June 23rd Thursday.

Still at the same place waiting for the river to fall. Today about 12 o'clock Brother Settle and all his family, except his daughter Susan, arrived in camps. They left her in the burial ground near Kentucky Town. We mourned for her loss but we expect to meet her in the land of Rest where there is no more parting. We rejoiced to see the balance of them once more.

June 25th Saturday.

Still here waiting for the river to fall. Yesterday John Haines was going to ride a wild horse of J. Gregg's and just as he was getting on the horse he laid down on his side and caught John's leg under him and hurt him pretty badly. Then Jack Pickle rode him, and he done some tall pitching, but Jack stuck the tighter. The river is falling very fast. Think we can get across tomorrow.

June 26th Sunday.

Still here. Getting very tired of these old camps.

June 27th Monday.

Pulled up stakes and started. Crossed the Brazos River and drove the cattle all across and did not lose many of them. We all got over safe and was very grateful to our Heavenly Father for his protection. Camped near Granberry.[10]

June 28 Tuesday.

This morning two yokes of our cattle are missing.

---

[10]Granbury, in Hood County, was settled in 1854 by Thomas Lambert who donated the townsite. In 1870, Granbury was a growing and prosperous settlement with attractive rock buildings many of which are still in use today. *Handbook of Texas*, 1: 715; Ewell, *History of Hood*, 7.

June 29th Wednesday.

Found our oxen. Drove on to Squaw Creek to camp.

June 30 Thursday.

Traveled on and camped on the waters of the Paluxy.

July 1st, Friday.

Arrived at Stephensville. Found some of our old acquaintances.[11] Moved on two miles and camped on the left of the road. Two of our men stayed in town til late and started for camps and missed us and went on to the first house, 10 miles distant, and stayed the night. That night we camped near a house and the gentleman came to the camps and stayed till late. His wife thought some wolves was Indians and she screamed louder than the wolves howled and frightened some of us considerably.

July 2nd Saturday.

Moved on ten or twelve miles and camped near where a man had a fight with an Indian. He was herding cattle and got off his horse and hobbled it and got down to watch his cattle. He heard something and looked at his horse and there was an Indian within thirty yards of him. He had unhobbled his horse. So then they went at it for the horse. The Indian shot an arrow at the man while he was getting his Navy [revolver] ready. He had a shield that he kept moving about to keep the balls from striking him.

We had to travel today, it being the first Sabbath we have traveled since we started. The grass was not good, and we went about 7 miles to find grass on the waters of the Leon. We met some men from Red River County in search of a murderer.

July 4th.

Crossed the Leon River and camped on the water of the same 2 miles from Camanche. The river was high enough to run into the lowest wagon beds and into our hack bed. That night we camped on the savannah where there was plenty of sand burrs.

---

[11]Stephenville, an early agricultural and ranching center in Erath County was settled in 1854. When the county was organized in 1856, Stephenville became the county seat. *Handbook of Texas*, 2: 668.

July 5th Tuesday.

Arrived at Camanche, a flourishing little town.[12] Traded some. Goods as cheap as they are in Hopkins County.

July 6th Wednesday.

Travelled through a fine farming country through the Caddo Mountains. The valleys are a mile to two or three miles wide. Grass is running mesquite mixed with the curly and a kind of blue grass.[13]

July 7th Thursday.

Crossed the Pecan Bayou and camped on the shore. Good grass but too much timber for lariating our horses. We have to guard our horses every night to keep the Indians from stealing them.

That night it rained a fine rain. We penned our cattle on the other side and the hands crossed them over in the rain. Before we left it was swimming depth to a horse.

July 8th Friday.

Traveled 6 miles and camped on a fine stream of good water and all hands went to cooking. Dinner over, we all went to washing. This is a beautiful country and all we need is settlers and railroads to make it one of the finest countries that I have seen in Texas.

July 9th Saturday.

Traveled about 10 miles and it commenced raining. We camped on the waters of the Jim Ned in Coleman County.[14] Plenty of timber and water and the range has been very good. There is too much stock here, but the cattle look in fine order. The cattle look almost a third larger

---

[12]Comanche, the county seat of Comanche County, was established in 1858. The town served as the principal supply center for surrounding ranches, but it was still a small frontier settlement in 1870. Stephen Powers, who visited the town in 1868, called it ''the uttermost end of human habitations.'' Powers, *Afoot and Alone*, 129.

[13]The Caddo Mountains are a series of small hills in southern Callahan and northern Brown counties. The principal peaks are West Caddo and East Caddo. *Handbook of Texas*, 1: 533.

[14]Coleman County was organized in 1858 with the county seat at Camp Colorado (note 15 below). The county was well known for its lush grass and running streams of which the Jim Ned was one of the largest. Several important trails, including the Van Dorn Military Road and John Chisum's ''Jinglebob'' Trail, passed through the

than they do in Eastern Texas. O, if the poor people in the Northern and Eastern states only knew what fine land and what good range we have here, I think they would not live on rented land any longer. Corn and wheat and vegetables and melons and pumpkins and squashes grow fine here in these valleys.

July 10th Sunday.

Crossed the Jim Ned, a bold, swift stream. Got to the prairie to Camp Colorado. This is an old fort, now abandoned.[15]

July 11th Monday.

All went to washing and remained at the same place. Today we have been on the road two months.

July 12th Tuesday.

We crossed the Jim Ned and went across the valley and ascended the hill on the south. O, what a beautiful scene presents itself to the eye. The full moon is rising in all her majesty in the east. The valley of the Jim Ned to the north and hills to the south and west and about half a mile down in the valley is a village of prairie dogs and here are our wagons and tents stretched out in a line. The children are playing on the green grass, some running races, some riding each other. One of the little boys has a saddle girted on him like a horse and when his rider mounts him he is pretty sure to pitch him over his head. Then you hear the joyous laugh from every little throat. Some of them are mimicing oxen while others drive them and some of the larger boys are trying their strength and activity by restling [sic] and jumping. O, if we all could enjoy the trip as well as the children do how happy the time would pass away.

---

county. Ibid., 1:372, 913. See also Beatrice G. Gay, *Into the Setting Sun* (Santa Anna, Texas: n.p., n.d.), 1-4.

[15]Camp Colorado was established in 1856 on the Colorado River in Coleman County and moved the following year to a new location on the Jim Ned near the Fort Belknap-Fort Mason road. The old post soon became a thriving community and the "center of Coleman County's settlements" until it was abandoned in 1861. *Handbook of Texas*, 1:279; Gay, *Into the Setting Sun*, 8-9, 34.

Camp Scene

July 13th Wednesday.

Still at the same camp. Brother Settle is hunting a yoke of cattle that got away a few nights ago and Eli is buying and branding some cattle and some others have bought some oxen.

July 14 Thursday.

Drove about 14 miles. Overtook some more immigrants, four families in all, 6 wagons. This is still a beautiful country. We passed Santa Anna's Mt. It looks like two immense potato hills leveled off at the top. The southern peak is the smallest.[16] We saw some antelopes today and hundreds of prairie dogs. They would stand up on their hind feet and bark as hard and fast as if they were large dogs when

---

[16]The Santa Anna Mountains are a small range in eastern Coleman County. Santa Anna's Mountain, the most prominent peak, has an elevation of 2,000 feet and is a well-known landmark. Many local legends and stories center on the mountain. *Handbook of Texas*, 2: 568; Gay, *Into the Setting Sun*, 167–74.

they are nothing but purps [sic]. One of the boys killed one and brought it into camps yesterday. They are a little larger than a fox squirrel with short legs and tail. They are of a brownish red and the tip of their tail has black hairs on it. They live on grass and herbs and when they eat out the range they move to better range. We saw owls and rattlesnakes in their habitations. The snakes are nearly white, from living underground I suppose.

July 15 Friday.

Traveled 12 miles and camped on a spring branch thirty yards wide in places and deep enough to swim a horse. I caught a trout that would weigh 5 lbs. and one turtle.

July 16th Saturday.

Camped on the Colorado River. Next morning some of our oxen were missing and we hunted about three hours and found them. Then 5 of the boys were out still looking for them and we was very uneasy until they got in, but they came in after all without a scratch.

July 17th Sunday.

We crossed the Colorado and traveled about three miles and crossed the Concho River. Went on five or six miles and camped within a mile of the river.

July 18th Monday.

Laid up on account of Cassa Weatherford being sick. Most of us went fishing and we caught several fine cats and had a fine fry.

July 19th Tuesday.

Some of our oxen missing. Could not find them and so we remained at the same campground. Some of the boys saw some elks today and a panther and we have seen some buffalos. Cassa is better.

July 20th Wednesday.,

Moved about two miles closer to the river. Four of the boys went back to hunt for the oxen. Ida Weatherford is sick today. Some of the men are fishing and some of the women are washing while some watches the camp and guards the horses.

July 21st Thursday.

Cassa and Ida are both better and we have got all our oxen and are ready for starting. Traveled about 12 miles and camped on the Concho. Saw two live wolves and several buffalo carcasses but no live ones.

July 22nd Friday.

Camped on the Concho within about 5 miles of Concho post.[17] Eddie Weatherford was very sick all day and that night and the next day.

July 23 Saturday.

Moved to the post or near it and camped on the Concho again. Here our cattle has to be inspected and our names and ages has to be given to an officer.

July 24th Sunday.

Remained at camps until 2 or 3 o'clock, then moved on two miles and camped on the Concho.

July 25th Monday.

Traveled 7 or 8 miles and camped near the mountains where the Negro soldiers and Indians had a fight a few days since.

July 26th Tuesday.

Camped on the Concho in a wide valley. Cassa's child is worse. Several not very well this evening.

July 28th Wednesday.

Mrs. Weatherford's child died about nine o'clock. We hauled him to the station to bury him.[18]

---

[17]The reference is to Fort Concho (see previous diary, note 23). At this point the train joined the route of the Goodnight-Loving cattle trail, the third most important trail in terms of the number of cattle driven over it. After reaching the Pecos, the trail turned north along the river to Fort Sumner, New Mexico. An excellent description of the route and a brief history of the trail is Donald Bubur, "The Goodnight-Loving Trail," in Wayne Gard, et al., *Along the Early Trails of the Southwest* (Austin: Pemberton Press, 1969), 133–52.

[18]The reference is probably to the Concho mail station three miles south of Fort Concho. Conkling, *The Butterfield Overland,* 1: 363.

July 28th Thursday.

Moved on 14 or 15 miles and camped on the Concho where we found good grass and plenty of water but found a yoke of our cattle was missing. Supposed they were left at the station, our last camp. Eli and Jake went back to look for them and have not got in yet.

July 29th Friday.

All better this morning except Mr. Shrode. Drove on 15 miles to another station at the head of the Concho River where we found a fine spring. That day passed an old fort or rather the ruins of a fort.[19] Went about 4 miles and camped where the Indians chased the mail coach 3 or 4 miles and then gave up the chase and went on with their drove of mules and cattle that they had stolen. But we have none of us seen or smelt an Indian yet.

July 30th Saturday.

Camped out on the plains 15 miles from the head of the Concho River. We are still in a valley surrounded by hills, but we are ascending gradually.

July 31st Sunday.

Have to drive 20 miles to water. Plenty of wood on the road for cooking purposes. Drove 8 miles and found a good pool of water and rested 3 hours and then drove on about 11 miles and found a pool of water. Camped about 3 o'clock and began to prepare for the desert. We still find wood plenty. The mesquit is all over these plains and looks like an old peach orchard. Turned out we are now within five miles of where we will have to haul water 40 miles and our stock will have to do without till we get to the Pecos River. We passed two graves yesterday and one today.

August 1st Monday.

This morning the stage passed us. It is something refreshing to see

---

[19]The "fort ruins" mentioned by the diarist were probably the ruins of one of the large, fortified Butterfield stage stops, possibly the one described by the Conklings as Llano Estacado station. Ibid., 1: 367–68.

even the mail coach away out here in these vast plains with only the driver and guard. Even an old broke down ox or a flock of snipes will break the monotony of the plains. Passed the Central Station (now abandoned) today and stopped 2 miles beyond and ate dinner and filled our vessels (not previously filled at the Concho),[20] Watered the oxen and cattle and started about 3 o'clock p.m. and traveled about 12 hours, then rested the oxen while we made coffee and ate our breakfasts. We then moved on for five hours more and stopped again and watered our horses and mules out of our barrels. We are near the Castle Mountains.

August 2nd Tuesday.

Still traveling. Not yet to the Pecos. These plains are not barren but have spots of grass and a low scrubby growth of mesquit and other growths and the Spanish dagger grows very large on the plains. I have seen some that would measure ten inches in diameter and six or eight feet high. A mile distant they resemble a man very much.[21]

Tuesday evening we got to the Pecos before we knew it. The river runs along in the prairie and half a mile off you would never think there was a stream of water there. We passed through the mountains today and there is the grandest scenery that I ever saw in my life. If it had not been for the bones of dead cattle strewed round in every direction I could have enjoyed the romantic scenery.[22]

August 3rd Wednesday.

Still in camps resting our teams and horses.

---

[20]Central Station was on the Finckling mail line from El Paso to San Antonio. It was located about thirty miles from the head of the Concho River near Castle Gap. *Texas Almanac, 1869,* 156. See also Bunyard, ''Diary,'' note 27.

[21]Travelers often noted the resemblance between the Spanish dagger plants and people. For example, Reid mistook ''a vast number of Spanish bayonets'' for attacking Indians. Reid, *Reid's Tramp,* 130.

[22]Although the Castle Mountains and the surrounding countryside, as described in both the southern route diaries, were considered to have spectacular scenery, the long drive from the Concho to the Pecos over some of the driest and most desolate country in Texas resulted in heavy stock losses to both cattle trains and emigrant trains. Bubur, ''The Goodnight-Loving Trail,'' 140–41; Conkling, *The Butterfield Overland,* 1: 365.

August 4th Thursday.

Traveled 12 miles up the Pecos. This stream is deep and the water is red and muddy, not unlike the Red River.

August 5th Friday.

Moved on 12 miles and camped on the Pecos again.

August 6th Saturday.

Moved on 2 miles, met two wagons and 15 men from New Mexico. One of the men turned back with us. Today we traveled 12 miles and camped about one mile from the river where there was mesquit brush and cactus with all kinds of thorns.

Today we had a good shower of rain which laid the dust and cooled the air and made traveling more pleasant. This climate is cool and very pleasant in the day and at night a blanket feels more comfortable with a good quilt on top of that.

August 7th Sunday.

Moved on a mile to the river and there saw a grand sight at the falls of the river. The water falls about 10 feet in six rods.[23] Here some of our cattle got into the alkali pools and drank of the water. One died and one horse died.

August 8th Monday.

Very cloudy, looks like we will have a storm. It rained a fine rain on before us and made plenty of water for our stock. We traveled about 18 miles and camped near a salt lake. The grass is salty and all the weeds have salt on them. Saw 5 men and a wagon from New Mexico.

August 9th Tuesday.

Passed the salt lake. The salt at the edges was almost pure and the water as salty as strong brine. There had been a rain the day before and the shore was nearly as smooth as glass. The children all got out and

---

[23]There were two falls on the Pecos between Horsehead Crossing and Pope's Crossing. The first, and largest, was near the present-day Grand Falls and is probably the one described by Mrs. Shrode. Conkling, *The Butterfield Overland*, 1: 376.

walked and ran foot races and capered along at a fine rate. Today a cool north wind, very pleasant traveling. Camped on the river by turning off the main road. Good grass and plenty of mesquit beans for our horses. They eat them as readily as corn.

August 10th Wednesday.

Laid by at the same ground to rest and graze our cattle and horses. Yesterday evening we killed a beef. The boys shot at it about 50 times before they got it. We think the Indians would be in great danger if they should attack us.

August 11th Thursday.

Today had 2 heavy rains on us as we traveled along. Today we have been on the road 3 months. Met two men from New Mexico. They came back and camped with us off the road in order to get grass. I sent a letter back home by them.

It rained a big rain after we camped and made the ground so boggy that the boys could not herd the cattle and horses so they turned them loose. Found one 3 year old heifer dead. Supposed lightning killed her. There was two or three caves near where we camped. I went to one of them. Could see 8 or 10 feet into it.

August 12th Friday.

Camped in the valley of the Pecos. That night it rained hard and thundered loud and lightned so sharp that I could not sleep. Finest morning. A wolf barked at Mr. Holcom like a dog. He would come up in two rods of him.

August 13th Saturday.

Traveled about 12 miles and camped near Pope's old fort where we found good grass and water.[24] The water difficult getting to it on account of steep rocky banks.

---

[24]Pope's "Old fort" or Pope's Camp was in Loving County near the Texas-New Mexico line. Established in 1855 by Captain John Pope, who laid out a wagon road from Horsehead Crossing to Delaware Creek, the site was a familiar point on the Pecos Road. Ibid., 1: 379–82; *Handbook of Texas*, 2: 392.

August 14th Sunday.

Some cow drivers passed us this morning with four wagons. O, what a rain fell on us last night. I have heard that it never rains here, but I tell you they have some very heavy dews here. Came to the river and could not cross. The river was too high and rising. I went to a bluff and found some pure rain water in some holes in the rocks and got a bucket full of good water. Once more camped on the river bank.

August 15th Monday.

Still on the river waiting for it to fall, so all have went to washing. Had good rain water to wash in. Men and women and children all went to washing. The Pecos water won't wash at all. Mr. Shrode was sick.

August 16th Tuesday.

Mr. Shrode is no better yet. Still in same camps. Several fine fish caught today. The river is rising very fast. Mr. Shrode is a little better this evening.

August 17th Wednesday.

Mr. Shrode is some better this morning. Traveled about 7 miles up the same side of the river. Could not cross on account of the river being so high. The range is splendid here. Looks like spring. Flowers blooming fresh. We found rose moss everywhere in this valley but no water for our stock.

August 18th Thursday.

Traveled 6 or 7 miles and our road ran into the river or so near that we could not follow it so we had to dig a pass along the foot of the mountains. All got over safe and no wagons broke in the passage. Camped in a valley near the river. The river is falling slowly. Mr. Shrode is nearly well. We camped on the other side of the river from where a Mr. Loving was killed three years since by the Indians and that has given it the name of the Loving Bend.[25]

---

[25]Loving Bend was named for cattleman Oliver Loving who, along with Charles Goodnight, opened the cattle trail from Fort Belknap to Fort Summer via the Pecos River route. In 1867, Loving and W. J. Wilson were attacked by Indians at this

August 19th Friday.

Moved on about 10 miles, met 6 wagons in the morning. They had made the road plain. They were from Bosque Grande in New Mexico.[26] We are now out of Texas and it is raining. O, how I wish we was at our journey's end.

August 20th Saturday.

Traveled about 10 miles and camped on the Pecos again. Mr. Shrode took his fish hooks to set them in the river and caught two large cat fish in a few minutes. They weighed about 12 lbs a piece.

August 21st Sunday.

Traveled on. Met some men and a family going back. When we stopped to water one yoke of oxen got in the river and swam across and they had to swim across and get them and the man came very near not making the other bank. He took the cramp. We then hitched up and drove on around a bend of the river close to a natural rock wall from ten to twenty feet high. One of the wagons bogged or rather the teams and one of our horses bogged we had to go so near the river where it had overflowed its banks. We then went about two miles and camped.

August 22nd Monday.

Moved on to the river about 6 miles. Some of the boys saw a train on the other side and talked with some of them. They said two of their men went out to look for oxen three days ago and had not got in. They supposed the Indians had killed them, but this evening they came up and the men got in but no oxen. Got to the river and could not cross.

---

point. Although both eventually escaped, Loving died several weeks later from gangrenous wounds. See "W. J. Wilson's Narrative" in J. Marvin Hunter, ed., *The Trail Drivers of Texas*, 2 vols. (New York: Argosy-Antiquarian Ltd., 1963), 1: 908–13 for an account of the incident. See also *Handbook of Texas*, 2:87.

[26]Bosque Grande, New Mexico, was on the Pecos River about fifty miles south of Fort Sumner. Considered as an "ideal holding spot" for cattle, the valley served as headquarters for the first herd John Chisum brought to the area in 1867. Bubur, "The Goodnight-Loving Trail," 148; T. M. Pearce, ed., *New Mexico Place Names: A Geographical Dictionary* (Albuquerque: University of New Mexico Press, 1965), 19.

August 23rd Tuesday.

Laid up in the same camps.

August 24th Wednesday.

Moved on about five miles and came to the river where the mountain was so close that they had to dig the side of it about 60 feet. Some of the wagons came very near going over into the river, but we all got safe across. Went about two miles and camped on the old river.

August 25th Thursday.

Traveled about four miles over a mountain and camped in the valley on the river.

August 26th Friday.

Laid by on account of Mrs. Carden being sick. Eli Hargrave caught 6 large cat fish, the largest weighed 16 lbs and another weighed 14½. This river is splendid for fishing in, but that is all. We are in sight of the Cottonwood Springs, but on the other side of the river.[27]

August 27th Saturday.

Still in same camps. Mrs. Carden is better but it rained last night and we have some lame cattle and they want rest. The salt and alkali make their feet sore and the wet weather makes it worse.

August 28th Sunday.

Traveled about ten miles over rough roads. About 12 o'clock had a severe hail storm on us with rain and wind. Some of the teams came very near upsetting the wagons in turning from the wind. The cattle and loose horses went back from it in a whoop. We picked up some of the hail in a cup and put it in a bucket of water and had some cool, nice water to drink.

This is the greatest country for firewood to have no timber growing on it that I ever saw in my life. There is mesquit brush growing everywhere. Some of it is dead and we dig the roots for firewood which

---

[27]These springs were probably located on Cottonwood Creek fifteen miles north of the Rio Penasco in present day Eddy County. Pearce, *New Mexico Place Names*, 41.

makes the best coals of anything. They are not hard to get. They are partly on top of the ground and can be knocked loose with an axe or hoe.

August 29th Monday.

Traveled about 12 miles over some very bad roads and came to a boggy slough and had to turn to the right to head it close to the mountains. Saw a monument of stones built up on one of the highest points. None of us went to it. Don't know whether it was for a guide or who built it. Met three men and Eli sent some letters to the office by them. We camped in the valley again where the musquitoes [sic] were very troublesome.

August 30th Tuesday.

Traveled about six miles and came to the river again where they filled up water vessels and watered the oxen and cattle and horses. Started for a fifteen mile strech [sic] without water. Moved on, crossed some spring branches, very strong sulphur, could smell it a hundred yards. Came to the hills and camped where there was fine range but no water for the stock. We traveled about 10 miles.

August 31st Wednesday.

Moved on two or three miles. Jennie fell out of the little wagon and both wheels ran over her arm and hand and one knee and bruised them considerably but did not brake [sic] any bones. About 12 o'clock came to Camanche Springs. They are very strong sulphur springs. The oxen would hardly any of them drink the water.[28] We traveled 18 or 20 miles and camped on a long ridge without any water for our stock.

September 1st Thursday.

This morning some of the oxen out. John Gregg and Mr. Haines and Dock Settle went to hunt for them. We went on to the river and crossed over and camped close to the river. The ox hunters got back. No oxen but they got a fine beef steer and a cow and yearling.

---

[28] Although there are several places by this name in New Mexico, none are near the location described by Shrode. Perhaps the name was misunderstood by the diarist or later changed and the orginal name forgotten.

September 2nd Friday.

Still in same camps. Five or six of the men have gone to hunt the lost oxen. Yesterday we bought some fine watermelons. They was very good as we had not had any this year and had been without vegetables for so long. The boys found all their oxen and four other head of cattle. The rule out here is when a herd man finds any stragling cattle to bring them on and if they find the owner they give them up and if not they keep them.[29]

September 3rd Saturday.

All right this morning. We crossed the Pecos at the Stanton Crossing where a man by the name of Berry Green was killed by John Hawkins while he was begging for his life.[30] He was buried about a mile above this crossing. Some of our men saw his grave. The wolves had nearly scratched down to the corpse. They covered it up again.

This morning we bade farewell to the Pecos without shedding a tear, not withstanding our long acquaintance, and started for the Hondo River. Traveled 12 miles and camped at Antelope Springs.[31] Mr. Shrode shot at an antelope but did not get it.

September 4th Sunday.

Traveled about 15 miles and camped on the Hondo near a grocery. This stream is about 20 feet wide, very rapid, fed by springs. An emigrant train of seven wagons and a herd of 1300 head of cattle passed us after we had camped. They were from Williamson and

---

[29]This "custom" of the trail was wide spread on all the overland trails and had come to have the force of law. See, for example, the Carpenter diary, and John Reid, "Paying for the Elephant: Property Rights and Civil Order on the Overland Trail," *Huntington Library Quarterly*, 41 (November 1977), 37–64.

[30]The Goodnight-Loving Trail crossed the Pecos at Pope's Camp and proceeded along the west bank of the river where water and grass were usually available. Evidently the Shrode train, unable to make the crossing because of the unusually heavy rains and rising river, crossed at Good Bend Crossing, ten miles south of modern Roswell. No reference to a "Fort Stanton Crossing" or the sad demise of Berry Green could be located.

[31]The Antelope Springs mentioned by Shrode are as elusive as her Comanche Springs. Again, there are several places with this name but none match the location of the train.

Burleson County. We passed four families camped on the road. Jennie has a fever today, I suppose caused from the bruises she got when the wagon ran over her. We got 28 head of cattle drowned in the Hondo.

September 5th Monday.

Remained in same camps. Jennie is a little better. Another train and herd passed today.

September 6th Tuesday.

Moved on two or three miles and came to a Mexican town called Missouri. The houses are all built of adobe or sun dried bricks and plastered and white washed inside and have glass windows.[32] Passed on 7 or 8 miles further and camped on the Hondo. We came very near getting some of our oxen drowned while they was drinking. Here Mr. Haines brought some cattle in that he had traded his mules for—19 head.

September 7th Wednesday.

Traveled over the roughest road yet and crossed the Hondo. Camped in the valley. Here they drove up a wild steer and roped him. He got loose and took after Helen with Lee in her arms. She ran with all her strength but stepped in a hole and fell. It was all that saved her. She was frightened almost to death and hurt by falling on a yoke.

September 8th Thursday.

Today is Lee's birthday. He is two years old. Traveled on up the creek. Sometimes the road so narrow that the wagons could not pass between the hills and the creek. One wagon slid down and came very near going into the creek. Crossed the creek three times. Traveled about 16 miles and camped near a mill. Found a fine spring. Here we bought some melons.

---

[32]Missouri Bottom or Missouri was located on the north side of the Rio Hondo about fifteen miles from present-day Roswell, New Mexico. It is sometimes shown on maps of the area as San José. See James D. Shinkle, *"Missouri Plaza," First Settled Community in Chaves County* (Roswell: Hall-Poorbaugh Press, 1972). Shinkle also mentions some of the other small towns in the area referred to in the following entries of the diary.

September 9th Friday.

Traveled about 12 miles and camped on a rocky hillside in between two corn fields. Had to watch our cattle and oxen out of the corn for they have no fences here. Their fields are all out of doors and some of their houses look like potatoe houses. They are built of poles set on end ten or twelve [inches] apart at the bottom and slant up like the rafters of a house and then covered with earth. Some has corn and melons growing on the tops of their houses. Some of them have a few cattle. As soon as they see us coming they run and drive their cattle up into the mountains or up out of the way and set down and watch them till we are out of sight.

One Mexican tried to get one of our cows yesterday. He first claimed her as his and then said Mr. Shrode had bought three bushels of him and was to give him the cow for it. O, how mad he got when he found his lies would not get the cow.

September 10th Saturday.

Today passed through a Mexican town of about 100 inhabitants. They ran out of their huts and some on top of them to look at us as we passed. The men's dress is like white men's but the women dress different from white women. Their home dress consists of a chemise and a shirt, a shawl over the head and shoulders, and no shoes or stockings. Their hair is long and plaited in two long plaits and hangs down the back. Most of them can talk a little broken English but will not as long as they can help it. They pretend like they can't talk any till they find not one to talk Mexican and then they can talk. Traveled about 12 miles, camped near Fort Stanton.[33]

September 11th Sunday.

Started on and came to Stanton, a very pretty little town. Yesterday

---

[33]Fort Stanton, near present Capitan, New Mexico, was established in May, 1855. It was abandoned at the beginning of the Civil War but was reoccupied by volunteer forces under Kit Carson who used the fort as a headquarters for expeditions against the Mescalero Apaches. The post was regarrisoned by Federal troops in 1868 and served as a protection against the Apaches until it was closed in 1896. Pearce, *New Mexico Place Names*, 59; Hart, *Old Forts*, 101–02; Frazer, *Forts of the West*, 103–04.

bought some fine pears, grapes and onions. Here we took the road to Fort Seldon. Traveled about 10 miles through the mountains.

September 12th Monday.

Found a hay wagon turned over and had to go around it on a steep hill. Camped near a mill on the Rio Docio, a mountain stream.[34] 10 miles.

September 13th Tuesday.

Traveled on through the mountains. Came to a spring branch in a cañon that was boggy. Mr. Settle's wagon came very near turning over. Found two fine springs. Got water for the day and then went on to a stream (Tulerosa) of water with a mill on it. Traveled about 18 miles. Camped near a Mexican farm. Bought some beans and cabbage.

September 14th Wednesday.

Traveled on down the valley of the Tulerosa about 7 miles and camped. Today suffered from the dust. Got nearly out of the mountains and are in sight of the Rocky Mountains. We came to another boggy place. One of Mr. Weatherford's oxen bogged down and had to be unyoked.

September 15th Thursday.

Laid by and divided the herd. About 3 o'clock started on. Traveled about 3 miles and camped on the Tulerosa.

September 16th Friday.

Traveled on. Came to the underground springs, 16 miles. These are a curiosity. There is a hole about 18 feet across and four feet deep with a branch of clear water running through it. It comes out of the ground at one side and runs into the ground on the other side. You can see two or three feet back. It looks like the mouth of a cave.

---

[34]Dowlin's Mills at the junction of Carrizo and Ruidoso Creeks several miles from Ruidoso, New Mexico.

September 17th Saturday.

Came to White Water Wells which take their name from the hills of white sand, almost as white as snow.[35] They are some of them barren of anything. Some have green bushes growing in spots on them. I never saw such a beautiful sight in all my life. Filled up our water barrels and watered our oxen but could not water the herd. Traveled on 3 or 4 miles and camped on the road about midnight. Tompkins came along once and it took all hands to keep the herds from mixing.

September 18th Sunday.

Traveled on to the water, about 18 miles. Found a large pond with plenty of water.

September 19th Monday

Laid by to rest our cattle and to let the other herds get out of the way.

September 20th Tuesday.

Moved on to San Augustine Springs.[36] The water is carried by troughs 3 miles down a mount and runs into tanks. They have troughs for cattle to drink out of. Here we filled up our water vessels and started over the San Augustine pass on the mountains, a very dangerous place on account of Indians. Traveled about 18 miles and camped on the plains.

September 21st Wednesday.

Arrived at Fort Seldon about sundown.[37] It was raining and we had

---

[35]White Water Wells were in present-day Otero County on the Fort Stanton-Fort Seldon road. Pearce, *New Mexico Place Names*, 180.

[36]San Augustine Springs was located in the San Augustine Pass in present-day Dona Ana County. The pass, near White Sands Proving Grounds, separates the Organ and San Andres Mountains. Ibid., 141.

[37]Fort Seldon, fifteen miles north of Las Cruces, was established in May, 1865, about one and a half miles east of the Rio Grande. The troops were withdrawn in 1877, but the post was re-garrisoned during the Geronimo breakout and remained in service until 1889. The nearby village of Leesburg had a "small store and grog shop and about 20 miserable huts." Ibid., 59; Hart, *Old Forts*, 132–34; Frazer, *Forts of the West*, 102–103.

to go on to water one mile and a half. Crossed the Rio Grande in the night and went one half mile and camped. We did not get the herd across the river, so some had to watch the herd all night. Mr. Greenup saw two Mexicans driving off 4 head of cattle while the wagons were crossing. He hailed them and when they did not stop, he went to shooting and emptied a six shooter at them. They left the cattle and ran off as fast as they could.

September 22nd Thursday.

Still in same camps in order to lay in supplies for our journey.

September 23rd Friday.

Today moved 8 miles up the cañon through the mountains. Said to be a very dangerous place on account of the Indians but I hope our Heavenly Father will still protect us by His powerful hand through as He has heretofore in dangerous places.

September 24th Saturday.

All right this morning. Moved on to a stage stand and bought water to water our stock at ten cents per head. All our vessels filled free of charge. Went a mile on the road and made a dry camp. We had to pay $145.00 for watering our stock. We are now on the Overland Mail Route from El Paso to Los Angeles.[38]

September 25th Sunday.

Traveled about 18 miles toward Fort Cummings. Camped near an old mail stand without water for our herd. A train of wagons passed us in the night with a small drove of sheep for the fort.

September 26th Monday.

Arrived at Fort Cummings, visited the graveyard. It is walled in with rough stones about 5 feet high, white washed, with a folding gate. Some of the graves are walled in with rock. I noticed 6 of them

---

[38] At this point, the Shrode train begins following the same route traveled by the Stewart train. Annotations will be given only for names or places not mentioned in the previous diary.

had been killed by the Apache Indians. There was only about 20 graves in all.

We watered our cattle and drove on a mile beyond the fort and camped. Several of the soldiers visited our camp that evening. They are very tired of a soldier life and say the soldiers are deserting every few days on account of being so lonesome. There are no citizens here and they have a lonesome time.[39]

September 27th Tuesday.

Traveled on through a very rocky cañon and got to Rio Mimbres and camped near the stream. Between two and three o'clock the guards found 7 of our horses were missing.

September 28th Wednesday.

No horses found yet, but we found the hobbles that had been cut off three of them. Some emigrants traveling behind us saw four Indians that evening and we have concluded that they stole them and ran them up into the mountains.

September 29th Thursday.

Still in same camps resting our cattle and horses as we have a long drive to make without water for our stock.

September 30th Friday.

Have not heard anything of our horses yet. All ready for starting on. Traveled on 6 or 7 miles and made a dry camp. Yesterday we killed a beef steer that we drove from Hopkins County and he made splendid beef. Mr. Holcomb bought a horse today, his being one that the Indians or Mexican stole. They left him afoot.

October 1st Saturday.

Went to Cow Springs. Found some adobe houses called St. John's Ranche [sic]. Some men in the house playing cards. Here we watered our cattle and horses paying 7 cents per head. The first cattle that was

---

[39]Many travelers comment on the difficulties endured by soldiers on frontier service. For example, see: Reid, *Reid's Tramp*, 114; Powers, *Afoot and Alone*, 155–57.

driven in drank, but the last found it so badly stirred that they would not drink it.[40] We then traveled on about 6 miles and camped.

October 2nd Sunday.

All right this morning. Traveled on to Soldiers Farewell.[41] This is an old station (now abandoned) and two or three springs of water. Here we found 7 wagons and we ate our dinners and watered our horses and oxen. Then traveled on about 10 miles and camped just on the other side of the Rocky Mountains. I had thought all along they would be the Elephant but they are nothing to compare with some we have crossed.

October 3rd Monday.

Traveled on to Barney's Station.[42] Watered everything, got our dinner and started on for another night drive. Drove on 10 miles and camped.

October 4th Tuesday.

This morning a yoke of Brother Settle's oxen missing. Supposed they were left at the last watering place 10 miles back. Traveled about 16 miles and camped at Stein's Peak where we found some good springs. Watered all our stock by digging them out and then digging holes for the water to run into.

---

[40]These buildings were probably named for Silas St. John, a construction engineer for the Butterfield Overland Mail who built many of the stations along this part of the line. Conkling, *The Butterfield Overland*, 2: 141–42. See also Bunyard, "Diary," note 52.

[41]Soldier's Farewell, located near the Continental Divide in present-day Grant County, was the next stage station. Bell described it as "a solitary ruin. . . ." "Two miserable water-holes are the great sources of attraction in this place," he continued. "While we looked at the thick green puddle, full of slime, and all sort of abominations from which we had to drink, a feeling of dread . . . crept over us." There are several theories as to the origin of the unusual name. Conkling, *The Butterfield Overland*, 2: 124; Bell, *New Tracks*, 2: 36.

[42]Barney's Station was nineteen miles southwest of Soldier's Farewell. According to Bell it was "also an uninhabited ruin like that we had left and, if anything, more dreary." Conkling, *The Butterfield Overland*, 2: 126; Bell, *New Tracks*, 2: 37.

October 5th Wednesday.

Started at 4 o'clock. Drove on through another cañon called Doubtful Pass in the Rocky Mountains.[43] It does look doubtful. Sometimes we could not see any place to get out at, but directly would see a narrow place just wide enough for the wagons to pass. Camped in two miles of San Simons Station, an old adobe wall.[44] Passed to the left and went up the branch 8 or 10 miles and found plenty of water and good grass and wood and camped there.

October 6th and 7th Thursday and Friday.

Still in the same camps. Mr. Shrode worked on some of the wagons and shod a horse. Some of us washed, some sewed and some darned up their stockings and some of the boys mended their whips and dressed raw hide hobbles, and etc.

October 8th Saturday.

Remain in the same camps resting our cattle and horses. Eli killed a duck this morning which was quite a treat for dinner. O, how slowly the time passes off when we are not traveling. I'm getting so tired of the road. Some of the train are writing letters to send back to their friends.

October 9th Sunday.

Still in same camps. Brother Settle preached today to the emigrants and Mr. Shrode concluded the services.

October 10th Monday.

All well this morning and fixing to move on. Last night was quite cool. A little ice in the water buckets. This morning we moved on about 14 miles and made a dry camp (that is we had no water only as

---

[43]Doubtful Canyon was a long narrow pass eight miles north of Stein's. Conkling notes that it was "appropriately named" and was "a notorious haunt of savage Apaches." Mrs. Shrode seems more concerned with the condition of the road than the presence of Indians. Conkling, *The Butterfield Overland*, 2: 128-29. See also: Powers, *Afoot and Alone*, 188-89; Bell, *New Tracks*, 2: 53; Duffen, "Way Diary," 156.

[44]San Simon's Station was the first stage stop in Arizona. It had an earthmade tank for storing water as well as a usually reliable supply from nearby San Simon Creek. Conkling, *The Butterfield Overland*, 2: 129-30; Bell, *New Tracks*, 2: 42.

we hauled it) about 12 miles from the Fort. We took a right hand road a mile from the pass and found water for our cattle at a spring in the cañon. Today been on the road 5 months.

October 12th Wednesday.

Still in same camps. Mr. Shrode traded for some bacon and we was not ready to start on.

October 13th Thursday.

Traveled on. Crossed the Apache Mountains and traveled on till 10 o'clock in the night. One of our men saw two Indians. They came down a cañon to get water.

October 14th Friday.

Moved on to the Springs, got water, and traveled on 5 or 6 miles in the night and camped.

October 15th Saturday.

Traveled about 14 miles. Passed about 20 soldiers at Colonel Stone's grave. They were taking up his bones for reinterment. He was killed by Indians about 12 months ago.[45] Camped on a dry branch.

October 16th Sunday.

Started early in order to get to water as soon as possible. Traveled over a hilly country. Went down a cañon so narrow that the wagons only just had room to pass. Got to the water about 12 o'clock. Crossed the San Pedro, a small running stream of clear water and camped on the other side from the Station. Here we overtook Mr. Tompkin's train and another train has come since we arrived here.

October 17th Monday.

Still in same camps resting our stock. Eli got hooked in the foot by an ox that we was holding down.

---

[45]Stone was evidently a local volunteer or militia officer. There is no mention of his career or death in the usually reliable Francis B. Heitman, *Historical Register and Dictionary of the United States Army from its Organization, September 29, 1789 to March 2, 1903.* 2 vols. (Washington D.C.: Government Printing Office, 1903).

October 18th Tuesday.

Started on about 1 o'clock. Traveled for 8 miles and made a dry camp in sight of Tompkin's before and McClelland behind.

October 19th Wednesday.

Traveled on. Saw the place where the Indians had burnt the stage and killed three men, cut open the mail, and scattered papers and letters. This was done 3 months ago. Went on a little further and John Gregg found a letter directed to him tied up to a tree from Mrs. Sara Hargrave informing us of the death of friends in Texas, among them my dear sister, Mrs. Compton.[46] Traveled 14 miles. Camped a mile beyond the Seneca.

October 20th Thursday.

Moved on at 12 o'clock. Traveled about 10 miles, made a dry camp. Not much grass.

October 21st Friday.

Moved on to Tucson. Camped in two miles of the city up the creek. This place is three hundred years old. It has about three thousand inhabitants.[47] R. Hargrave met us 8 miles before we got there and piloted us a nearer way to the water.

October 22nd Saturday.

Still in same camps resting. Got some letters from home and some from California today. Mr. Price has just drove into camps. He is going on with us and five other gentlemen joined us today.

October 23rd Sunday.

Moved on through the city. It is of adobe. Some nice buildings of

---

[46]This method of "delivering" mail was a common practice on most of the emigrant routes.

[47]Mrs. Shrode is somewhat inaccurate in her estimates. Tucson was nearly two hundred, not three hundred, years old. Her population figure is more accurate. The 1870 census reported Tucson's population as 3,224. See John Spring, *John Spring's Arizona*, A. M. Gustafson, ed. (Tucson: University of Arizona Press, 1966), 144. For other descriptions of the town see Bunyard, "Diary," note 61.

the sort. Some full stores. Inhabitants mostly Mexicans. Did not see any white women in the city.

October 24th Monday.

Still in same camps. Lost some cattle and some of the boys have gone back to hunt for them.

October 25th Tuesday.

The boys found 10 head of their cattle in a Mexican herd. Made him turn them over to Mr. Holcomb. Mr. Gregg and Mr. Shrode bought a herd of cattle and they are receiving them. Moved back about a mile.

October 26th Wednesday.

Moved on about 5 miles.

October 27th Thursday.

Today Mr. Settles folks left us and went on. Some of our cattle got into a frost bitten bean patch and eat some beans and vines and the old Mexican sued for $150 damage. We are going back above Tucson till it is settled.

October 28th Friday.

Moved on back to the Santa Cruz and camped on the same ground that we had camped on.

October 29th Saturday.

Moved on at two o'clock. Traveled about 7 miles and camped. One of the men found a beef steer tied up by the foot. He had crippled his foot till we had to butcher him on the road.

October 30th Sunday.

Traveled on to Point Mountain Wells.[48] Watered our teams at 10 cents per head and filled our vessels. Went on about 10 miles and camped.

---

[48]Point Mountain Wells was a Butterfield stage stop eighteen miles northwest of Tucson. The correct name was Pointer Mountain. Conkling, *The Butterfield Overland*, 2: 161; previous diary note 62.

October 31st Monday.

Traveled on 10 miles and had dinner in the Picach Gap (called Pecatch). This is very dry country. Dust in the road 6 inches deep. You can see the dust 20 miles when herds or trains are traveling. If the country was level enough we could see it farther. We have not been out of sight of mountains since we struck them on the Pecos River.

Ate our suppers and traveled till 12 o'clock in the night. Came to Blue Water Station. Watered our oxen and horses and laid down to sleep a little. The herd went on to the Gila. The boys with the herd never slept any that night and we but very little.

November 1st Tuesday.

Started on at 8 o'clock for the Gila River. Arrived there about seven o'clock in the night. Not much grass but plenty of brush.

November 2nd Wednesday.

Laid by. About 50 Pimo Indians in camps.

November 5th Saturday.

Started on to Salt River. Traveled about 6 miles and camped near a Pemah [sic] Indian village. They are a friendly tribe and Uncle Sam is trying to teach them to work. O, what a field for the good missionary is here and good persevering teachers. Some of them only half clad and the little ones go entirely naked.

November 6th Sunday.

Moved on through the Indian village. They build their huts of willow brush and daub them with mortar. Something twists the willow twigs in so close that the rain will not penetrate them. Camped in two miles of the Maricopa Station.

November 7th Monday.

Traveled on to the Gila, crossed over, and stopped to brouse our oxen on willow brush for there is no grass here worth naming. We read in the papers of the fine rains in California which cheered us up considerably today. Traveled back, found grass and camped near the Gila Bend Road.

November 8th Tuesday.

Moved 2 miles to better grass. The old Mexican chief was here to-day. Jake and Major are sick.

November 9th Wednesday.

Indians in camps this morning. Jake and Major are better.

November 10th Thursday.

All well this morning. Still in same camps.

November 11th Friday.

Today we have been on the road six months. O, how I will rejoice to get to a place that I can call home once more.

November 13th Sunday.

Still in same camps. Haines started on Thursday, 10th and Tompkins on Friday, 11th.

November 14th Monday.

Still here in the same camps. The boys are going to make a corral to pen the cattle of nights. We will leave some here with the herd and the families will go on in a few days.

November 17th Thursday.

We started for California leaving the herd behind. We got started at four o'clock. Traveled till 10 o'clock.

November 18th Friday.

Traveled all day. Camped close to the gap.

November 19th Saturday.

Started on. Got to the river about noon. Found a train of emigrants there. That evening about 40 soldiers came up and camped near us.

November 20th Sunday.

Moved on 8 miles to hard scrabble water. Old Broad gave out and

"Jornado del Muerto"

laid down and refused to get up. For an hour turned everything out to the willows for there is no grass here.

November 21st Monday.

Moved on. Met 20 wagons loaded with goods and mining implements. Traveled 3 miles and had to leave one of our oxen that had give up and we could not get him any farther. Camped at Kenyon Station. Here we met a Methodist missionary going out to Salt River. His name is Alex Groves. He is from California.

November 22nd Tuesday.

Still in the same camps browsing our oxen.

November 23rd Wednesday.

Moved on about 8 miles over a rough road. Found a little grass and camped.

November 24th Thursday.

Moved on to Oatman Flat Station, 5 miles. Found some grass. Today Jake is 21 years old.

November 25th Friday.

Laid by and the men all went hunting. Mr. Shrode killed a fine fat black tailed buck. The fat was over an inch thick on the hams. It looked like a fat mutton. It weighed 23 lbs.

November 26th Saturday.

Moved on about 7 miles over very rough roads. Passed the graves of Mr. and Mrs. Oatman. They were killed by the Indians 17 years ago.[49] Here Mr. Price buried his child. We traveled 7 miles, found some grass and camped.

November 27th Sunday.

Moved on. Got to Burk's Station. There we got a letter from Brother Settle. Traveled on after watering. One of J. H. Gregg's oxen laid down while going along and I fear he will give out before we get much farther. The dust in this valley is from 6 to 12 inches deep in the road and the wind blows and drives it in our faces till we look like mulatoes [sic.]. O, this road to California is a hard road to travel.

We went 3 or 4 miles and found comfortable vacant houses to stop in which was very acceptable as it is blowing a cold north wind. Sprinkled rain after dark.

November 28th Monday.

Still in the houses. Like them very much, the first we have slept in

---

[49]This well-publicized attack, in which Oatman, his wife and one child were killed, occurred in 1851. The Oatman's son, Lorenzo, was severely beaten and left for dead, and their two girls were taken captive. Lorenzo and one of his sisters were eventually rescued. The "massacre" attracted widespread attention, and almost every traveler on the road commented on the incident. See, for example, Browne, *Adventures*, 88–89; Reid, *Reid's Tramp*, 231; Powers, *Afoot and Alone*, 231. Susan Parrish and her family traveled part of the way to California with the Oatmans and later cared for the two surviving children. See her diary in Root, *Following the Pot of Gold*.

for nearly 7 months. Here we found Mrs. Mary Nash. She came to see us and brought us some sweet potatoes, some milk and potato pumpkins.

December 1st Thursday.

Still here. The train has not come on yet. Mr. Shrode wrote a letter to J. Gregg and one of the boys at the wells.

December 2nd Friday.

Still in these old houses waiting (with patience worn thread bare) for the train of wagons.

December 3rd and 4th Saturday and Sunday.

Still here. Today I went across the river visiting to Colonel Woolseys.

December 5th Monday.

The train we were looking for come on but we did not go with them.

December 6th Tuesday.

Today is Viola's birthday. She is six years of age. We have left a part of our baggage in care of Colonel Woolsey and lady and we are going to Yuma. Started about 10 o'clock and traveled 14 miles. Found a grand place to camp, plenty of wood, water, and willow brush. No grass.

December 7th Wednesday.

Started at sundown. Got to teamster's camp about 10 o'clock. Found grass between where we camped and that place. Traveled on to where the Gila and the mountains came close together and camped. We feel quite lonely after having so much company on the road. We traveled 21 miles today.

December 8th Thursday.

Camped at Antelope Peak. Traveled 19 miles.

December 9th Friday.

Camped at Swifts Ranche. Traveled 20 miles.

December 10th Saturday.

Traveled on to Oroville (which in Spanish is Golden City).[50] There we ate dinner after looking at the steam pump that they are forcing water over 2000 feet high into the mountains to wash the gold dust out. Traveled 27 miles. Camped within 3 miles of the city.

December 11th Sunday.

Today have been on the road 7 months. Arrived in Arizona City about 10 o'clock.

December 15th Thursday.

Started down to Smith's ferry.[51]

December 16th Friday.

Arrived there about 11 o'clock. Crossed over and found Brother Settles folks and others that had started on.

December 17th Saturday.

Moved on over a rough road to a well on the plains. Are camped after traveling 22 miles.

December 18th Sunday.

Moved on to Gardner's Wells and ate dinner two miles from there. Traveled on to Alamo Station, 19 miles.[52]

---

[50]Oroville, a few miles east of Gila City, was a mining boom town. In the late 1860s it was larger and more important than Arizona City. Rosalie Crowe and Sidney R. Brinckerhoff, *Early Yuma: A Graphic History of Life on the American Nile* (Flagstaff: Northland Press, 1976), 5, 25.

[51]Several ferries were established on the Colorado River at Arizona City. One, at Pilot Knob south of the Gila, was run by local Indians. Another was started by Lieutenant Cave Couts and later sold to G. W. Lincoln and later still to John Glanton, a cut-throat scalp hunter who was killed by his Indian competitors. The best-known ferry was that operated by L. J. F. Jager, or Yaeger, at a point several miles below present-day Yuma. Conkling, *The Butterfield Overland*, 2:200–204; Hoover, *Historic Spots*, 109.

[52]Alamo Station, or Alamo Mocho, derived its name from the cottonwood which evidently flourished there at one time. The station was located on the Alamo River

December 19th Monday.

Traveled 14 miles over bad sand. Camped at New River Station.

December 20th Tuesday.

Traveled about 10 miles over the best roads. Stopped at point of mountains and ate our dinners where we found a little grass. All around looked like a lake of water reflecting the shadows of mountains and bushes. The bushes look like tall trees. Traveled 18 miles and camped near Laguna Station at a well down in a dry branch.[53] Water salty.

December 21st Wednesday.

Traveled over a sandy road. Found a little grass.

December 22nd Thursday.

Moved on to Mountain Springs where we found white folks and a John Chinaman for cook.[54]

December 23rd Friday.

Started on up the Milqutay Mountains. Found a very good road for 2 miles. Took a right hand road in order to cut off 6 or 7 miles and wished we had gone the other way. Had to unload twice the hills were so steep. Got to Walker's Station where we camped on a spring branch. Plenty of grass and water.[55]

---

just south of the U.S.-Mexico boundary. Conkling, *The Butterfield Overland*, 2: 221–22; Browne, *Adventures*, 50.

[53]Laguna Station was another of the stage stops in present-day Imperial County California. It was located approximately five miles west of the present town of Silsbee, California. Conkling, *The Butterfield Overland*, 2: 225.

[54]Mountain Spring Station was another stage stop, although not on the Butterfield line. It was located at Mountain Spring Pass near the present Imperial-San Diego county line. Hoover, *Historic Spots*, 108.

[55]The reference is evidently to Guatay Mountain named from the Indian word for a large house, probably because it "looked like an enormous wigwam." No reference to Walker's Station could be found. Evidently it was another stage stop whose name and location have been forgotten. Hoover, *Historic Spots*, 108–109; Federal Writers' Program, *California*, 643.

December 24th Saturday.

Traveled on. Camped at an old ranch belonging to a Mr. Hayden.

December 25th Sunday.

Went on towards Bottoms. Met him on the road. He knew us some distance. Hollowed Christmas Gift.[56] Got to the mountains here to send for a yoke of cattle to pull our wagon up the hill. Got to Bottoms all right. Found them all well and looking for us. Had a good dinner prepared for us which was very acceptable. Staid there a week, moved down the valley 12 miles. Here our mules were stolen by the Mexicans and they refused to give them up.

The diary ends at this point although later pages in the book are filled with household accounts and children's school lessons. The Shrodes stayed in the area for several months before relocating near San Diego as noted in the introduction.

Personnel

Captain John Tompkins, Senior, and wife, Granma Tompkins, Charley Tompkins, Harriet T., Maila T., John T., George T., Ella T., Joe T.

Alfred Carden and wife, Charles C., Wm. R. C.

Wm. Beard and wife and child

Lafayette Haines and wife, Albert H., Olivia H., John H., M. Jenks H., Amy Haines, Theodore and Lander Haines, nephews of Lafayette Haines

Mr. Whitfield, Charley Berkley, John Bata

These were from Corryell County

Rev. M. G. Settle and wife, Mark S., Dock S., Lafayette S., Mattie S.

Sam'l Brown and wife and 5 children

D. T. Shrode and wife and 4 children

---

[56]"Christmas Gift" is a traditional southern Christmas greeting often used on Christmas Day in place of the more familiar Merry Christmas.

Mrs. Anthony, Billy W. Weatherford and wife and 2 children

J. H. Gregg and wife and 3 children

Joe Montgomery, Taylar Hancock

Nellie Hargrave

D. S. Shrode and wife and 8 children and Frank Shrode

Eli Hargrove, Peter Holcomb, Will Greenup, Jack Pickle, Bill Carter

McDummick and black Frank

Mr. McClellen and son, Bill. John Panka, Jim Wms.

Mr. Murray and seven daughters, Millie, Matilda, Anna, Etha, Dora, Meriella and Tila Lee

Ben Griffin & wife and child, Fannie

Bibliography

MANUSCRIPT JOURNALS

Ashley, Angeline Jackson. "Crossing the Plains in 1852." Henry E. Huntington Library, San Marino, California.

Bailey, Mary Stuart. "A Journal of Mary Stuart Bailey, 1852." Henry E. Huntington Library, San Marino, California.

Bunyard, Harriet. "Diary of a Young Girl from Collin County, Texas." Henry E. Huntington Library, San Marino, California.

Carpenter, Helen. "A Journal Across the Plains in An Ox Cart, 1857." Henry E. Huntington Library, San Marino, California.

Fitzgerald, Ida F. "Account of Life of Plummer Edward Jefferis including Voyages from New York to California in 1850 and 1854." Henry E. Huntington Library, San Marino, California.

French, Barsina Rogers. "Journal of a Wagon Trip from Evansville, Indiana to Prescott, Arizona, April 8–September 3, 1867." Henry E. Huntington Library, San Marino, California.

Hall, Maggie. "The Story of Maggie." Bancroft Library, Berkeley, California.

Haun, Catherine. "A Woman's Trip Across the Plains in 1849." Henry E. Huntington Library, San Marino, California.

McDougal, Jane A. "Diary Kept by Mrs. Jane McDougal, 1849." Henry E. Huntington Library, San Marino, California.

"Returns from U.S. Military Posts, 1800–1916." National Archives Microcopy, 617. "Fort Griffin, Texas, July 1867–May 1881," Roll 429. National Archives and Records Service, Washington, D.C.

Sawyer, Francis. "Overland to California, Notes from a Journal . . . May 9 to August 17, 1852." Newberry Library, Chicago, Ilinois.

Shrode, Maria. "Journal, 1870." Henry E. Huntington Library, San Marino, California.

PUBLISHED JOURNALS

Ackley, Mary E. *Crossing the Plains and Early Days in California: Memories of Girlhood Days in California's Golden Age.* San Francisco: privately printed, 1928.

Akin, James. "The Journey of James Akin." Dale Morgan, ed. *University of Oklahoma Bulletin,* (1919).

Bailey, L. R., ed. *Survey of a Route . . . The A. B. Gray Report.* Los Angeles: Westernlore Press, 1963.

Bartlett, John R. *Personal Narrative of Explorations. . . .* 2 volumes. New York: D. Appleton, 1854.

Bates, Mrs. D. B. *Incidents on Land and Water or Four Years on the Pacific Coast.* Boston: published for the author, 1860.

Barker, Charles A., ed. *Memoirs of Elisha Oscar Crosby.* San Marino: Huntington Library, 1945.

Becker, Robert, ed. *Thomas Christy's Road: Across the Plains, A Guide to the Route . . . to the City of Sacramento.* Denver: Old West Publishing Company, 1969.

Bell, James G. "A Log of the Texas-California Cattle Trail." *Southwestern Historical Quarterly,* 35 (January–April, 1932), 208–37.

Bell, William. *New Tracks in North America: A Journal of Travel and Adventure.* 2 volumes. London: Chapman and Hall, 1869.

Berry, Louise, ed. "Overland to the Gold Fields of California in 1852: The Journal of George Hawkins Clark." *Kansas Historical Quarterly,* 11 (August, 1942), 227–96.

Bieber, Ralph, ed. *Exploring Southwestern Trails.* Glendale: Arthur H. Clark, 1935.

Browne, J. Ross. *Adventures in the Apache Country, or A Tour Through Arizona, 1864.* Donald M. Powell, ed. Tucson: University of Arizona Press, 1974.

Bryant, Edwin. *What I Saw in California.* London: Richard Bently, 1849.

Carter, R. G. *On the Border with McKenzie or Winning West Texas from the Comanches.* Washington, D.C.: Eynon Printing Company, 1935.

Carter, William A. "Diary of Judge William A. Carter." *Annals of Wyoming,* 11 (April 1939), 75–110.

Chandless, William. *A Visit to Salt Lake . . . and a Residence in the Mormon Settlements at Utah.* London: Smith, Elder and Company, 1857.

Clark, William. "A Trip Across the Plains in 1857." *Iowa Journal of History and Politics,* 20 (April 1922), 163–223.

Cleland, Robert G., ed. *Apron Full of Gold: The Letters of Mary Jane Megquier from San Francisco, 1849–1856.* San Marino: Huntington Library, 1949.

Coles, Gilbert L. *In the Early Days Along the Overland Trail in Nebraska Territory in 1852.* Kansas City: Frankline Hudson Publishing Company, 1905.

Conway, Cornelius. *The Utah Expedition Containing a General Account of the Mormon Campaign.* Cincinnati: Safety Fund Reporter Office, 1858.

Cooke, Lucy. *Crossing the Plains in 1852: Narrative of a Trip from Iowa to the "Land of Gold" As Told in Letters Written During the Journey.* Modesto, California: n.p., 1923.

Couts, Cave J. *From San Diego to the Colorado in 1849.* William McPherson, ed. Los Angeles: Arthur M. Ellis, 1932.

Cunynghame, Arthur, "Travel on the Illinois and Michigan Canal." Paul M. Angle, ed. *Prairie State: Impressions of Illinois, 1673-1967 By Traders and Other Observers.* Chicago: University of Chicago Press, 1968.

Dale, Edward E. *The Cross Timbers, Memories of a North Texas Boyhood.* Austin: University of Texas Press, 1966.

Dawson, Glen, ed. *Lorenzo D. Aldrich: A Journal of the Overland Route.* Los Angeles: Dawson's Book Shop, 1950.

"Diary of Miss Harriet Bunyard." Percival J. Cooney, ed. *Historical Society of Southern California Quarterly,* 13 (1924), 92–124.

Duffen, William A., ed. "Overland via 'Jackass Mail' in 1858: The Diary of Phocion R. Way." *Arizona and the West,* 2 (Spring–Summer, 1960), 35–53; 147–64.

Dunbar, Edward. *The Romance of the Age or the Discovery of Gold in California.* New York: D. Appleton, 1867.

Dunham, E. Allene Taylor. *Across the Plains in a Covered Wagon.* n.p., n.d.

Foreman, Grant, ed. *Marcy and the Gold-Seekers.* Norman: University of Oklahoma Press, 1937.

Frink, Margaret. *A Journal . . . of a Party of California Gold Seekers.* Oakland, California: n.p., 1897.

Frizzell, Lodisa. *Across the Plains to California in 1852.* New York: New York Public Library, 1915.

Harris, Benjamin. *The Gila Trail: The Texas Argonauts and the California Gold Rush.* Richard Dillon, ed. Norman: University of Oklahoma Press, 1960.

Herndon, Sarah R. *Days on the Road: Crossing the Plains in 1865.* New York: Burr Printing House, 1902.

Horton, Emily. *Our Family with a Glimpse of Their Pioneer Life.* n.p., 1922.

Hutcheson, Austin E. "Overland in 1852: The McQuirk Diary." *Pacific Historical Review,* 13 (December 1944), 426–32.

Ingalls, Eleazer S. *Journal of a Trip to California by the Overland Route Across the Plains in 1850–51.* Waukegan: Tobey & Company, 1852.

Ivins, Virginia. *Pen Pictures of Early Western Days.* n.p., 1908.

Lee, Arthur T. *Fort Davis and the Texas Frontier.* College Station: Texas A&M University Press, 1976.

Lowe, Percival G. *Five Years a Dragoon ('49 to '54) and Other Adventures on the Plains.* Kansas City: F. Hudson, 1906.

Maxwell, William A. *Crossing the Plains, Days of '57.* San Francisco: Sunset Publishing House, 1915.

McCollum, William. *California as I Saw It.* Dale Morgan, ed. Los Gatos, California: Talisman Press, 1960.

McConnell, H. H. *Five Years a Cavalryman or Regular Army Life on the Texas Frontier.* Jacksboro, Texas: J. N. Rogers & Company, 1889.

McDougall, William H. "A Woman's Log of 1849, From the Diary of Mrs. John McDougall." *Overland Monthly*, 2nd series, 16 (September 1890), 273-80.

Morgan, Dale, ed. "Letters by Fortyniners Written from Great Salt Lake City in 1849." *Western Humanities Review*, 3 (April 1949), 98-116.

———. *The Overland Diary of James A. Pritchard from Kentucky to California in 1849*. Denver: Old West Publishing Company, 1945.

Ormsby, Waterman L. *The Butterfield Overland Mail*. L. H. Wright and J. M. Bynum, eds. San Marino: Huntington Library, 1942.

Osbun, Albert. *To California and the South Seas, The Diary of Albert G. Osbun*. J. H. Kemble, ed. San Marino: Huntington Library, 1966.

Pierce, George F. "Parson's Progress to California." *Historical Society of Southern California Quarterly*, 21 (1939), 45-78.

Pomfret, John E., ed. *California Gold Rush Vouages, 1848-1849: Three Original Narratives*. San Marino: Huntington Library, 1954.

Porter, Lavinia. *By Ox Team to California: A Narrative Crossing the Plains in 1860*. Oakland: Oakland Enquirer Office, 1910.

Potter, David, ed. *Trail to California: The Overland Journal of Vincent Geiger and Wakeman Bryarly*. New Haven: Yale University Press, 1945.

Powers, Stephen. *Afoot and Alone: A Walk from Sea to Sea by the Southern Route*. Hartford, Conn.: Columbian Book Company, 1872.

Reid, John C. *Reid's Tramp or A Journal of the Incidents of Ten Months Travel*. Selma, Alabama: John Hardy and Company, 1858.

Root, Virginia V. *Following the Pot of Gold at the Rainbow's End in the Days of 1850*. Leonore Rowland, ed. Downey, California: Elena Quinn, 1960.

Royce, Sarah. *A Frontier Lady: Recollections of the Gold Rush and Early California*. New Haven: Yale University Press, 1932.

Shrode, Maria. "Overland by Ox Train in 1870." *Historical Society of Southern California Quarterly*, 26 (March 1944), 9-37.

Spring, John. *John Spring's Arizona*. A. M. Gustafson, ed. Tucson: University of Arizona Press, 1966.

Steele, Eliza R. "By Packet from Peoria to Alton and the Towns Along the Way." In Paul M. Angle, ed. *Prairie State: Impressions of Illinois, 1673-1967 By Traders and Other Observers*. Chicago: University of Chicago Press, 1968.

Stowell, Levi. "Bound for the Land of Canaan, Ho! Diary of Levi Stowell." Marco G. Thorne, ed. *California Historical Society Quarterly*, 27 (March 1948), 33-50; 157-64; 259-66; 361-70.

Taylor, Bayard. *Eldorado or Adventures in the Path of Empire*. 2 volumes. New York: George Putnam, 1850.

Tyler, Lyman S., ed. *The Montana Gold Rush Diary of Kate Dunlap.* Denver: Old West Publishing Company, 1969.

Ward, Harriet S. *Prairie Schooner Lady: The Journal of Harriet Sherrill Ward.* Ward G. and Florence Dewitt, eds. Los Angeles: Westernlore Press, 1959.

Waters, Lydia M. "Account of a Trip Across the Plains in 1855." *Quarterly of the Society of California Pioneers,* 6 (March 1929), 59–79.

GUIDEBOOKS AND DIRECTORIES

Brown, Nat P. and John K. Dallison. *Brown & Dallison's Nevada, Grass Valley and Rough and Ready Directory.* San Francisco: Town Talk Office, 1856.

Child, Andrew. *Overland Route to California.* Reprint edition. Los Angeles: N. A. Kovach, 1946.

Dacus, J. A. and James W. Buel. *A Tour of Saint Louis or the Inside Life of a Great City.* Saint Louis: Western Publishing Company, 1878.

Gunn, O. B. *New Map and Handbook of Kansas and the Gold Mines.* Pittsburg: W. A. Haven, 1859.

Parker, Nathan. *Stranger's Guide to Saint Louis.* Saint Louis: G. B. Wintle, 1867.

Platt, P. L. and N. Slater. *Traveler's Guide Across the Plains Upon the Overland Route to California.* Reprint edition, Dale Morgan, ed. San Francisco: John Howell, 1963.

The Texas Almanac and Emigrants Guide. Galveston: W. Richardson & Company, 1867.

The Texas Almanac and Guide to Texas for 1869. Galveston: W. Richardson & Company, 1869.

Thompson, Hugh B. *Directory of the City of Nevada and Grass Valley.* Nevada City: Charles F. Robbins, 1861.

Ware, Joseph E. *The Emigrants Guide to California.* Reprint edition, John Caughey, ed. Princeton: Princeton University Press, 1932.

Secondary Works

ARTICLES

Faragher, Johnny and Christine Stansell, "Women and Their Families on the Overland Trail to California and Oregon, 1842–1867." *Feminist Studies,* 2 (1975), 150–66.

Carley, Maurine, "Oregon Trail Trek No. Four." *Annals of Wyoming,* 29 (April 1957), 78–82.

Harris, Earl R. "Courthouse and Jail Rocks: Landmarks on the Oregon Trail." *Nebraska History*, 43 (March 1962), 29–51.

Mantor, Lyle E. "Fort Kearny and the Westward Movement." *Nebraska History*, 29 (September 1948), 175–207.

Mattes, Merrill J. "Chimney Rock on the Oregon Trail." *Nebraska History*, 35 (March 1955), 1–26.

————. "Robidoux's Trading Post at 'Scott's Bluffs,' and the California Gold Rush." *Nebraska History*, 30 (June 1949), 95–138.

Nasatir, A. P. "International Rivalry for California and the Establishment of the British Consulate." *California Historical Society Quarterly*, 46 (March 1967), 53–70.

Pickett, Karen. "John McDougal." Typescript, California State Library.

Reid, John. "Dividing the Elephant: The Separation of Mess and Joint Stock Property on the Overland Trail." *Hastings Law Review*, 28 (September 1976), 79–92.

————. "Paying for the Elephant: Property Rights and Civil Order on the Overland Trail." *Huntington Library Quarterly*, 41 (November 1977), 37–64.

Riley, Glenda. "Images of the Frontierswoman: Iowa as a Case Study." *Western Historical Quarterly*, 8 (April 1977), 189–202.

Schlissel, Lillian. "Women's Diaries on the Western Frontier." *American Studies*, 18 (Spring 1977), 87–100.

Stoeltje, Beverly J. "'A Helpmate for Man Indeed,' The Image of the Frontier Woman." *Journal of American Folklore*, 88 (January–March 1975), 25–41.

Watkins, Albert. "History of Fort Kearny." *Nebraska Historial Society Publications*, 16 (1911), 227–67.

Willman, Lilian M. "The History of Fort Kearney." *Nebraska State Historical Society Publications*, 21 (1930), 211–318.

BOOKS

Bancroft, H. H. *California InterPocula.* San Francisco: History Publishing Company, 1888.

————. *History of California.* 7 volumes. San Francisco: History Publishing Company, 1888.

Bates, Ed F. *History and Reminiscences of Denton County.* Denton, Texas: McNitzky Printing Co., 1918.

Berthold, Victor. *The Pioneer Steamer California, 1848–1849.* Boston: Houghton Mifflin, 1932.

Bless, Bertha. *Weston: Queen of the Platte Purchase.* Weston, Missouri: The Weston Chronicle, 1969.

Boynton, Searles R. *The Painter Lady: Grace Carpenter Hudson.* Eureka: Interface California Corp., 1978.

Cates, Clifford D. *Pioneer History of Wise County.* Decatur, Texas: n.p., 1907.

Caughey, John W., ed. *Rushing for Gold.* Berkeley: University of California Press, 1949.

Chittenden, Hiram M. *History of Early Steamboat Navigation on the Missouri River.* 2 volumes. New York: Francis P. Harper, 1903.

Conkling, Roscow and Margaret. *The Butterfield Overland Mail, 1857–1869.* 2 volumes. Glendale: Arthur H. Clark, 1947.

Crowe, Rosalie and Sidney R. Brinckerhoff. *Early Yuma: A Graphic History of Life on the American Nile.* Flagstaff: Northland Press, 1976.

Dangberg, Grace. *Carson Valley, Historical Sketches of Nevada's First Settlement.* Reno: Carson Valley Historical Society, 1972.

Davis, H. P. *Gold Rush Days in Nevada City.* Nevada City: Berliner and McGinnis, 1948.

Ewell, T. T. *History of Hood County, Texas from Its Earliest Settlement to the Present.* Granbury, Texas: Granbury News, 1895.

Faragher, John M. *Women and Men on the Overland Trail.* New Haven: Yale University Press, 1979.

Faulk, Odie. *Destiny Road: The Gila Trail and the Opening of the West.* New York: Oxford University Press, 1973.

Federal Writers Program. *Arizona: A State Guide.* New York: Hastings House, 1940.

————. *California: A Guide to the Golden State.* Revised edition. New York: Hastings House, 1967.

————. *Indiana: A Guide to the Hoosier State.* New York: Oxford University Press, 1941.

————. *Missouri: A Guide to the "Show Me" State.* New York: Duell, Sloan and Pearce, 1941.

————. *Nevada: A Guide to the Silver State.* Portland: Binfords and Mort, 1940.

————. *Texas: A Guide to the Lone Star State.* New York: Hastings House, 1940.

————. *Wyoming: A Guide to Its History, Highways and People.* New York: Oxford University Press, 1941.

Federal Writers Project. *Illinois: A Descriptive and Historical Guide.* Chicago: A. C. McClurg and Company, 1939.

————. *New Mexico: A Guide to the Colorful State*. New York: Hastings House, 1953.

Frazer, Robert W. *Forts of the West: Military Forts and Presidios . . . to 1898*. Norman: University of Oklahoma Press, 1965.

Gard, Wayne, et. al. *Along the Early Trails of the Southwest*. Austin: Pemberton Press, 1969.

Gay, Beatrice G. *Into the Setting Sun*. Santa Anna, Texas: n.p., n.d.

Gibson, Arrell M. *The Life and Death of Colonel Albert Jennings Fountain*. Norman: University of Oklahoma Press, 1965.

Gregg, Rosalie, ed. *Wise County History, A Link with the Past*. Quanah, Texas: Nortex Press, 1975.

Gudde, Erwin G. *California Gold Camps, A Geographical and Historical Dictionary*. Elisabeth K. Gudde, ed. Berkeley: University of California Press, 1975.

Hafen, LeRoy R. *The Overland Mail, 1849-1869*. New York: AMS Press, 1969.

————. *Fort Laramie and the Pageant of the West, 1834-1890*. Glendale: Arthur H. Clark, 1938.

Haley, J. Evetts. *Fort Concho and the Texas Frontier*. San Angelo: San Angelo Standard Times, 1952.

Hare, D. H. *The Tell of Time: People, Places and Things of Sulphur Bluffs and Hopkins County Texas*. Hereford, Texas: Pioneer Book Publishers, 1972.

Hart, Herbert M. *Old Forts of the Southwest*. New York: Bonanza Books, 1964.

Heitman, Francis B. *Historical Register and Dictionary of the United States Army from Its Organization, September 29, 1789 to March 2, 1903*. 2 volumes. Washington, D.C.: Government Printing Office, 1903.

Hill, Joseph T. *The History of Warner's Ranch and Its Environs*. Los Angeles: privately printed, 1927.

Hittell, Theodore H. *History of California*. 4 volumes. San Francisco: N. J. Stone & Co., 1898.

Hoover, Mildred Brooke, H. E. Rench and Ethel Rench. *Historic Spots in California*. 3rd edition. Stanford: Stanford University Press, 1966.

Hunter, J. Marvin, ed. *The Trail Drivers of Texs*. 2 volumes. New York: Argosy-Antiquarian Limited, 1963.

Kemble, John. H. *The Panama Route, 1848-1868*. Berkeley: University of California Press, 1943.

Lamar, Howard, ed. *The Reader's Encyclopedia of the American West*. New York: Crowell, 1978.

Lewis, Oscar. *Sea Routes to the Gold Fields, The Migration by Water to California, 1849-1852*. New York: Knopf, 1949.

Lucas, Mattie Davison and Mita H. Hall. *A History of Grayson County, Texas.* Sherman, Texas: Scruggs Printing Co., 1936.

Madsen, Brigham D. *The Bannock of Idaho.* Caldwell, Idaho: Caxton, 1958.

Mattes, Merrill J. *Fort Laramie and the Forty Niners.* Estes Park, Colorado: Rocky Mountain Nature Association, 1949.

_____. *The Great Platte River Road: The Covered Wagon Mainline via Fort Kearny to Fort Laramie.* Nebraska State Historical Society Publications, 25. Lincoln: Nebraska State Historical Society, 1969.

_____. *Scott's Bluff National Monument, Nebraska.* Historical Handbook Series #28. Washington, D.C.: National Park Service, 1958.

McConnell, J. C. *The West Texas Frontier.* 2 volumes. Palo Pincto, Texas: n.p., 1935–39.

Morgan, Dale. *The Humboldt, Highroad of the West.* New York: Farrar and Rinehart, 1943.

Monaghan, Jay. *Civil War on the Western Border, 1854–1865.* Boston: Little, Brown, 1950.

Newcomb, W. W. *The Indians of Texas from Prehistoric to Modern Times.* Austin: University of Texas Press, 1961.

Paden, Irene. *The Wake of the Prairie Schooner.* New York: MacMillan, 1943.

Paul, Rodman. *California Gold: The Beginning of Mining in the Far West.* Cambridge: Harvard University Press, 1947.

Pearce, T. M., ed. *New Mexico Place Names: A Geographical Dictionary.* Albuquerque: University of New Mexico Press, 1965.

Pride, Woodbury F. *The History of Fort Riley.* Fort Riley, Kansas: n.p., 1926.

Putnam, J. W. *The Illinois and Michigan Canal, A Study in Economic History.* Chicago: University of Chicago Press, 1918.

Raht, Carlysle G. *The Romance of the Davis Mountains and the Big Bend Country.* El Paso: Rahtbook Co., 1919.

Reiter, Joan. *The Women.* Alexandria, Virginia: Time-Life Books, 1978.

Riley, Glenda. *The Frontierswoman: Iowa as a Case Study.* Des Moines: University of Iowa, in press.

_____. *Women on the American Frontier.* The Forum Series. Saint Louis: Forum Press, 1977.

Rister, Carl Coke. *Fort Griffin and the Texas Frontier.* Norman: University of Oklahoma Press, 1936.

Severson, Thor. *Sacramento, An Illustrated History, 1839–1874.* Sacramento: California Historical Society, 1973.

Shinkle, James D. *"Missouri Plaza," First Settled Community in Chaves County.* Roswell, New Mexico: Hall-Poorbaugh Press, 1972.

Sinnott, James. *History of Sierra County.* 3 volumes. Volcano, California: The California Traveler, 1952.

Smythe, H. *Historical Sketch of Parker County and Weatherford, Texas.* Saint Louis: Louis C. Lavat, 1877.

Society of First Steamship Pioneers. *First Steamship Pioneers.* San Francisco: H. S. Crocker & Company, printers, 1874.

Sonnichen, C. L. *Pass of the North.* El Paso: Texas Western Press, 1968.

Stewart, George. *The California Trail.* New York: McGraw Hill, 1962.

Swanson, Leslie. *Canals of Mid-America.* Moline, Illinois: n.p., 1964.

Tarpley, Fred. *Place Names of Northeast Texas.* Commerce, Texas: East Texas State University, 1969.

Unruh, John. *The Plains Across: The Overland Immigrants and the Trans-Mississippi West.* Urbana: University of Illinois, 1979.

Utley, Robert M. *Fort Davis National Historic Site, Texas.* Historic Handbook Series #38. Washington, D.C.: National Park Service, 1965.

———. *Frontiersmen in Blue: The United States Army and the Indian, 1848-1865.* New York: MacMillan, 1967.

Webb, Walter Prescott and H. Bailey Carrol, eds. *The Handbook of Texas.* 3 volumes. Austin: Texas State Historical Association, 1952-1976.

Index

Errata

This book has been photographically reproduced from the original. The following is a correction.

Helen Carpenter diary
P. 149, n. 33: "Columbia" should read "Snake."

ADDITIONAL
HUNTINGTON LIBRARY CLASSICS

The Butterfield Overland Mail
by Waterman L. Ormsby,
edited by Lyle H. Wright and Josephine M. Bynum
paper, $12.95

The Boom of the Eighties in Southern California
by Glenn S. Dumke
cloth, $24.95

The Cattle on a Thousand Hills: Southern California, 1850–1880
by Robert Glass Cleland
cloth, $24.95, paper, $12.95

Juan Rodríguez Cabrillo
by Harry Kelsey
paper, $12.95

A Victorian Gentlewoman in the Far West: The Reminiscences
of Mary Hallock Foote
edited and with an introduction by Rodman W. Paul
paper, $14.95

NEW WESTERN HISTORY TITLE

Voyage to California Written at Sea, 1852: The Journal
of Lucy Kendall Herrick
edited by Amy R. Russell, Marcia R. Good, and Mary G. Lindgren
and with an introduction by Andrew Rolle
cloth, $24.95

Visit our web site: http://huntington.org/HLPress/HEHPubs.html